Middleware Management with Oracle Enterprise Manager Grid Control 10*g* R5

Monitor, diagnose, and maximize the system performance of Oracle Fusion Middleware solutions

Debu Panda

Arvind Maheshwari

[PACKT] PUBLISHING

BIRMINGHAM - MUMBAI

Middleware Management with Oracle Enterprise Manager Grid Control 10g R5

First published: November 2009

Production Reference: 2241109

Published by Packt Publishing Ltd.
32 Lincoln Road
Olton
Birmingham, B27 6PA, UK.

ISBN 978-1-847198-34-1

www.packtpub.com

Cover Image by Karl Moore (karl.moore@ukonline.co.uk)

Credits

Authors
Debu Panda

Arvind Maheshwari

Reviewers
Joseph S. Gomez

Ulises Lazarini

Peter McLarty

Acquisition Editor
James Lumsden

Development Editor
Darshana D. Shinde

Technical Editor
Arani Roy

Indexer
Hemangini Bari

Editorial Team Leader
Abhijeet Deobhakta

Project Team Leader
Lata Basantani

Project Coordinator
Srimoyee Ghoshal

Proofreader
Andie Scothern

Graphics
Nilesh R. Mohite

Production Coordinator
Shantanu Zagade

Cover Work
Shantanu Zagade

Foreword

Middleware market is a fast growing market with a variety of vendors ranging from enterprise grade middleware products such as Oracle's Fusion Middleware to open source efforts such as JBoss and Apache Tomcat. Oracle Fusion Middleware is the number one middleware in the market with over 90,000 customers. Enterprise Manager provides an integrated management solution for Oracle Fusion Middleware. It is a complete management solution for the Oracle stack, which includes Oracle Fusion Middleware, Oracle Database, Oracle Enterprise Linux, Oracle VM, and packaged applications such as Oracle eBusiness Suite, Siebel CRM, and PeopleSoft. It also leverages the built-in management capabilities in the Oracle stack to provide an integrated and end-to-end management solution for the Oracle eco-system.

In a typical datacenter, there are multiple Middleware platforms. Monitoring, application performance management, configuration management, and life cycle operations of diverse middleware platforms is very expensive. Most of the new JEE applications are composite applications built with multi-tiered architecture and hence management of such applications needs specialized tools. As Information Technology becomes the core to the success of any business, there is a greater need of business-IT alignment. This book will show you how Enterprise Manager from Oracle meets these new challenges in the data center and can help reduce the total cost of ownership as well allow IT to contribute to a greater business success.

Enterprise Manager Grid Control 10*g* R5 was released in March 2009. This version of Enterprise manager provides management capability for Oracle and non-Oracle middleware platform that includes Oracle WebLogic Server, Oracle Application Server, Oracle Coherence, Oracle SOA Suite, IBM Web Sphere, and JBoss Application Server, and many more. This book will help you understand how Enterprise Manager Grid Control provides for better business-IT alignment and allows IT to not just manage middleware but also manage business processes implemented using SOA architecture.

The authors have first-hand experience in creating, delivering and rolling-out several releases of Oracle Fusion Middleware and Oracle Enterprise Manager Grid Control. This book covers the management challenges faced by Middleware administrators in the evolving Middleware market. The book includes the authors' practical experience in adopting Enterprise Manager Grid Control in managing Oracle Fusion Middleware. It is a must read for anyone using Enterprise Manager Grid Control for managing middleware and JEE applications deployed in the data center.

Ali Siddiqui,
Vice President—Product Development Fusion Middleware Management,
Oracle Corporation

About the Authors

Debu Panda, lead author of the best selling EJB 3 in Action (Manning Publications), is a Product Management Director on the Oracle Fusion Middleware Management development team, where he drives development of the middleware management aspects of Oracle Enterprise Manager. He has more than 17 years of experience in the IT industry and has published more than 30 articles on enterprise Java technologies and has presented at leading technology conferences such as Oracle Open World, Java One, and so on. Debu maintains an active blog on middleware technologies at http://www.debupanda.com.

I would like to thank my wife, Renuka, for her immense support and continuous encouragement and for her patience with all the late nights and weekend hours I have spent on the book in the past 9 months. I would also like to thank my kids, Nistha and Nisheet, who did not demand my attention while I wrote this book.

Many thanks to Rajiv Taori, Senior Director of Product Management and Ali Siddiqui, Vice President of Oracle Application and Systems Management Products for allowing me to fit this book into my busy schedule, and for their constant encouragement.

Thanks to Rajiv K. Maheshwari, Rao Bethanabotla, Madhav Sathe, Nicole Haba, Rahul Goyal, Senthil Saivam, Sandeep Pandita, Ajay Jagannatha Rao and the entire Enterprise Manager Middleware Management development team at Oracle for their help while writing the book.

Many thanks to James Lumsden, Srimoyee Ghoshal, Darshana Shinde, and Arani Roy, and the entire team at Packt Publishing for turning our drafts to a book! I would also like to extend my thanks to all the reviewers of the book.

Finally, I would like to thank my co-author Arvind Maheshwari for his hard work and help in completing the book.

Arvind Maheshwari, is a senior Software Development Manager for the Oracle Enterprise Manager development team, is focused on building management solutions for middleware. He has 15 years of experience in the IT industry and has played the role of Developer, Consultant, Architect, and Manager in the Financial, Manufacturing, and Telecom industries, developing enterprise solutions that are deployed in high-availability architectures.

I thank my wife Seema, kids Ashutosh and Anusha, for letting me use precious family time to work on this book.

I thank my management chain—Ali Siddiqui, Rajiv Maheshwari, and Rahul Goyal for supporting the idea of writing a book about Middleware management.

I thank Senthil Saivam, Manish Bisarya, Rishi Saraswat, Venkatesh Audinarayan, Govinda Sambamurthy, Sandeep Pandita, Rajiv Kuriakose, Ravi Ummadi, Suresh Kotha, Anil Kumar, Priya Ulaganathan, Rajesh Vemana, and all of my colleagues for their help and support while writing the book.

I thank my co-author Debu Panda—who provided guidance at every step of this project.

I thank Srimoyee Ghoshal and James Lumsden at Packt Publishing for coordinating this project and ensuring that this book sees the light of day.

About the Reviewers

Joseph S. Gomez, has been in the IT field for 13+ years and loves every minute of it. Originally educated as a Graphic Designer, Joe was working at an art studio (as most Graphic Designers do) when his sister mentioned that there were several local companies willing to hire people and give them paid training to prepare them for the Y2K boom. That was all that it took and Joe hasn't looked back since. Joe is now the technical lead for his employer's OLAP Center of Excellence and is currently working on the Business Intelligence team as well.

In addition to enjoying his work in IT, Joe is also an author himself having co-authored the book, Oracle Essbase 9 Implementation Guide, with his good friend Sarma Anantapantula.

Ulises Lazarini, is the President of Consultoria Informatica Lazarini, and partner of Oracle with more than ten years of experience working with Oracle databases and an OCP member since Oracle 7.3.4., 8. 8i 9i, and 10g.

He has been an Oracle instructor in the kernel field for more than 12 years now. He has been a speaker on Oracle Open World. (September 2008, "Migration from Siebel 7.8 running on SQL Server to Oracle 10g RAC"), DBA Consultant of two Database Successful Oracle Cases. Ulises has been very active in the installation and monitoring of RAC environments for OLTP and DataWarehouses Databases.

He has been responsible for the high availability for global's databases.

Peter McLarty, is a Senior Consultant working in Brisbane, Australia. Peter has worked with technology all his life. He is presently employed by Pacific DBMS Pty Ltd.

He works with Oracle database, Middleware Fusion and Enterprise Manager with clients in Brisbane. Peter's career spans 25 years in technology and 13 years in database management.

Peter has worked mainly in Australia and Asia. Peter's other interests include studying Asia and its cultures and of course its food, sailing and football. He can be found supporting his team each season at the stadium.

He has a wife and two children who say that they have to suffer through the times of editing books, amongst other projects. Peter would like to thank them for their understanding and allowing dad to do his stuff at times!

Peter can be reached on the Internet at `peter.mclarty@pameacs.com`.

Table of Contents

Preface

Rob's Blackberry screams in the middle of the night. He picks it up with hesitation. He gets a text message from an automated system, telling him that there are serious issues in the applications that he supports, and users in Australia are facing problems as well. Rob is an administrator for middleware applications. He opens his laptop and starts looking at the issue. After hours of investigation he finds that the external web service their application depends on is not responding.

This might sound familiar. It's typical in the life of many of today's administrators. Welcome to the world of middleware management, where life starts with service violations and ends with the diagnostics of performance issues.

Most modern applications have become global, and run 24X7 and if you are a middleware administrator then probably your work has become 24X7 too. Today's applications are very complex and depend on several components that you, as an administrator, do not have control over. But you have the responsibility to make sure that the application meets availability and performance criteria. You probably want to avoid situations like Rob's and do away with sleepless nights. You probably want to be proactive and implement the right tools and methodologies so that you can avoid many of the interruptions to your applications.

Throughout this book, we will discuss how you can use Oracle Enterprise Manager to proactively monitor your middleware applications and the underlying infrastructure.

Before we do that, let us first drill down and examine the various complexities in modern applications.

Complexities in modern applications

Modern day applications are way more complex than predecessors such as client-server or mainframe applications. Technologies such as the Internet, Java Enterprise Edition (Java EE) and Service Oriented Architecture (SOA) have revolutionized the way that applications are built and integrated. They are multi-tier and run on heterogeneous platforms. They depend upon several resources within and outside of organizations. Today's resources may include an application running on a mainframe system, or an ERP system, or resources made available by a partner through the Internet, intranet, or extranet. As an administrator, you may not have control over these resources, or applications—however, you are responsible for their performance.

Some of the typical characteristics of modern applications are:

- Deployed on an application server or middleware
- Depends on databases and messaging providers
- May depend on applications running on mainframe systems or legacy systems
- May depend on external services available over the internet or extranet
- May depend upon complex and long running business processes
- May have complex routing or workflow requirements
- May depend on a clustered caching service for faster data access

Also, today's applications have complex requirements with associated and specific requirements such as:

- Availability
- Service Level
- Compliance and security

If you are a middleware administrator, you know that you have a lot of things to do! You have to wear several hats from time to time.

Middleware administrator—a man with several hats

Unlike a database administrator or UNIX system administrator—a middleware administrator has to be knowledgeable in several areas and perform a lot of tasks to keep applications up and available. You have to know how the application works and understand its dependencies. The most trivial applications have database access, and hence you must be proficient in database technologies such as JDBC and SQL. You have to understand messaging systems and key technologies such as various web services and **Service Oriented Architecture (SOA)**. Most applications employ different security mechanisms, such as using an LDAP Server, thus you have to know the basics of security infrastructure.

With modern application complexities, you have to be agile and you need the right sets of tools and practices.

If you are a middleware administrator then you know how your life goes! Some of the typical tasks that middleware administrators perform are as follows:

- Monitors performance of production environment middleware and associated applications
- Diagnoses production issues
- Plans for production deployment
- Installs/provisions software
- Tracks and applies patches
- Performs trend analysis and capacity planning for future growth
- Brings into compliance standards such as the Information Technology Infrastructure Library (ITIL)

You may ask the question—how do you juggle between these tasks? What is the optimal ratio of these tasks? There are no right answers here. This is actually based on your organization. We have seen administrators just struggling to keep up with monitoring the production middleware platform and making it highly available. This typically happens if you do not use the right tools and practices. Administrators spend most of their morning running several scripts to verify the health of their middleware platform. If you spend your entire morning checking the health of your middleware platform, then it is highly unlikely that you will be able to perform all of your tasks in your eight hour daily job!

Another challenge is that many organizations do not have full-time people who are middleware administrators. In some organizations, the database administrators or developers take on additional responsibilities for middleware administration. If you are part of such an organization then it is really challenging for you to perform all aspects of middleware management without the appropriate management tools.

Key challenges faced by administrators

To compete, organizations are trying to keep their costs low. This is putting greater burdens on the IT infrastructure, which must remain agile to make the company's applications highly available. As a middleware administrator, you have more responsibilities and less resources for keeping your infrastructure running and maintaining the service levels of your applications. Middleware administrators, in particular, are faced with a number of challenges that come with managing a complex application architecture. Some of the key challenges are:

- Inability to manage multiple installs of a middleware package from a single management console
- Lack of visibility to other tiers in the applications
- Managing application performance to meet service levels and application diagnostics
- Compliance to standard practices such as Information Technology Infrastructure Library (ITIL)

To cope with these challenges, you have to choose the right management tools to manage your middleware infrastructure. There are several tools available in the marketplace. However, if you are using Oracle Fusion Middleware; Oracle Enterprise Manager is the right choice to manage your complete application infrastructure. Oracle Enterprise Manager not only provides great tools to manage your Oracle databases but it also provides comprehensive functionalities to manage your middleware infrastructure and enterprise applications.

Throughout this book, we will provide an insight on how to manage applications running on Oracle Fusion Middleware and third-party application servers.

What this book covers

This book will help you to manage your middleware infrastructure and applications effectively and efficiently using Oracle Enterprise Manager. You will learn how you can proactively monitor your production middleware applications running on Oracle Application Server, Oracle WebLogic Server, Oracle SOA suite such as Oracle BPEL Process manager, Oracle Server Bus, Oracle Coherence, and so on. You will learn different aspects of proactive monitoring and alert notifications, service level management and incident management, diagnostics of production applications, lifecycle automation using out-of-the-box deployment procedures, patching mechanisms, and so on. You will learn the best practices that you can use to make your middleware infrastructure highly available.

Chapter 1: *Enterprise Manager Grid Control* will introduce the key concepts of Oracle Enterprise Manager Grid control. You will learn about the Grid Control architecture and terminology, basic concepts, and entities. The lifecycle of a managed target in Grid Control.

Chapter 2: *Installing Enterprise Manager Grid Control* discusses installing Grid Control and its key components. You will also learn about various Grid Control versions, platform support, and installation options, tricks for mass deployment of Grid Control, high availability setup for Grid Control, and some guidelines on what install/setup mode the user should use.

Chapter 3: *Enterprise Manager Key Concepts and Subsystems* expands further on key entities, subsystems that we introduced in Chapter 1. Besides expanding on those we'll use these subsystems to answer work areas that we outlined in Chapter 1.

We'll also provide the reader with some best practices for using each subsystem.

Chapter 4: *Managing Oracle WebLogic Server* defines the typical management needs for WebLogic environments and will apply solution areas learned from Chapter 3.

We will have some example exercises on how to set up monitoring and management for WebLogic Server's environment.

We'll also list some of the best practices on how to manage a WebLogic Server.

Chapter 5: *Managing Oracle Application Server* defines the typical management needs for an Oracle Application Server environment and will apply solution areas learned from Chapter 3.

We will have some exercises on how to set up monitoring and management for an Oracle Application Server environment. We will discuss some of the key features such as deployment and patch automation.

We will also list some of the best practices on how to manage monitoring and management for the Oracle Application Server environment.

Chapter 6: *Managing Forms and Reports Services and Applications* provides an introduction to Forms and Reports Monitoring. You will learn about both Forms Server and Forms Application Monitoring. You will also learn about Forms Server Cloning using Enterprise Manager Deployment Procedures.

Chapter 7: *SOA Management – BPEL Management* firstly discusses the business/IT alignment introduction. Then the chapter explains what additional management requirements it puts on middleware administrators.

Also, in this chapter we'll define the typical management needs for SOA/BPEL environments and will apply solution techniques learned from Chapter 3. We'll also explain how to handle additional management requirements coming from the business/IT alignments.

We'll have some exercises on how to set up monitoring and management for SOA/BPEL.

Chapter 8: *SOA Management – OSB (aka ALSB) Management* will provide an introduction to Oracle Service Bus and managing Oracle Service Bus. We will learn automated deployment of OSB applications and managing configurations for OSB environment. We will also list some of the best practices for managing SOA/OSB environments.

Chapter 9: *Managing Identity Manager Suite* discusses Oracle Fusion Middleware Identity Manager Suite that enables the users to manage identity and access for enterprise applications. In this chapter, we'll discuss how to manage Oracle's Identity Manager Suite with Enterprise Manager.

Chapter 10: *Managing Coherence Cluster* discusses Oracle Coherence that is an in-memory caching solution that enables organizations to predictably scale mission-critical applications. In this chapter, we'll discuss the monitoring, configuration management, and provisioning aspects of Coherence Cluster.

Chapter 11: *Managing Non-Oracle Middleware* discusses managing third-party middleware. We will learn about discovering and monitoring of IBM WebSphere, JBoss, Apache HTTP Server, ApacheTomcat, and Microsoft middleware such as Microsoft IIS. We will also learn how to do service level management of applications running on third-party middleware.

Chapter 12: *Java and Composite Applications Monitoring and Diagnostics* discusses how to diagnose Java applications using Oracle's Enterprise Manager product family such as Application Diagnostics for Java (AD4J) and Composite Application Monitor and Modeler (CAMM). CAMM allows you to diagnose performance issues in composite applications whereas AD4J allows you to diagnose issues such as memory leak and application in Java applications and the underlying JVM.

Chapter 13: *Building your Monitoring Plug-in* contains detailed steps on how to extend Grid Control functionality. It'll have a step-by-step instructions for building a monitoring plug-in for Sun System Web Server.

Chapter 14: *Best Practices for Managing Middleware Components Using Enterprise Manager* discusses some of the best practices for middleware management that you can apply while using Enterprise Manager Grid Control to manage your middleware applications.

Who this book is for

Most people think of Oracle Enterprise Manager Grid Control as a database administration tool and are not aware of the middleware management capabilities it offers. This book helps you learn the middleware management functions and the features offered by Oracle Enterprise Manager. If you are a middleware administrator or aspire to be one, then this book is for you. This book will help database administrators, developers, and system administrators who are supporting applications that run on Oracle Fusion Middleware. If you are a system architect, application developer or application support person then this book will help you to learn different perspectives on middleware and application infrastructures.

Conventions

In this book, you will find a number of styles of text that distinguish between different kinds of information. Here are some examples of these styles, and an explanation of their meaning.

Code words in text are shown as follows: "We can include other contexts through the use of the `include` directive."

A block of code is set as follows:

```
<ColumnDescriptor NAME="Status" TYPE="NUMBER" IS_KEY="FALSE">
  <Display>
    <Label NLSID="apache_resp_stat">UpDown Status</Label>
  </Display>
</ColumnDescriptor>
```

Any command-line input or output is written as follows:

```
$AD4J_HOME/jamserv/bin/apachectl start
```

New terms and **important words** are shown in bold. Words that you see on the screen, in menus or dialog boxes for example, appear in the text like this: "clicking the **Next** button moves you to the next screen".

> Warnings or important notes appear in a box like this.

> Tips and tricks appear like this.

Reader feedback

Feedback from our readers is always welcome. Let us know what you think about this book—what you liked or may have disliked. Reader feedback is important for us to develop titles that you really get the most out of.

To send us general feedback, simply send an email to feedback@packtpub.com, and mention the book title via the subject of your message.

If there is a book that you need and would like to see us publish, please send us a note in the **SUGGEST A TITLE** form on www.packtpub.com or email suggest@packtpub.com.

If there is a topic that you have expertise in and you are interested in either writing or contributing to a book on, see our author guide on www.packtpub.com/authors.

Customer support

Now that you are the proud owner of a Packt book, we have a number of things to help you to get the most from your purchase.

> **Downloading the example code for the book**
> Visit http://www.packtpub.com/files/code/8341_Code.zip to directly download the example code.
> The downloadable files contain instructions on how to use them.

Errata

Although we have taken every care to ensure the accuracy of our content, mistakes do happen. If you find a mistake in one of our books — maybe a mistake in the text or the code — we would be grateful if you would report this to us. By doing so, you can save other readers from frustration, and help us to improve subsequent versions of this book. If you find any errata, please report them by visiting `http://www.packtpub.com/support`, selecting your book, clicking on the **let us know** link, and entering the details of your errata. Once your errata are verified, your submission will be accepted and the errata added to any list of existing errata. Any existing errata can be viewed by selecting your title from `http://www.packtpub.com/support`.

Piracy

Piracy of copyright material on the Internet is an ongoing problem across all media. At Packt, we take the protection of our copyright and licenses very seriously. If you come across any illegal copies of our works, in any form, on the Internet, please provide us with the location address or web site name immediately so that we can pursue a remedy.

Please contact us at `copyright@packtpub.com` with a link to the suspected pirated material.

We appreciate your help in protecting our authors, and our ability to bring you valuable content.

Questions

You can contact us at `questions@packtpub.com` if you are having a problem with any aspect of the book, and we will do our best to address it.

1
Enterprise Manager Grid Control

The typical data center for a medium or large enterprise is composed of a myriad of technologies. One can see different types of hardware, operating systems, databases, middleware, integration servers, storage devices, and networking devices in any such data center. Such diversity of technologies and operating systems can be attributed to many factors, and some of them are:

- Evolution of IT systems: As architectural patterns moved from monolithic systems to distributed systems, not all IT systems were moved to the newest patterns. Some new systems were built with new technologies and patterns whereas existing systems that were performing well enough continued on earlier technologies.

- Best of breed approach: With multi-tiered architectures, enterprises had the choice of building each tier using best of breed technology for that tier. For example, one system could be built using a J2EE container from vendor A, but a database from vendor B.

- Avoiding single vendors and technologies: Enterprises wanted to avoid dependence on any single vendor and technology. This led to systems being built using different technologies. For example, an order-booking system built using .NET technologies on Windows servers, but an order shipment system built using J2EE platform on Linux servers.

- Acquisitions and Mergers: Through acquisitions and mergers, enterprises have inherited IT systems that were built using different technologies. Frequently, new systems were added to integrate the systems of two enterprises but the new systems were totally different from the existing systems. For example, using BPEL process manager to integrate a CRM system with a transportation management system.

We see that each factor for diversity in the data center has some business or strategic value. At the same time, such diversity makes management of the data center more complex. To manage such data centers we need a special product like Oracle's Enterprise Manager Grid Control that can provide a unified and centralized management solution for the wide array of products.

In any given data center, there are lots of repetitive operations that need to be executed on multiple servers (like applying security patches on all Oracle Databases). As data centers move away from high-end servers to a grid of inexpensive servers, the number of IT resources increases in the data center and so does the cost of executing repetitive operations on the grid. Enterprise Manager Grid Control provides solutions to reduce the cost of any grid by automating repetitive operations that can be simultaneously executed on multiple servers. Enterprise Manager Grid Control works as a force multiplier by providing support for executing the same operations on multiple servers at the cost of one operation.

As organizations put more emphasis on business and IT alignment, that requires a view of IT resources overlaid with business processes and applications is required. Enterprise Manager Grid Control provides such a view and improves the visibility of IT and business processes in a given data center. By using Enterprise Manager Grid Control, administrators can see IT issues in the context of business processes and they can understand how business processes are affected by IT performance.

In this chapter, we will get to know more about Oracle's Enterprise Manager Grid Control by covering the following aspects:

- Key features of Enterprise Manager Grid Control:
    - Comprehensive view of data center
    - Unmanned monitoring
    - Historical data analysis
    - Configuration management
    - Managing multiple entities as one
    - Service level management
    - Scheduling
    - Automating provisioning
    - Information publishing
    - Synthetic transaction
    - Manage from anywhere
- Enterprise Manager Product family

- Range of products managed by Enterprise Manager:
  - ° Range of products
  - ° EM extensibility
- Enterprise Manager Grid Control architecture.
  - ° Multi-tier architecture
  - ° Major components
  - ° High availability
- Summary of learning

Key features of Enterprise Manager Grid Control

Typical applications in today's world are built with multi-tiered architecture; to manage such applications a system administrator has to navigate through multiple management tools and consoles that come along with each product. Some of the tools have a browser interface, some have a thick client interface, or even a command line interface. Navigating through multiple management tools often involves doing some actions from a browser or running some scripts or launching a thick client from the command line.

For example, to find bottlenecks in a J2EE application in the production environment, an administrator has to navigate through the management console for the HTTP server, the management console for the J2EE container, and the management console for the database.

Enterprise Manager Grid Control is a systems management product for the monitoring and management of all of the products in the data center. For the scenario explained above, Enterprise Manager provides a common management interface to manage an HTTP server, J2EE server and database. Enterprise Manager provides this unified solution for all products in a data center.

In addition to basic monitoring, Enterprise Manager provides a unified interface for many other administration tasks like patching, configuration compliance, backup-recovery, and so on.

Some key features of Enterprise Manager are explained here.

Comprehensive view of the data center

Enterprise Manager provides a comprehensive view of the data center, where an administrator can see all of the applications, servers, databases, network devices, storage devices, and so on, along with performance and configuration data. As the number of all such resources is very high, this Enterprise Manager highlights the resources that need immediate attention or that may need attention in near future. For example, a critical security patch is available that needs to be applied on some Fusion Middleware servers, or a server that has 90% CPU utilization.

The following figure shows one such view of a data center, where users can see all entities that are monitored, that are up, that are down, that have performance alerts, that have configuration violations and so on. The user can drill down to fine-grained views from this top-level view.

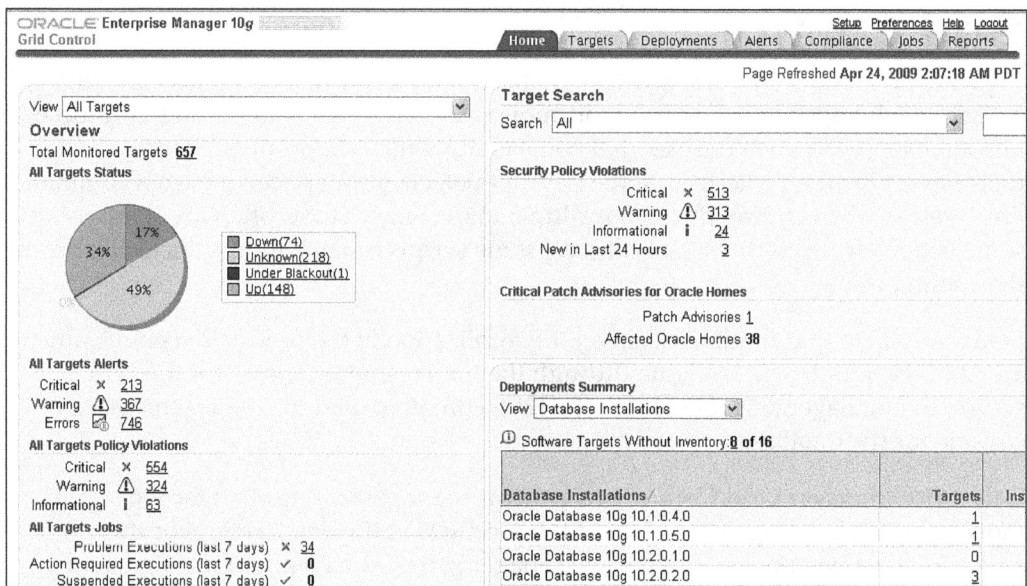

The data in the top-level view and the fine-grained drill-down view can be broadly summarized in the following categories:

Performance data

Data that shows how an IT resource is performing, that includes the current status, overall availability over a period of time, and other performance indicators that are specific to the resource like the average response time for a J2EE server. Any violation of acceptable performance thresholds is highlighted in this view.

Configuration data

Configuration data is the configuration parameters or, configuration files captured from an IT resource. Besides the current configuration, changes in configuration are also tracked and available from Enterprise Manager. Any violation of configuration conformance is also available. For example, if a data center policy mandates that only port 80 should be open on all servers, Enterprise Manager captures any violation of that policy.

Status of scheduled operations

In any data center there are some scheduled operations, these operations could be something like a system administration task such as taking a backup of a database server or some batch process that moves data across systems, for example, moving orders from fulfillment to shipping. Enterprise Manager provides a consolidated view of the status of all such scheduled operations.

Inventory

Enterprise Manager provides a listing of all hardware and software resources with details like version numbers. All of these resources are also categorized in different buckets – for example, Oracle Application Server, WebLogic application Server, WebSphere application are all categorized in the middleware bucket. This categorization helps the user to find resources of the same or similar type. Enterprise Manager. It also captures the finer details of software resources – like patches applied.

The following figure shows one such view where the user can see all middleware entities like Oracle WebLogic Server, IBM WebSphere Server, Oracle Application Server, and so on.

Unmanned monitoring

Enterprise Manager monitors IT resources around the clock and it gathers all performance indicators at every fixed interval. Whenever a performance indicator goes beyond the defined acceptable limit, Enterprise Manager records that occurrence. For example, if the acceptable limit of CPU utilization for a server is 70%, then whenever CPU utilization of the server goes above 70% then that occurrence is recorded. Enterprise Manager can also send notification of any such occurrence through common notification mechanisms like email, pager, SNMP trap, and so on.

Historical data analysis

All of the performance indicators captured by Enterprise Manager are saved in the repository. Enterprise Manager provides some useful views of the data using the system administrator that can analyze data over a period of time. Besides the fine-grained data that is collected at every fixed interval, it also provides coarse views by rolling up the data every hour and every 24 hours.

Configuration management

Enterprise Manager gathers configuration data for IT resources at regular intervals and checks for any configuration compliance violation. Any such violation is captured and can be sent out as a notification. Enterprise Manager comes with many out-of-the-box configuration compliance rules that represent best practices; in addition to that, system administrators can configure their own rules.

All of the configuration data is also saved in the Enterprise Manager repository. Using data, the system administrator can compare the configuration of two similar IT resources or compare the configuration of the same IT resource at two different points in time. The system administrator can also see the configuration change history.

Managing multiple entities as one

Most of the more recent applications are built with multi-tiered architecture and each tier may run on different IT resources. For example, an order booking application can have all of its presentation and business logic running on a J2EE server, all business data persisted in a database, all authentication and authorization performed through an LDAP server, and all of the traffic to the application routed through an HTTP server.

To monitor such applications, all of the underlying resources need to be monitored. Enterprise Manager provides support for grouping such related IT resources. Using this support, the system administrator can monitor all related resources as one entity and all performance indicators for all related entities can be monitored from one interface.

Service level management

Enterprise Manager provides necessary constructs and interfaces for managing service level agreements that are based on the performance of IT resources. Using these constructs, the user can define indicators to measure service levels and expected service levels. For example, a service representing a web application can have the same average JSP response time as a service indicator, the expected service level for this service is to have the service indicator below three seconds for 90% of the time during business hours.

Enterprise Manager keeps track of all such indicators and violations in the context of a service and at any time the user can see the status of such service level agreements over a defined time period.

Scheduling

Many data center operations are repeated at fixed interval and on multiple IT resources. For example, database backup is performed every day at midnight for all of the database servers in a data center. Typically, system administrators write some scripts and use some scheduling mechanism like crontabs to perform these operations. Monitoring of such operations across multiple servers is expensive; the system administrator needs to check logs on each server and maintain scripts on each server and so on.

Enterprise Manager also provides a scheduling mechanism and, using that mechanism, the user can execute an operation on multiple resources as per the defined schedule. The outcome of all such operations, across multiple resources, is saved in the Enterprise Manager repository and the system administrator can see all of the results from one central console. Besides that, events like the success or failure of an operation can be sent out as notifications via standard notification mechanisms like email, SNMP trap, and so on.

Automating provisioning

Initial provisioning of new IT resources is an expensive operation; the system administrator needs to install the Operating System, all required software like the database, J2EE server, all required patches, and the business applications. After this, the system administrator needs to configure the software and applications. Enterprise Manager provides support for building gold images from existing IT resources, and provisioning new IT resources from the gold image. Using the gold image, the system administrator can easily provision a new IT resource by cloning it from an existing IT resource.

Enterprise Manager also provides a software library where the gold images of Operating Systems, software, and so on, can be stored for future use.

Information publishing

System administrators do need to publish data related to their data center; like resource utilization data, configuration compliance data, inventory of resources, and so on. Also, a lot of the data publishing activity has to be repeated at every fixed interval, for example, resource utilization data needs to be published at the end of every month.

Enterprise Manager has a reporting and publishing framework to build and publish reports in HTML format that summarize the data available in the Enterprise Manager repository. Report generation can be scheduled and the generated reports are also saved in the repository. These reports can be automatically sent out by emails as per the schedule defined by the system administrators.

There are many useful out-of-the-box reports that the system administrator can use to publish performance data, configuration compliance data, and so on. System administrators can also customize or build new reports through the intuitive user interface.

Synthetic transaction

There are times when all of the performance indicators are within acceptable ranges, but users still complain for about application performance. To troubleshoot such issues, system administrators often log in to the application to try to simulate what the real users do. Sometimes such problems are related to some specific geographic regions only, for example, customers in Europe cannot check out the shopping cart but customers in other countries are fine.

Recording typical user actions and repeating those instructions from different geographical regions can provide proactive monitoring for such issues. Enterprise Manager provides a framework for such support where typical user behavior can be recorded and repeated from various geographical locations. In the example above, Enterprise Manager can record the web transaction for checking out of the shopping cart and can repeat this synthetic transaction from various locations.

Web transactions can be used for checking availability for web applications. Enterprise Manager provides other mechanisms to check the availability of other resources like TNSPING to check the availability of a database.

Manage from anywhere

Enterprise Manager has a multi-tiered architecture; with the presentation layer on a J2EE server and content that is presented in HTML format. The Enterprise Manager console can be accessed through a browser that the system administrator can access remotely. Enterprise Manager is certified for all major browsers like Internet Explorer, Firefox, Netscape, Mozilla, and so on.

Enterprise Manager product family

The Oracle Enterprise Manager product family is a group of similar systems management products and it includes:

- **Oracle Enterprise Manager Database Control**: This flavor of Enterprise Manager gets installed with the installation of a database. This product can manage one database, associated listeners and the host where database is installed.

- **Oracle Enterprise Manager Application Server Control**: This flavor of Enterprise Manager gets installed with the installation of an Application Server. This product can manage one Application Server or an Application Server Cluster or an Application Server Farm and the host where it is installed.

- **Oracle Enterprise Manager Grid Control**: This flavor of Enterprise Manager needs its own installation. This product can manage all of the resources in a data center. In this book we'll learn more details about this particular flavor of Enterprise Manager product.

Products managed by Enterprise Manager

Enterprise manager is a system management product from the Oracle Corporation that provides a set of features for the comprehensive management of Oracle products like Oracle Database, Oracle WebLogic Server, Oracle SOA suite, Oracle Applications, and so on. Enterprise Manager also provides management support for non-Oracle products including databases like SQL Server, middleware platforms such as JBoss Application Server, IBM WebSphere MQ, and storage management system such as NetApp.

As mentioned in the initial introduction, data centers contain many types of IT resources from different vendors, and different technology platforms. There may also be homegrown products or applications in data centers. Enterprise Manager provides management support for most of the common resources, but there could be some resources for which there is no support out-of-box. Enterprise Manager provides a framework to extend management support for such resources. Using this, users and third party vendors can build custom management support. In Chapter 12, we'll cover this extensibility in more detail. Functionality for such support is packaged as plug-ins that can be deployed on top of Enterprise Manager. For example, there are some plug-ins available for .NET and BizTalk server. For a complete list of available plug-ins, please refer to the Oracle web site.

Enterprise Manager also provides connectors to integrate with help desk products like BMC Remedy or HP Service Center. By integrating EM with these products, alerts on the EM side can be converted to tickets on the help desk side and resolution of those tickets can clear alerts generated on the EM side.

The following illustration shows the range of products supported by Enterprise Manager Grid Control:

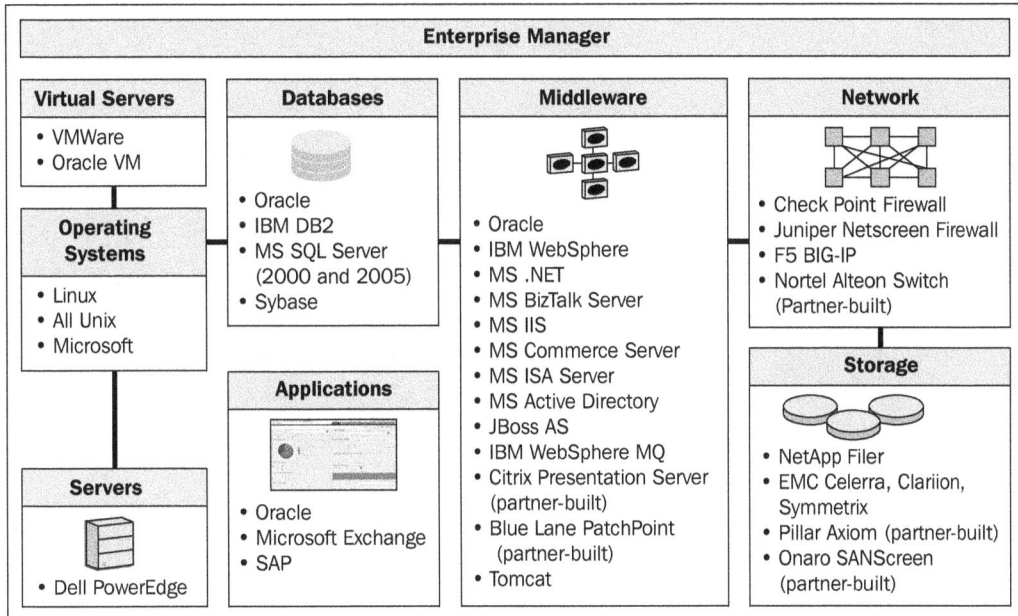

Enterprise Manager Architecture

The Enterprise Manager product is built using Java technology and an Oracle database. The Enterprise Manager product runs on top of Oracle Application Server and uses an Oracle Database as its persistence store. Enterprise Manager has three main components:

- Oracle Management Service (OMS)
- Oracle Management Agent (OMA)
- Oracle Management Repository (OMR)

For user interactions there is a centralized console that operates upon the Management Repository and uses services provided by the Management Server. This is a browser-based console.

In a typical setup, one management agent needs to be installed (on each host to be managed) that uploads data to the Management Server and that, in turn, persists the data in the repository. A system administrator can access this data or initiate or schedule an operation though the console. The next diagram shows a sample setup of the Enterprise Manager:

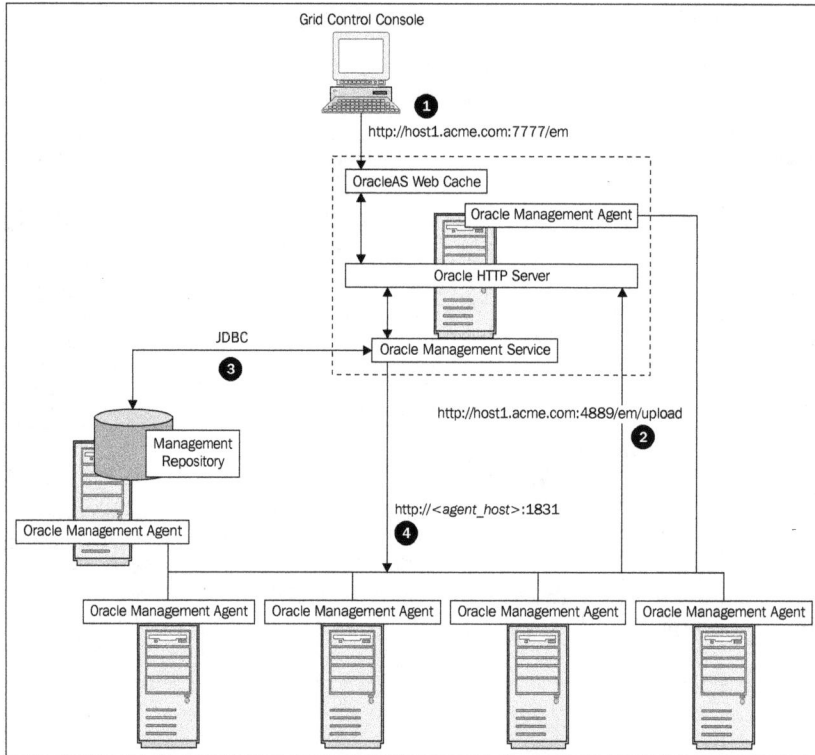

Before we get into the details of each component, one Enterprise Manager term, **target**, should be introduced. Target is very central for the EM system and everything moves around various target models.

Target

Target is a generic term that refers to any managed entity that is managed by Enterprise Manager. For each target there is a model of the target stored in the Enterprise Manager repository. There are various target types available out-of-the-box like target types for a WebLogic server, or target types for BPEL Process Manager. The target model contains all the properties needed for managing the target. For example, a model for the WebLogic server contains JMX URL and credentials to connect to JMX server. The target model also defines what metrics should be collected for a target, the associated thresholds for those metrics and the collection frequency for those metrics.

At a broad level, targets are of two types—the agent target, and the repository only target. Agent targets are the target models that get created as the end result of the discovery process. The agent and the repository maintain the definition and model of such targets. Metrics for such targets are collected by the agent and uploaded to the repository. The repository only targets are targets that get created only in the repository—they may get created as part of the discovery process or they may be created manually. All of the metric calculations of such targets are done in the repository. For example, WebLogic Managed Server is modeled as an agent target and WebLogic Domain and WebLogic Cluster are modeled as repository only targets.

Oracle Management Service (OMS)

OMS is a central process for Enterprise Manager. It provides a set of common services that help in the monitoring and management of a target. Some of those services are job scheduling, notification, and so on. OMS collects data from all of the agents and, after processing, persists it into the repository. For other system management operations like backup recovery, OMS orchestrates the sequence of events that need to be triggered on the agent for a given target.

OMS also communicates with the agent over HTTP/HTTPS protocol and uses JDBC to persist data in the repository.

Oracle Management Agent (OMA)

The Oracle Management Agent process is a proxy process for Enterprise Manager that collects data from targets and sends it to the Management repository. Generally it is co-located on the same host where a target is running. In this book we will use the terms OMA and agent interchangeably.

The agent keeps the target model synchronized with the actual target. It also collects monitoring and configuration information as per the target model, and uploads it into the Management repository via services exposed by the Management service. This collection of information is done as per the collection frequency defined by the target model. During collection, metrics are evaluated against the thresholds defined in the target model. In case metric values violate the thresholds, the agent generates an alert and sends it to the Management Server.

The agent executes all of the operations that are triggered from OMS, at the end of the operation the agent returns the status and output of such operations, for example, a "start WebLogic server command" triggered from OMS is delegated to the agent, after completion the agent sends the status and output of such commands back to OMS.

Besides monitoring, the agent executes all of the operations that are scheduled from OMS, and returns the status and output of such operations, for example, the agent executes a start-stop operation scheduled from OMS and returns the status and output of that operation.

Agents use a heartbeat mechanism to keep the Management Server informed about the health of agent. The agent communicates with the Management Server over HTTP/HTTPS protocol. In more secure setups, agents need one password to communicate with the management service.

Oracle Management Repository (OMR)

OMR is the persistence store for all EM data. All data related to target models, performance metrics and configuration metrics are persisted in the OMR. OMR also keeps historical data that can be used for analyzing the performance of the system over a period of time. Historical data related to configuration can be used to track configuration changes. OMR is built using an Oracle Database.

Some data from the Oracle Management Repository is exposed via public views and can be used for integration with external systems. The repository can be installed in a pre-existing database or a new database.

In this book, we will use the terms Oracle Management Repository and repository interchangeably.

Enterprise Manager Console

The Enterprise Manager Console is a browser-based interface where the user can view all the data from the management repository in useful formats like performance analysis charts, availability reports, and so on. Using the same console, administrators can schedule and monitor various operations like backup recovery, patching, and so on.

Enterprise Manager High Availability

As Enterprise Manager becomes a central point for managing and monitoring a complete IT infrastructure, the availability of Enterprise Manager itself is extremely critical. To support the high availability of OMS, Enterprise Manager supports a configuration where two or more OMSs are configured in active mode. To support high availability of the persistence store Management Repository can be setup to work with Oracle Real Application Cluster (RAC) database.

Summary

In this chapter, we learnt about diversity in a data center and the challenges posed by such diversity. We introduced Enterprise Manager Grid Control features and its architecture.

Here are the key takeaways from this chapter:

- In typical data centers we see different types of hardware, Operating Systems, databases, middleware servers, storage devices, network devices, and so on. Enterprise Manager is a systems management product used to manage such diverse IT entities

- Key monitoring features of Enterprise Manager include—centralized management interface, unmanned monitoring, historical data analysis, and so on

- Key management features of Enterprise Manager include—configuration management, service level management, scheduling, and so on

- Enterprise Manager provides a feature to publish aggregated performance, configuration and inventory data for a data center

- Enterprise Manager provides support for a wide range of IT products

- Enterprise Manager has an extensibility framework for homegrown applications and products not supported out-of-the-box

- Target is one major entity in Enterprise Manager

- Enterprise Manager has a multi-tiered distributed architecture
- The main components of Enterprise Manager are—Oracle Management Server (OMS), Oracle Management Repository (OMR), and Oracle Management Agent (OMA)
- Enterprise Manager Console provides a browser-based interface for all monitoring and management operations

Now that we know the key features of Enterprise Manager Grid Control and know about the main components of Enterprise Manager. It's time to install and start playing with Oracle Enterprise Manager. The next chapter provides details on where to get the latest version of Enterprise Manager software and how to install it.

2
Installing Enterprise Manager Grid Control

We introduced Rob, the Middleware administrator, at the beginning of the book. After sleepless nights and many escalations from the user community, Rob felt the heat. He convinced his management and fellow administrators to implement proactive monitoring within their IT organization. He decided to do away with his pride and an *all scripts* approach. The majority of Rob's applications ran on Oracle Fusion Middleware and therefore, Oracle Enterprise Manager Grid Control was the obvious choice.

In the last chapter, we introduced the architecture of Oracle Enterprise Manager Grid Control. In this chapter, we will help you get started with the installation process. The actual installation steps are very well documented in the Enterprise Manual and we will not bore you to death by duplicating all those steps in this chapter. Our primary goal is to help you get started with the installation of Enterprise Manager Grid Control with the simplest configuration that you can use, in conjunction with this book.

In this chapter, we will discuss the following:

- Downloading and installing Oracle Management Service
- Installation of Oracle Management Agent
- Starting and stopping of Oracle Management Service
- Starting and stopping of Oracle Management Agent

Of course, the proof of the pudding is in the eating! So let us get started with the installation of Enterprise Manager Grid Control 10g R5 (10.2.0.5).

Installation procedure

In the last chapter, you learnt that Enterprise Manager Grid Control has three main components:

- The Oracle Management Service
- The Oracle Management Repository
- The Oracle Management Agent

Thus, the actual installation procedure may sound a bit overwhelming when you think of a three-tier install. However, the reality is that the installation process is a very straight-forward and well-documented procedure. To make it simple, we recommend that you choose the default install type and install all components (at least the OMS and repository) on a single machine. But, before you get started with the install, you will need to download the binaries that follow.

Pre-requisite

Before you get started with the install, you will have to make sure that you have the right resources on the machine that you are installing Grid Control on to. The following table shows the minimum recommended resource requirement for Linux or Windows environment. You will need to check the install guide for resource requirements if you are using a different platform.

Component	CPU speed	Required disk space	Required Memory
OMS	3 GHz	2GB	2GB
Repository	3 GHz	10GB	2GB
Agent	3 GHz	500 MB	N.A.

If you are installing both OMS and Management Repository on the same machine, we recommend that you have at least 4GB of RAM for better performance. You must be wondering why Enterprise Manager Grid Control requires so much resource! You have to understand that Oracle Enterprise Manager Grid Control is not a development tool but an administration tool for managing production targets such as databases and middleware. OMS runs an instance of Oracle Application Server 10g and the repository is based on an Oracle database.

Operating system requirements

Once you have ensured that you have sufficient resources on the machine on which you plan to install Oracle Enterprise Manager Grid Control, you have to then make sure that you meet the operating system's requirements. We recommend that you check the release notes available at Oracle Technology Network for your platform for the required patch level for your operating system.

If you are using a UNIX environment, the installation process requires a super user or (root) privileges on your box to run a script during the installation process. If you do not have system administration privileges on your machine, you will have to work with the system administrator to run the script before you can complete the installation. Here are some other operating system's requirements that your system must meet:

- Make sure that the operating system user that you are using belongs to the `oinstall`, `dba`, and `osuser` groups.
- Make sure that you can ping your server with the fully qualified host name (`hostname.domainname`). If you cannot ping your server using DNS, make sure that you enter this name in the host's file (`/etc/hosts` UNIX).

Downloading the software

The Oracle Enterprise Manager Grid Control software can be downloaded from Oracle Technology Network at the following location: `http://www.oracle.com/technology/software/products/oem/index.html`.

> Note that you cannot install Grid Control OMS 10*g*R5 directly. You will have to install Grid Control 10*g*R1 on Unix platform or 10*g*R2 on Windows and then upgrade by applying the 10*g*R5 (10.2.0.5) patchset.

This book primarily covers 10*g*R5 features and hence, we recommend that you install this version. In order to install 10.2.0.5, you will need to download 10*g*R1 and the 10.2.0.5 patchset.

Both these binaries are large files and you will need around 15 GB of storage space to store the downloaded ZIP files, unzipped version of binaries, and actual installed binaries for the OMS, and the repository and storage space for the repository.

Installing OMS and repository

In this section, we will present you with some guidelines that you can use along with the install guide. We are assuming that you are installing Grid Control for the first time for a learning or testing purpose. Hence, we will focus on the simple install type where both OMS and Repository are installed on the same machine. Also, we assume that you will choose a new database for the management repository. This is the fastest way to install Grid Control. This will install database software and create the repository database.

Installing Grid Control 10*g*R1 or 10*g*R2

To get started with the install of Grid Control 10*g*R5, you will have to install 10*g*R1 on Linux 32 or 10*g*R2 on the Windows environment. Make sure that you have downloaded the binaries to your server. Let us assume that you are installing on a Linux 32 machine.

You can start Oracle Universal Installer by running the `runInstaller` (or `setup.exe` on Microsoft Windows) from the top-level directory of the software binaries.

The installer verifies the pre-requisites (O/S version, patch level, memory, and so on) when they get invoked. Some of the pre-requisite checks may fail and the installer may ask you to proceed or cancel the install.

As you proceed with the install, you will be prompted to choose the install type. For simplicity and for testing/training purposes we recommend that you choose the **Enterprise Manager 10g Grid Control Using a New Database** option, as shown in the following screenshot:

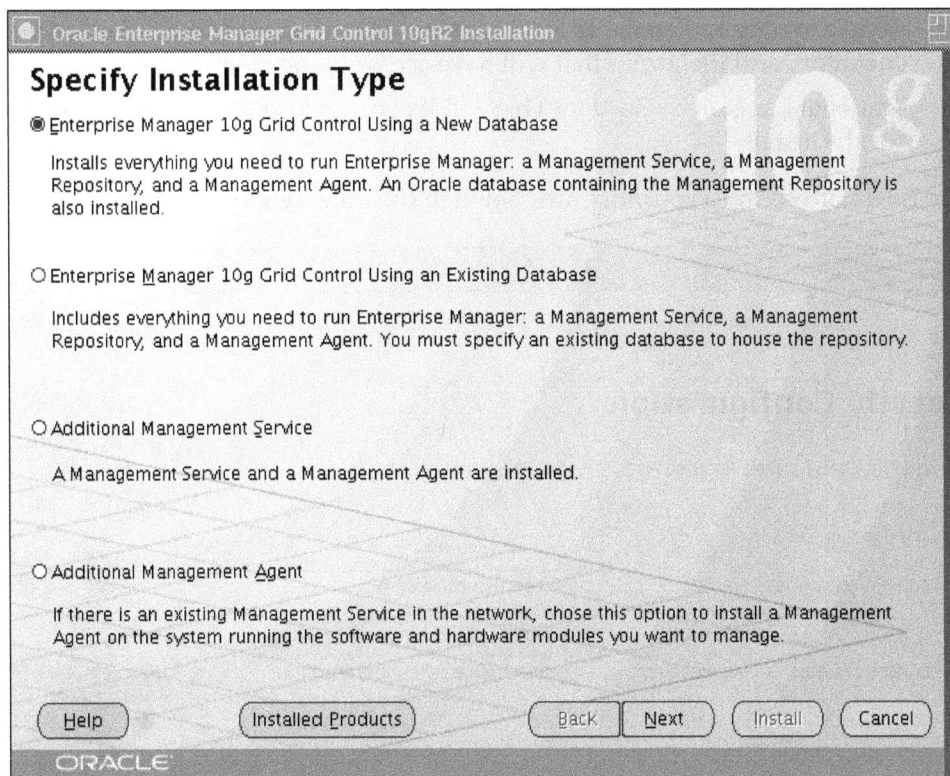

After this screen you will be prompted to enter the following information in three subsequent screens:

- Install location: This will contain directories where the OMS and repository database will get installed
- Oracle Inventory details: This will contain the directory to store the Oracle Inventory and the group that will have access to the Oracle Inventory
- National Language selection: This will let you choose the language to be used for the install

Database details for the repository are shown in the following screenshot:

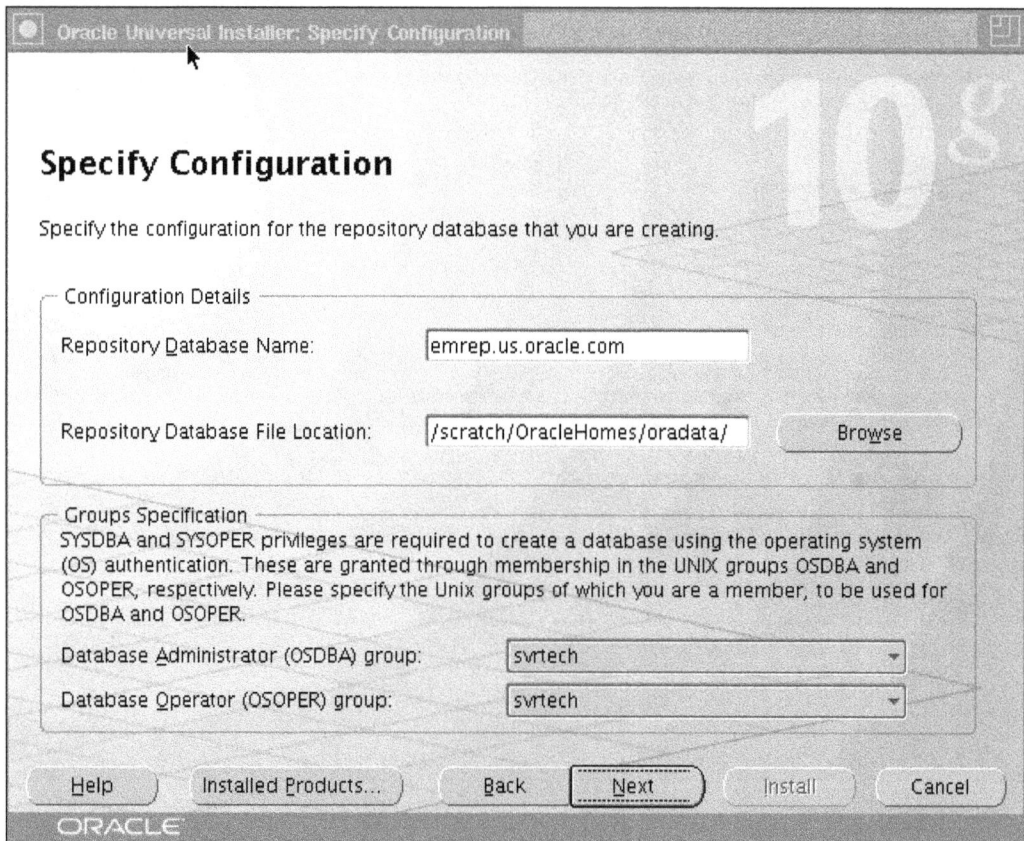

You will also be asked to provide credentials for the database repository and super user (sysman) for the OMS, as shown in the following screenshot:

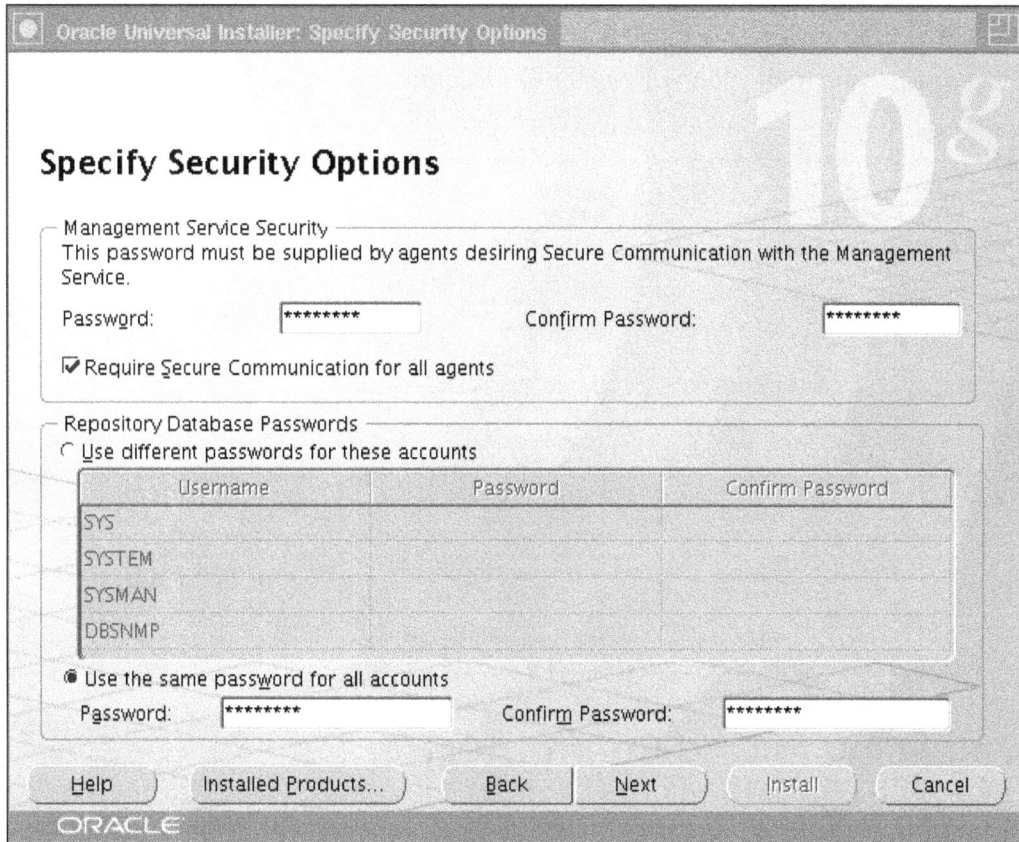

Make sure that you make a note of these passwords as you will need them in the future, to logon to the OMS or to manage the repository database.

The installer will first install the binaries and then run the Configuration Wizard to configure the OMS and the repository database. Before the Configuration Assistants are run, the installer will prompt you to run some configuration scripts and you need administration or (root) privileges to run these scripts. The Configuration Wizard will fail if you do not run these scripts.

After the install is successfully completed, the installer will provide you with the URL for the management console.

The default http port for the OMS is `4889`, and you can access Grid Control by using the URL in the following format `http://hostname:port/em`. You will have to enter **SYSMAN** as your user ID and the password that you entered during the install process.

After a successful login, you will see the Grid Control, as in the following screenshot:

Upgrading to Grid Control 10*g*R5

Oracle Enterprise Manager Grid Control 10*g*R5 is the latest version available and includes several middleware management features. As mentioned, we really recommend that you upgrade to 10*g*R5 to make the most of the benefits. You can download the 10*g*R5 patch set from Oracle Technology Network. Follow the instructions in the 10*g*R5 Release Notes for your platform. The patch installer will upgrade your OMS and the repository database to 10*g*R5.

Installing Management Agent

You can either upgrade your existing Agent to 10gR5 or download 10gR5 Agent and install it on your target machine. Unlike the OMS, the agent does not require you to first install 10gR1. You can directly install the 10gR5 Agent. There are several ways to install the Agent, yet for simplicity, the OUI method is recommended. You will have to select the right option as shown:

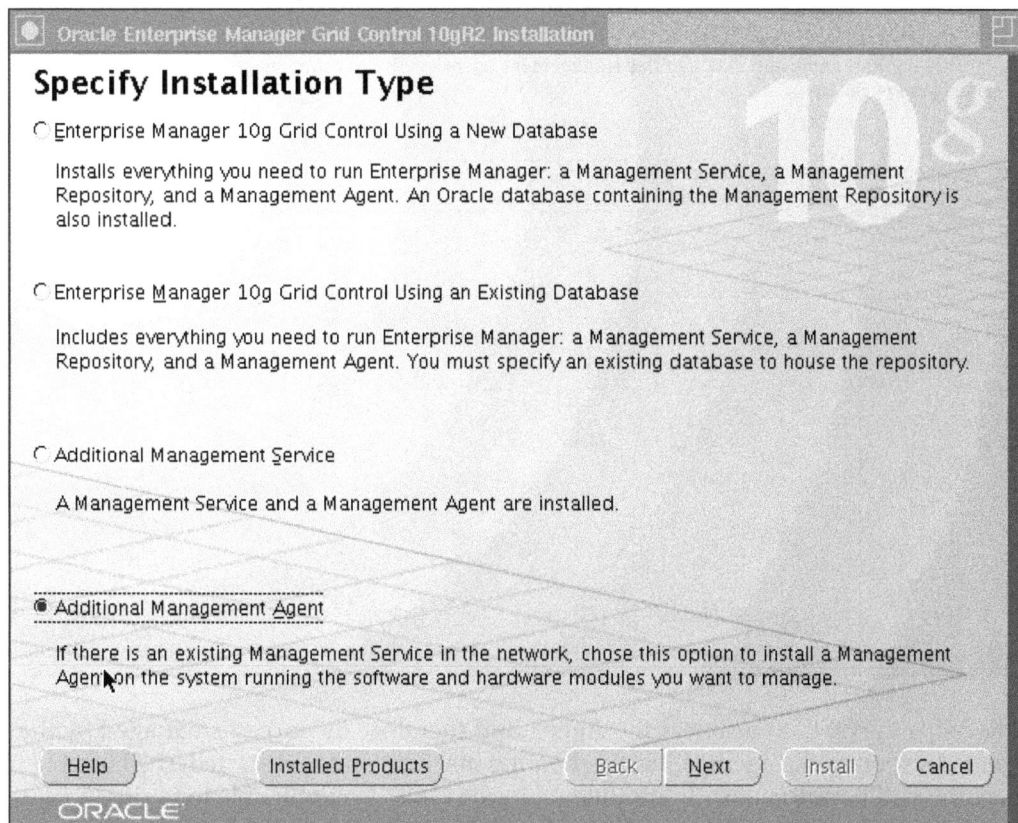

The most important step in the Agent install is **wiring** or pointing your Agent to your OMS as in the following screenshot:

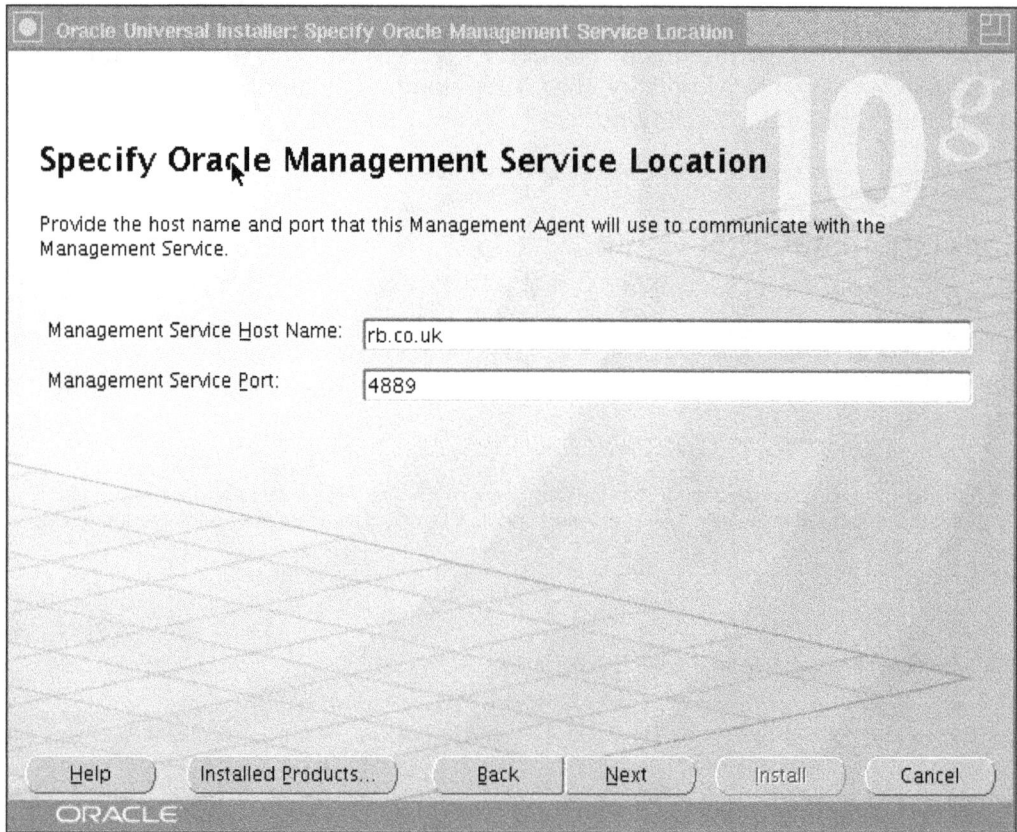

This helps the OMS to discover the Agent, and therefore the targets, managed by the agent. As soon as the agent is installed on the machine and it is started, the target machine will be automatically discovered in the OMS. You will able to verify that simply by logging into Enterprise Manager Grid Control and clicking on targets. We will discuss this further in Chapter 4, *Managing Oracle WebLogic Server*, when we discover an Oracle WebLogic Server.

Starting and stopping Grid Control

Now that we have completed the installation of Oracle Enterprise Manager Grid Control, we will discuss how to start and stop the various components. For a more detailed explanation of these commands or more detailed options, we recommend that you follow the *Oracle Enterprise Manager 10g Grid Control Advanced Configuration Guide*.

Starting and stopping OMS

Before logging in to Oracle Enterprise Manager Grid Control you will have to start the OMS and ensure that you are in the `$OMS_HOME/bin` directory to execute these commands. `$OMS_HOME` is the directory where you have installed OMS. However, if you are using Microsoft Windows then you can start the Windows Service for OMS.

- To automatically start the OMS and the underlying application server processes, you will have to execute the following command:

  ```
  emctl start oms
  ```

- You will see the following message:

  ```
  Oracle Enterprise Manager 10g Release 5 Grid Control
  Copyright (c) 1996, 2009 Oracle Corporation.  All rights reserved.
  opmnctl: opmn started
  Starting HTTP Server ...
  Starting Oracle Management Server ...
  Checking Oracle Management Server Status ...
  Oracle Management Server is Up.
  ```

- To check the status of the OMS, you will have to use the following command:

  ```
  emctl status oms
  ```

- To stop the OMS, you will use:

  ```
  emctl stop oms
  ```

Although starting the OMS automatically starts the underlying Oracle Application Server, it is worth knowing the commands to start, stop, and check the status of the underlying server that powers the OMS.

Ensure that you are in `$OMS_HOME/oms/bin` when you execute these commands.

- You can start the Application Server by entering the following code:

  ```
  opmnctl startall
  ```

- To check the status of Application Server, you can use the command:

  ```
  opmnctl status
  ```

- You can stop the Application Server by executing:

  ```
  opmnctl stopall
  ```

> Note that the OMS is not started automatically when you reboot a Linux/UNIX machine. However, it is automatically restarted on a Windows machine.

Starting and stopping the repository database

As discussed earlier, the Oracle Management Repository is an Oracle database that stores information about the managed targets. You may need to start/stop the repository database. If you are using Windows then you can start/stop the Windows service to start/stop the DB instance.

However, here are the commands to start the repository database in a UNIX environment:

```
setenv ORACLE_HOME /scratch/OracleHomes/db10g
setenv ORACLE_SID emrep
setenv PATH $ORACLE_HOME/bin:$PATH
sqlplus /nolog
SQL*Plus: Release 10.1.0.4.0 - Production on Mon Apr 20 14:28:37 2009
Copyright (c) 1982, 2005, Oracle.  All rights reserved.
SQL> connect sys as sysoper
Enter password:
Connected to an idle instance.
SQL> startup
```

The Oracle database is automatically restarted when you reboot the host machine; you do not have to restart the database repository.

Starting and stopping the Agent

Finally, we will discuss how to start/stop the Agent, and how to verify whether the Agent is responding properly. In UNIX environments, you will have to start the Agent after the host machine is rebooted. In a Windows environment, the Agent is a Windows service and will be started automatically.

- To start the Agent, you have to use the following commands:

  ```
  emctl start agent
  ```

- To stop the Agent:

  ```
  emctl stop agent
  ```

- To verify the health of the Agent

  ```
  emctl status agent
  ```

Summary

By exploring the various stages of installing Oracle Enterprise Manager Grid Control, we should now be aware of the following:

- Where to go to download Oracle Enterprise Manager 10*g* Grid Control and the installation procedure for each component

- That installation with the new database is the simplest and fastest way to get started with EM Grid Control

- How to execute basic commands to start/stop and check the status of the different components of Oracle Enterprise Manager Grid Control Control

In the next chapter, we will be discussing basic concepts in enterprise applications and systems management. You will learn more about targets modeling and discovery. You will learn more about how you can be proactive by implementing alerts and event notification mechanisms and service level monitoring. Also we will introduce you to how you can automate mundane administration tasks such as jobs, provisioning, and configuration management. So tighten your seat belt while we take you on the exciting ride of management concepts!

3
Enterprise Manager Key Concepts and Subsystems

Generally enterprise software is composed of many technical and functional subsystems. Many of the technical and functional subsystems need to be tweaked or customized according to the needs of a particular enterprise. Good enterprise software is one that provides useful out-of-the-box features that need minimal or no customizations of the subsystems, and at the same time provides flexibility for customizations.

Most often we see that, while using enterprise software, System Administrators discover an un-documented feature, or use an existing feature or a subsystem in an innovative way. This helps to get better returns on the investment made on the enterprise software. Hence, it's very important that the System Administrators and IT Managers are aware of major processes and subsystems in any given enterprise software.

In this chapter, we'll learn about major processes and subsystems of Enterprise Manager Grid Control, and the concepts behind those subsystems.

The subsystems that we'll be covering in this chapter are as follows:

- Target
- Monitoring
- Configuration Management
- Jobs
- Notification
- Provisioning
- Service Level Management
- Information publishing

Target

As seen in Chapter 1, the term 'target' refers to an entity that is managed via Enterprise Manager Grid Control. Target is the most important entity in Enterprise Manager Grid Control. All other processes and subsystems revolve around the target subsystem. For each target there is a model of the target that is saved in the Enterprise Manager Repository. In this book, we will use the terms target and target model interchangeably.

Major building blocks of the target subsystem are:

Target definition

All targets are organized into different categories, just like the actual entity that they represent, for example there is WebLogic Server target, Oracle Database target, and so on. These categories are called target types.

For each target type there is a definition in XML format that is available with the agent as well as with the repository. This definition includes:

- Target Attributes: There are some attributes that are common across all target types, and there are some attributes specific to a particular target type. The example of a common attribute is the target name, which uniquely identifies a managed entity. The example of a target type specific attribute is the name of a WebLogic Domain for a WebLogic Server target. Some of the attributes provide connection details for connecting to the monitored entity, such as the WebLogic Domain host and port. Some other attributes contain authentication information to authenticate and connect to the monitored entity.

- Target associations: Target type definition includes the association between related targets, for example an OC4J target will have its association defined with a corresponding Oracle Application Server.

- Target Metrics: This includes all the metrics that need to be collected for a given target and the source for those metrics. We'll cover this in greater detail in the Metrics subsystem.

Every target that is managed through the EM belongs to one, and only one, target type category. For any new entity that needs to be managed by the Enterprise Manager, an instance of appropriate target type is created and persisted in the repository.

Out-of-the-box Enterprise Manager provides the definition for most common target types such as the Host, Oracle Database, Oracle WebLogic Server, Seibel suite, SQLServer, SAP, .NET platform, IBM Websphere application server, Jboss application server, MQSeries, and so on. For a complete list of out-of-the-box targets please refer to the Oracle website.

Now that we have a good idea about the target definition, it's time we get to know more about the target lifecycle.

Target lifecycle

As the target is very central to the Enterprise Manager—it's very important that we understand each stage in the target life cycle.

Please note that not all the stages of the lifecycle may be needed for each target. However, to proceed further we need to understand each step in the target lifecycle. Enterprise Manager automates many of these stages, so in a real life scenario many of these steps may be transparent to the user. For example, Discovery and Configuration for monitoring stages are completely automated for the Oracle Application Server.

Discovery of a target

Discovery is the first step in the target lifecycle. Discovery is a process that finds the entities that need to be managed, builds the required target model for those entities, and persists the model in the management repository. For example, the discovery process executed on a Linux server learns that there are OC4J containers on that server, it builds target models for the OC4Js and the Linux server, and it persists the target models in the repository.

The agent has various discovery scripts and those scripts are used to identify various target types. Besides discovery, these scripts build a model for the discovered target and fill in all of the attributes for that target. We learnt about target attributes in the previous section.

Some discovery scripts are executed automatically as a part of the agent installation and therefore, no user inputs are needed for discovery. For example, a discovery script for the Oracle Application Server is automatically triggered when an agent is installed. On the other hand, there are some discovery scripts where the user needs to provide some input parameters. An example for this is the WebLogic server, where the user needs to provide the port number of the WebLogic Administration Server and credentials to authenticate and connect to it. The Enterprise Manager console provides interface for such discovery.

Discovery of targets can happen in two modes—local mode and remote mode. In local mode, the agent is running locally on the same host as the target. In remote discovery mode, the agent can be running on a different host. All of the targets can be discovered in local mode and there are some targets that can be discovered in remote mode. For example, discovery of WebLogic servers can happen in local as well as remote mode.

> One important point to note is that the agent that discovered the target does the monitoring of that target. For example, if a WebLogic Server target is discovered through a remote agent it gets monitored through *that same* remote agent.

The next screenshot shows the screen where the user needs to provide inputs for the WebLogic discovery:

Configuration for monitoring

After discovery the target needs to be configured for monitoring. The user will need to provide some parameters for the agent to use to connect to the target and get the metrics. These parameters include monitoring credentials, host, and port information, using which, the agent can connect to the target to fetch the metrics. The Enterprise Manager uses these parameters to connect, authenticate, and collect metrics from the targets. For example, to monitor an Oracle database the end user needs to provide the user ID and password, which can be used for authentication when collecting performance metrics using SNMP protocol.

Enterprise Manager Console provides an interface for configuring these parameters.

For some targets such as Application server, this step is not needed, as all the metrics can be fetched anonymously. For some other targets such as Oracle BPEL Process Manager, this step is needed only for detailed metrics; basic metrics are available without any monitoring configuration, but for advanced metrics monitoring, credentials needs to be provided by the end user. In this case, monitoring credentials are the user ID and password, used to authenticate when connecting to BPEL Process Manager for collecting performance metrics.

Updates to a target

Over a period of time, some target properties, attributes, and associations with other targets change — the EM target model that represents the target should be updated to reflect the changes. It is very important that end-users see the correct model from Enterprise Manager to ensure that all targets are monitored correctly. For example, in a given WebLogic Cluster, if a new WebLogic Server is added and an existing WebLogic Server is removed — Enterprise Manager's target model needs to reflect that. Or, if credentials to connect to WebLogic Admin Server are changed — the target model should be updated with new credentials. The Enterprise Manager console provides UI interface to update such properties.

If the target model is not updated there is a risk that some entity may not be monitored, for example if a new WebLogic server is added but the target model of domain is not updated, the new WebLogic server will not be monitored.

Stopping monitoring of a target

Each IT resource has some maintenance window or planned 'down-time'. During such time it's desirable to stop monitoring a target and collecting metrics for that resource. This can be achieved by putting that target into a blackout state. In a blackout state, agents do not collect monitoring data for a target and they do not generate alerts. After the maintenance activity is over, the blackout can be cleared from a target and routine monitoring can start again. Enterprise Manager Console provides an interface for creating and removing blackout state for one or more targets.

Monitoring

Enterprise Manager performs round-the-clock monitoring of targets by collecting the performance data. Unmanned monitoring is one of the key features of Enterprise Manager Grid Control. Monitoring subsystem is a crucial piece in unmanned monitoring of targets. Let's learn about monitoring subsystem.

We will now see the major building blocks of the monitoring subsystem in greater detail.

Fetchlets

A managed resource can expose performance indicators through various interfaces like JMX, SNMP, and so on. For example, WebLogic Server performance indicators are exposed through a JMX interface. Enterprise Manager provides executables that can access performance data from most of the standard interfaces. These executables are called **fetchlets**. There is one fetchlet for each data access mechanism. Some useful fetchlets are SNMP, JMX, and URLXML fetchlets, which can be used to access data from SNMP interface; JMX interface, and URL interfaces respectively.

For a complete list of available fetchlets, please refer to the Enterprise Manager documentation.

Metrics definition

Metrics is the performance data that is collected from each target at fixed intervals and can also be collected on demand. The metrics definition for a target type defines all performance indicators that need to be collected and what fetchlet should be used to collect those indicators. This is defined in a template file. This template file is very important and we'll be referring to this file by the term **target metadata**.

For a given target type, the collection frequency of the metrics is defined in another template and we refer to that as a **target collection** file.

Metric collection and aggregation

To monitor performance indicators of a given target, metrics are collected by an agent, as per the definition in the target metadata file, and are collected as per the frequency defined in the target collection file.

After collection, the data is kept at a staging location; from there it is uploaded into the repository at fixed intervals. All performance metric data is persisted in the repository and can be used to analyze a system's performance over a period of time. For coarse views, these metrics are rolled up every hour and every 24 hours. Data aggregated every hour is kept for 31 days and data aggregated for 24 hours is kept for 365 days. Raw data received from the agent is only kept for seven days. Data purge policies can be configured to suit user needs.

The following screenshot shows one such example, detailing the average execution for one of the web services deployed on a WebLogic Server. From this view, the user can see real-time data or historical data.

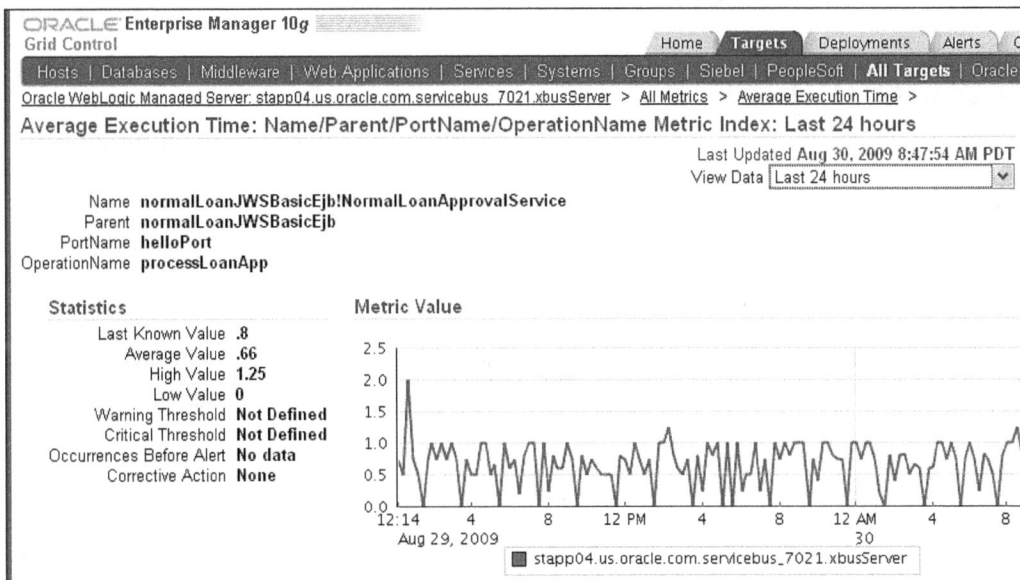

Metric alerts

Enterprise Manager can use metric data that is persisted in the repository in two ways. Firstly, the user can see and analyze data over a period of time. Secondly, any time a particular data value crosses acceptable limits; Enterprise Manager can keep track of such instances.

The user can define thresholds to in turn define the acceptable limits of performance metrics. Enterprise Manager supports two levels of thresholds for the metrics — warning and critical threshold. For example, a CPU % usage metric can have 70% as warning and 90% as critical threshold. Enterprise Manager provides default thresholds for many metrics that the user can customize. For metrics where no thresholds are defined, the users can define them.

Whenever a metric data value crosses the threshold, an alert is generated and stored in the Management repository. If a warning threshold is violated; a warning alert is generated, and if a critical threshold is violated; a critical alert is generated. These alerts can be used for generating some form of notification.

Monitoring templates

Monitoring template is a construction, using which, one can define the thresholds for a target type, and can apply this template to multiple targets of the same type. When there are multiple targets of same type, setting thresholds for all such targets can be a tedious task. Monitoring templates can make it simpler by providing one central place to define thresholds for all targets of the same type.

System Administrator can also define default-monitoring template for a given target type. Once a template is marked as default for a target type, all new targets of the same type will automatically get the same thresholds as defined in the template.

> Recommendation: Define default-monitoring template for all target types in the datacenter and add metric thresholds to the template. This will ensure that all targets of the same type will have the same thresholds.

Configuration management

Enterprise Manager collects configuration data of targets to provide configuration management support. For collection of configuration data, Enterprise Manager uses the same mechanism as performance metrics, that is; all the configuration to be collected and mechanisms to collect are defined in **target metadata**, and frequency of configuration collection is defined in **target collection**. Agent collects configuration data and uploads it into the repository.

Though the data collection mechanism is the same for performance and configuration data, the usage of configuration data is very different from the usage of performance data. Configuration data is used for ensuring configuration compliance and configuration change tracking.

Let us look into building blocks that provide configuration compliance and change tracking.

Policy

Enterprise Manager Grid Control provides **policy** subsystem for configuration and security compliance.

Policy is a construct to define configurations and security recommendations for a given target type. For example, a security policy for OC4J recommends that all data sources should not have passwords in clear text; a configuration policy for WebLogic server recommends that the server should be running in production mode. The Enterprise Manager uses these policies to periodically check for conformance across multiple targets in a given datacenter.

Enterprise Manager comes with lots of out-of-the-box policies and users can customize those policies and define new policies; Enterprise Manager Console provides interface to customize or define new policies.

Policies are defined for a target type and can be enforced for all targets of a given type or only for some targets of a given type. The end user can configure what policies need to be enforced for a given target. For example, if there is a policy for a host target type that mandates that only port 80 should be open on all servers—the System Administrator may decide not to enforce that policy for a new server that is used for developmental activity.

Each policy definition is associated with a severity level. There are three severity levels, which are **Informational**, **Warning**, and **Critical**. Enterprise Manager evaluates these policies against the configuration data that is collected from the targets. Any violation of these policies is saved in the repository and can be used for sending out notifications.

We learnt in an earlier section how monitoring template can be used to set thresholds across multiple same targets. Policies can also be added to a monitoring template along with a metric threshold.

> Recommendation: Define default-monitoring template for all target types in datacenter and add policies to the default template. This will ensure that all targets of the same type have the same configuration and security compliance.

Configuration snapshot

Configuration snapshot of a target is a set of all configuration parameters at one point in time. Enterprise Manager keeps all related configuration for a target as configuration snapshot.

Enterprise Manager keeps a track of configuration changes by using configuration snapshots. When uploading a new configuration snapshot, it compares the new configuration snapshot with the existing snapshot, and the changes are saved separately in the repository.

Besides keeping track of changes, configuration snapshot can be used to compare the configuration of one target with multiple targets of the same type.

Comparing configurations is a critical part of any IT operations and troubleshooting. It is common to find that an application will work in one environment and not work in another environment. The fastest way to troubleshoot this is to compare the configuration between two environments, but configuration comparison can be a dreary job and issues are likely to be missed by the human eye, as configuration is spread out in multiple files across servers.

The following screenshot shows one such comparison of configuration snapshots of two WebLogic servers, where you can see the difference in heap parameters:

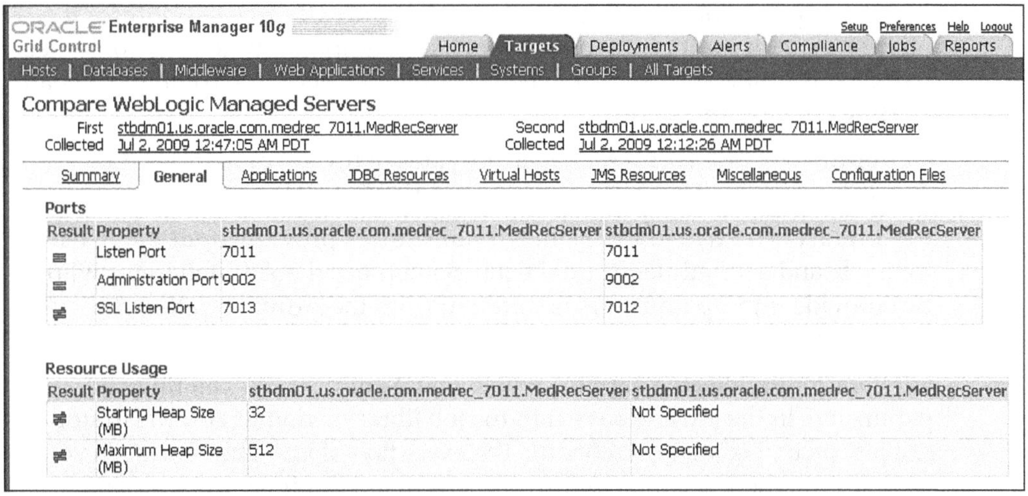

Job

Job system of Enterprise Manager provides support for scheduling the operations and executing an operation as per the schedule. Enterprise Manager provides a framework where a unit of work to be done is defined as a **job**, these jobs can be scheduled to run on multiple targets and the outcome of that is persisted in the repository. For the scheduling of a job, Enterprise Manager console provides an interface, using which the user can specify the parameters to be passed on to the job and the targets where the job needs to be executed.

For example, the Database backup job contains all the details on how to perform database backup. Enterprise Manager console provides an interface to select on which database this operation needs to be run, what is the backup mode (online, offline), and what is the schedule to run this job.

Success or failure of the job execution can also be sent out as a notification.

Major building blocks of job system are as follows:

- **Job Definition**: Job definition contains the parameters required by the job and the sequence of steps to be performed. It provides rich support for the orchestration of multiple steps in a job, like conditionally running some steps based on the outcome of earlier steps, waiting for one step to complete before starting the next and so on.

  Out-of-the-box Enterprise Manager provides many job definitions, like Oracle Application Server backup, WebLogic start/stop, and so on.

- **Job Library**: To run a job, System Administrators provide input parameters for a job, and a schedule to run the job. Sometimes the Administrator who can provide input parameters is different from the Administrator who schedules the job.

  Job library provides the support where one Administrator can fill in all parameters in the job and save it in the job library; another Administrator can just pick up a job and schedule the execution of job. This feature is very useful when there are multiple levels of System Administrators, super Administrators can define the jobs parameters and save in the job library, and Operators can execute/schedule the jobs.

- **Multi-tasking jobs**: Often, Administrators need to schedule multiple jobs in a particular sequence. Enterprise Manager provides "Multi-task job", using this, the Administrator can combine multiple jobs and run them as one job. Enterprise Manager console UI provides an interface for defining multi-task jobs where the user can define what jobs need to be run and in what order.

  Multi-task jobs can also be saved in job library.

Notification system

As we saw in the earlier sections, Enterprise Manager collects monitoring and configuration information round-the-clock, and schedules the job at a specified time. All of these activities continue to happen even when nobody is actively looking at Enterprise Manager. Whenever required, System Administrators can see the history of metric alert, policy violation or job results. But there are some alerts, policy violations, or job results that need immediate attention. Enterprise Manager provides notification framework, and by using this, notifications for alerts, policy violations, and job failures can be sent out.

Major building blocks of Notification system are:

- Notification Methods

  Enterprise Manager provides support for various notification methods that include SNMP trap, emails, and so on. Enterprise Manager console provides an interface for configuring the notification methods. For example, console provides an interface to configure SNMP notifications, where the user can provide details like SNMP community, SNMP host, SNMP port, and so on.

- Notification Rules

  System Administrator should get paged only for the critical resources and only for the critical performance indicators or policy violations. Enterprise Manager provides support for Notification rules AND using that, Administrators can define for what type of events a notification should be sent out and which notification method should be used.

Provisioning

The provisioning subsystem provides support for *automating* provisioning of software on multiple targets. Using provisioning subsystem, the System Administrator can do initial provisioning of software, for example provisioning of Linux operating system and RAC database on a new host. Provisioning system also provides support for provisioning software from a reference installation, where Enterprise Manager can clone software from reference environment to new environment. For example, if a database instance is running on host1, Enterprise Manager can provision a new database instance on host2 by cloning the database instance on host1.

Major building blocks of provisioning subsystem are:

Deployment procedures

Deployment procedures define the steps that need to be executed to achieve a particular objective. For example, the deployment procedure for J2EE server installation defines all of the steps that need to be executed to install a J2EE server. The provisioning subsystem provides out-of-the-box deployment procedures for most common provisioning operations, it also provides support to customize existing deployment procedures or to define a new deployment procedure.

Provisioning subsystem also provides support for scheduling and executing these deployment procedures. Enterprise Manager console provides an interface for scheduling deployment procedure and monitoring the status of scheduled deployment procedure.

Software library

Software Library is a central repository to keep installable software and gold images of software. Provisioning framework uses Software Library for storing gold images and provisioning new software from the images. For example, the provisioning subsystem can build a gold image from an existing Linux setup and store it in the software library. At some later point in time the provisioning subsystem can use the stored gold image to provision a new Linux host.

Software library also provides support for versioning, maturity levels (beta, production) for installable software and gold images. Enterprise Manager Console provides interface to browse the contents of software library, and update the version, maturity level of software, and gold images.

Service Level Management

We saw in earlier sections that using target subsystem and monitoring subsystem we can monitor any resource in a datacenter. We can see the availability of any IT resource by looking at the history of status metrics. In the traditional approach, the history of status metric is good enough to measure system performance.

In most of the datacenters today, IT systems performance is measured by **Service Level Agreements (SLA)**. SLA includes the performance indicators to be used, thresholds for the performance indicators, and expected availability of the IT resource in terms of the performance indicators. For example, one sample SLA for a Linux host includes CPU usage and IO rate as performance indicator; it also includes acceptable thresholds for CPU and IO rate. This SLA measures the availability of Linux servers in terms of CPU usage and IO rate.

Enterprise Manager provides support for defining and monitoring service level agreements. It provides necessary backend support and console UI, using that, SLA can be defined and stored in the repository. It also provides a console interface to monitor SLA performance over a period of time.

The next screenshot shows the interface for defining the SLAs. You can see that a user can select the performance indicators to be included in SLA definition.

Edit Service Level Rule

Service Level is a measure of service quality. Service Level is calculated as percentage of time during business hours a service meets specified availability and performance criteria. The actual Service Level will be calculated for different time periods, but the same criteria will apply for all these time periods.   (Cancel) (OK)

Expected Service Level

Specify the percentage of time during business hours that you expect your service to meet the availability and performance criteria described below.

Expected Service Level [85.0]

Actual Service Level

| Business Hours | | | Availability Criteria |

Business Hours

Days
☑ Monday ☑ Tuesday ☑ Wednesday
☑ Thursday ☑ Friday ☐ Saturday
☐ Sunday

Start Time [00 ▾] : [00 ▾]   End Time [24 ▾] : [00 ▾]

Service Time Zone **(UTC+00:00) (GMT)**

Availability Criteria

For Service Level calculations, specify the availability states during which the Service will be considered UP.

☑ Up   ☐ Under Blackout

☑ Unknown (Pending, Agent Unreachable, Metric Error)

Performance Criteria

Optionally select performance metrics that will be evaluated when computing Service Level. A critical alert on any of the selected metrics will count as a Service Level violation.

Available Performance Metrics

Selected Performance Metrics

> Move
>> Move All
< Remove

CPU Utilization (%)
Free Memory (%)

Information publishing

There is lot of useful data stored in the enterprise repository; the information-publishing system provides a means to publish this data in various useful formats. Report is a construct that is used for publishing data from the Enterprise Management repository.

Enterprise Manager provides a lot of out-of-the-box reports, that the user can customize or use as-is. For example, a report on all policy violations, or a report on all metric alerts, or a report on all configuration changes. Besides these reports, the user can create new reports through the Enterprise Manager console.

We will now learn about the major building blocks for Information Publishing System.

Report definition

Report definition contains details like what data should be shown, how to get that data, layout of the report, parameters for the report, and at what frequency the report should be generated. For example, a particular report provides details about the performance of a BPEL process, the data for this report is shown in tabular format and one pie chart and this report is generated every 24 hours, this report is also emailed out to some specific email ids.

Report element

Report elements are reusable components that users can include in the report definition when defining new reports. For example "Table from SQL" element can be used to extract data from repository, and to use this element the user needs to provide a query. At runtime this query is executed against the repository and the data is inserted into the report.

Information publishing system provides support for scheduling of the reports, using that the user can define a schedule from the console to generate the reports. Generated reports are saved in the repository. Also, these reports can be sent out by emails.

Summary

In this chapter, we learnt about the key subsystems of Enterprise Manager Grid Control. We learnt about the major building blocks for each of the subsystems. Here are the key takeaways from this chapter.

- Users should be aware of subsystems of enterprise software.

- Target subsystem provides support for target type definition and target lifecycle. Target type definition contains attributes, metric definition, and associations with other targets.

- Monitoring subsystem provides support for collecting metrics, aggregating metrics, and raising alerts.

- Configuration management provides support for policy definitions and conformance of policies in datacenter; any non-conformance is raised as policy violation.

- As best practice, you should use monitoring templates to define the metrics threshold and policies across targets.

- Job system provides scheduling mechanism. Job library provides ready-run jobs where the parameters are already filled in and any operator can execute the jobs. You can use Multi-task jobs to chain multiple jobs and run them as one job.

- You can define the alerts, policy violations, and job statuses for which you want notifications to be sent out for.

- Provision subsystem can be used to provision software from installation media or reference installations.

- Service Level Agreements (SLA) can be defined and saved in the repository. Enterprise Manager provides a view of SLA performance over a period of time.

- You can use information publishing system to publish pre-defined reports or create your own reports. Enterprise Manager console provides GUI to define new reports. Reports can be scheduled, and all generated reports can be persisted in the repository. Additionally these reports can be sent out via email.

We have covered the key subsystems of Enterprise Manager Grid Control, so now we have a good insight into how these subsystems work and how we can customize them. It's time we apply this knowledge to see how Enterprise Manager manages middleware targets. In the next chapter we'll be learning about managing and monitoring Oracle WebLogic Server using the Enterprise Manager.

4
Managing Oracle WebLogic Server

Oracle WebLogic Server is the leading Java application server in the market. Oracle completed the acquisition of BEA Systems in June 2008. WebLogic Server was the flagship product offered by BEA systems and is used by many organizations to deploy their enterprise Java and SOA applications. In this chapter, you will learn about the following:

- Introduction to Oracle WebLogic Server and it's architecture
- Discovering WebLogic Server Domains
- Monitoring and configuration management of WebLogic Server Domains and applications, and service level management of applications running on WebLogic Server

Introducing WebLogic Server

WebLogic Server is a Java EE application server where you run enterprise Java applications. Most organizations want their production applications to be highly scalable and available. Hence, most often you will run more than one instance of WebLogic Server in your environment.

The following diagram depicts the architecture for a WebLogic Server Domain.

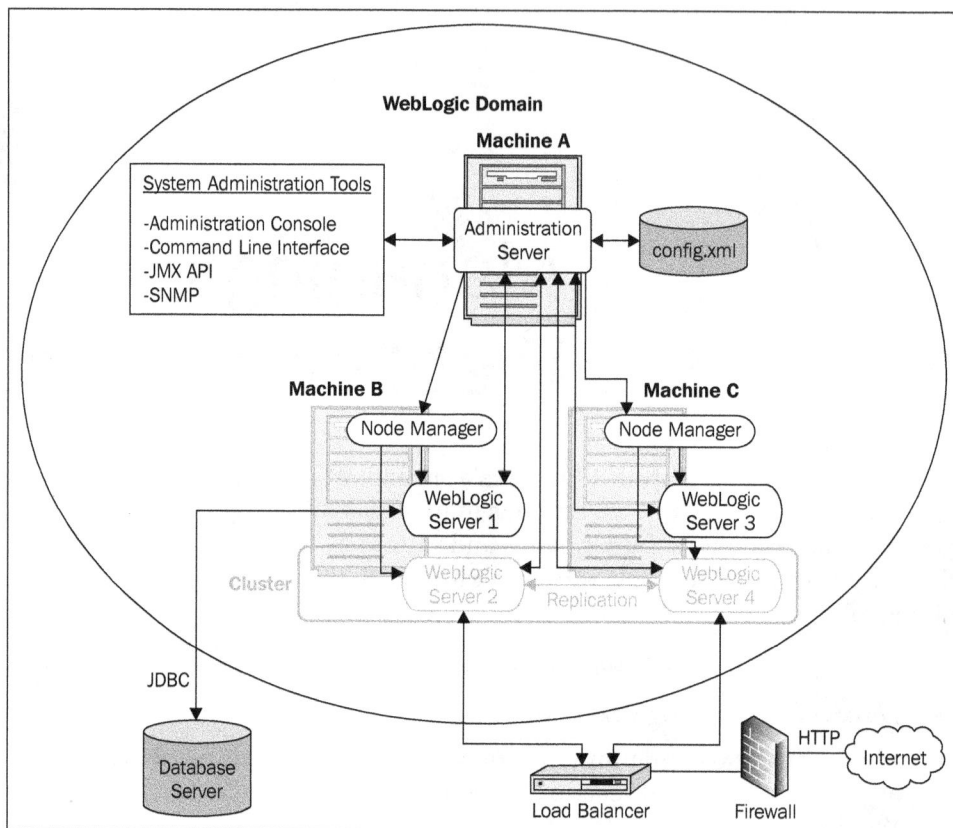

A WebLogic Server domain is a collection of WebLogic Servers that are managed together. A WebLogic Server Domain may consist of one Administration Server, one or more managed servers, one or more clusters, and one or more node managers. The Administration Server is used for administration purposes and has to be available for any configuration changes such as the deployment of applications. The Administration Server is a WebLogic Server instance that hosts the Administration Console and contact point for command line interface. You can deploy custom applications to the administration server like any other managed server, however, we do not recommend you do that.

An Oracle WebLogic Managed Server is a server instance that is managed as a part of a domain and not the Administration Server. A managed server is used for deploying customer applications. A managed server may be running on the same or a remote server machine where the Administration Server is running. The Administration Server manages the lifecycle of the managed server with node manager. A node manager is a separate server process that runs on a server machine to facilitate the administration of the managed servers.

A WebLogic Server Cluster consists of multiple Oracle WebLogic Managed Server instances running simultaneously and working together to provide increased scalability and reliability.

For more information about WebLogic Server please refer to WebLogic Server documentation at `http://download.oracle.com/docs/cd/E13160_01/wli/docs10gr3/index.html`.

> Oracle Enterprise Manager manages an Oracle WebLogic Server domain as a single entity. You can monitor multiple domains of WebLogic Server from a single instance of Oracle Enterprise manager Grid Control.

Supported versions

You can manage different versions of WebLogic Servers from a single install of Oracle Enterprise Manager Grid Control. Following is the support matrix for Oracle Enterprise Manager for Oracle WebLogic Server:

EM Version	WebLogic 10.3.x	WebLogic 10.0	WebLogic 9.x	WebLogic 8.1	WebLogic 7.x
10.2.0.5	Yes	Yes	Yes	Yes	Yes
10.2.0.4	No	Yes	Yes	Yes	Yes
10.2.0.3	No	No	Yes	Yes	Yes

Discovering WebLogic Server

A target such as WebLogic Server Domain has to be added into Enterprise Manager for management purposes. This process is called target discovery. As you remember from our discussion in Chapters 1 and 3, the agent facilitates the discovery and management of a target. Hence, you need an Oracle Management Agent to discover/monitor a WebLogic Server Domain. The agent talks to the Administration Server using Java Management Extension (JMX) API. The agent can either be in the same server host that the Administration Server is running on, or can be on a remote machine. We recommend that you use a local agent. You can monitor multiple WebLogic Server domains from a single agent. However, it is recommended that you do not monitor more than five domains or 30 managed servers using a single domain. Similarly, we recommend that you do not monitor different versions of WebLogic Servers using a single agent.

> The agent requires access to the WebLogic Server binaries for discovery and monitoring purposes. If you are using a remote discovery then you have to copy WebLogic JAR files such as `weblogic.jar` or `wlclient.jar` file from your WebLogic Server install to the server host where agent is running. If you are using a local agent then ensure the agent user has access to the WebLogic Server binaries (weblogic.jar) and the BEA_HOME environment variable is set if you are using UNIX/Linux environment.

Adding a new WebLogic Server Domain

Let us now discuss the steps required to discover or add a WebLogic Server Domain into Enterprise Manager Grid Control.

In order to discover a new WebLogic Domain from Grid Control follow these steps after logging into Grid Control as an administrator:

- Click on **Targets** on the top menu bar and select **Middleware** and you will see the current list of middleware targets. If you have not discovered any middleware then you will need the Oracle Application Server target on which the Enterprise Manager Grid Control runs on.

- From the drop-down list on the right, select Oracle WebLogic Server and click on Add and you will get the following screen:

Add Oracle WebLogic Server Domain: Host

In order to add a Oracle WebLogic Server Domain to Enterprise Manager, you must first specify details of the host on which the Oracle WebLogic Administration Server is running. If only one domain is found, the Select Domain step will be skipped.

∗ Administration Server Host	staec36.us.oracle.com
∗ Version	10.x
Port	7001
Trusted Keystore Filename	
	Specify the absolute path of the Trusted Keystore file name. This is required if the port is SSL enabled.
∗ Administration Server Username	weblogic
∗ Password	********
	☑ Save as Preferred Credentials.
	☐ Agent is running on a host other than the Administration Server.
Agent Host	
Administration Server Home Directory	
	Specify the absolute path of the directory where the weblogic.jar file is located.

☑ **TIP** The Administration Server credentials are used to collect metric data for this target, and will be stored as Monitoring Properties for the target. If you want to change the password, click the Monitoring Configuration link on the respective server home page.

Home | **Targets** | Deployments | Alerts | Compliance | Jobs | Reports | Setup | Preferences | Help | Logout

- Enter the relevant information such as the host machine name where WebLogic Administration Server is running, admin port, and WebLogic Server credentials.

  If the agent is running on the same machine then it automatically finds the WebLogic Server home if the BEA_HOME environment is set. If the Oracle Agent is located in a remote server then you have to supply agent details and the location where WebLogic Client libraries are located.

  Most people use the default WebLogic user to manage WebLogic Server. However, WebLogic Server provides role-based access control. You may be in a highly secured environment and you want to monitor your WebLogic Server domain with a low privileged user. EM Grid Control allows you to monitor WebLogic Servers with Monitors privilege.

  While discovering your WebLogic Server Domain, you can specify the low privileged username. Note, that the users in the Monitors Group do not have privileges to start/stop WebLogic Server instances and hence you will not be able to recycle managed servers from Grid Control.

- On the next page, you will be prompted to supply the host/machine credentials for the host where Oracle Agent is running. After supplying the host credentials and clicking Next, Enterprise Manager will find the managed servers and clusters in the domain and you can select the servers/clusters that you want to manage/monitor from EM.

- Finally, you will be prompted to confirm your selection. Once you confirm your selection, the WebLogic Domain with the servers and clusters will be discovered and you are good to go! You have to ensure that all managed servers and clusters that you plan to manage from Enterprise Manager are up and running during the discovery process. If a server is not started up then Enterprise Manager does not find during discovery process.

> Enterprise Manager does not automatically discover if any managed server is not up during discovery or newly added server/cluster. If there is a change in your domain then you have to refresh the domain using the **Refresh Domain** button in the **WebLogic Server Domain Home Page**.

Monitoring WebLogic Server

You can monitor both the availability and performance of WebLogic Server Domains from Enterprise Manager. You can view both real time and historical metrics of your WebLogic Server Domains. As we discussed earlier, WebLogic Server has three distinct entities such as WebLogic Server Domain, cluster and managed server. Each of these are modeled as separate targets in Enterprise Manager. Thus each domain, managed server and cluster has separate homepages, status, and so on.

Availability and state

You can monitor the status of WebLogic Server. WebLogic Server has several states such as RUNNING, ADMIN, SHUTDOWN, STARTING, and so on. However, an Enterprise Manager target can have only two statuses either UP or DOWN. In a production monitoring purpose it makes sense because your applications are unavailable when the WebLogic Server is in a state other than RUNNING. Enterprise Manager shows the status as UP only when the state of the WebLogic Server is RUNNING and if the server is in some other state such as ADMIN, STARTING, and so on, then Enterprise Manager reports the status as DOWN.

The clusters and domain are the collection of one and more managed servers and they do not have their own status. The status for the managed servers are aggregated and shown for clusters and domains. Hence if a domain has 5 managed servers and a cluster with 4 managed servers and the Administration Server, and one managed server is down, then the status of the domains will be reported as 4 Up 1 Down and 3 Up 1 Down. Similarly, other information such as metrics alerts and policy violations are all aggregated for the domain and clusters and shown in the Domain and Cluster Homepage.

You can use Enterprise Manager to view the historical availability status of your server, cluster, and so on. For example, the WebLogic Server homepage provides the availability status for the last 24 hours and you can click on the availability link to view the history for down time.

The default view shows the availability for the past 24 hours and you can customize by clicking the view data drop-down at the top of the page.

Performance monitoring

Enterprise Manager provides a variety of performance metrics for the WebLogic Server and applications. You can view both real time and historical performance metrics for resources such as Data Sources and JMS, or applications metrics such as EJB, Web services, JSP/Servlets, and so on. We will not bore you to death by telling you how to navigate pages to do this, but we will spend time on looking at how to proactively monitor for specific performance metrics and get notifications. A question may come to your mind, Enterprise Manager provides a lot of metrics (under the **All Metrics** page), but not all of these are exposed in the Graph. How do I create some custom graphs for using these metrics? You can do this by building a new service. We will also discuss the creation of service later in this chapter.

Event notifications and setting metric thresholds

In a production environment you want to be proactive and want to be alerted when a problem occurs or a metric threshold is reached. Many Administrators write scripts to check for thresholds at regular intervals and check them manually. Enterprise Manager helps to automate proactive monitoring. You may remember from our discussion on alerts in Chapter 3 that Enterprise Manager lets you set thresholds for metrics that you want to monitor, and it alerts you when the threshold is reached. For example, you are using JRockit JVM and you want to be alerted when the physical memory usage reaches a specific level such as 100MB, or you want to be alerted when the invocation time for any Servlets/JSPs is higher than your expectation level.

In order to setup a metric alert you have to follow these steps:

- Navigate to the **Home** page of your WebLogic Server.

- Click **Metric and Policy Settings** on the WebLogic Server **Home** page and you will get the follow screen. This will display the page that will show any existing metric threshold settings.

Metric	Comparison Operator	Warning Threshold	Critical Threshold	Corrective Actions	Collection Schedule
JRockit - Used Heap	>	60	100	None	Every 15 Minutes
JRockit - Used Physical Memory	>	60	120	None	Every 15 Minutes
Status			Down	None	Every 1 Minute

Oracle WebLogic Managed Server: staec36.us.oracle.com:medrec_7001:medreccluster:Server2 >
Metric and Policy Settings

Metric Thresholds | Policies

View [Metrics with thresholds]

TIP Empty Thresholds will disable alerts for that metric.

Metric Thresholds Links

- Change the **View** to **All Metrics** and then you will get the screen to set thresholds for new metrics. You can change the warning and critical thresholds of metrics that you want to monitor as follows and click **OK** and you will get a confirmation that the update was successful.

The alerts will be shown in the WebLogic Server homepage (under metric alert) when such an event occurs as shown in the following figure:

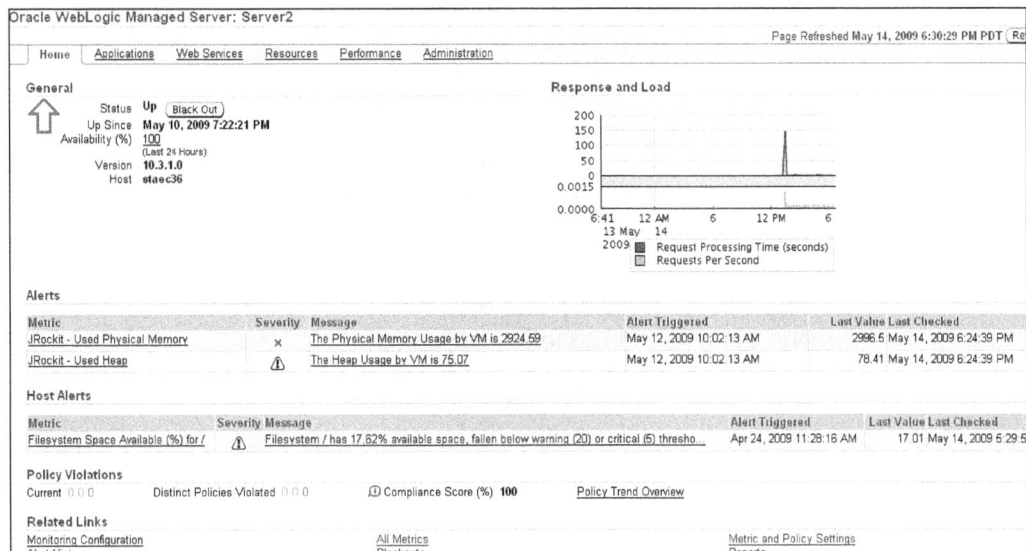

You can drill down a particular event by clicking on the alert text and you can see the details of the metric alert as follows:

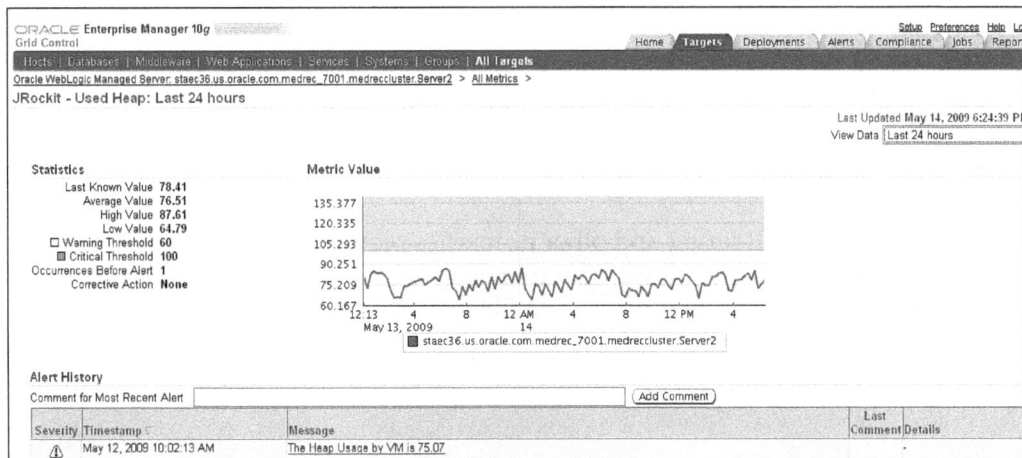

You can acknowledge and clear the event or add a comment from this page. Adding a comment or acknowledging an alert really helps when multiple administrators monitor the same set of WebLogic Servers. The other administrators know that you are investigating the problem.

Setting up notification methods

The real benefit for alert notification is that the management system notifies you when an event occurs. Enterprise Manager supports several notification mechanisms such as e-mail, web page, SNMP trab, running a corrective action job or even integration with ticketing systems such as Remedy or Siebel Helpdesk.

Let us dive down into how to setup a notification when an alert is raised. For example, you want to get an e-mail when an alert is raised.

You have to perform the following steps to set up e-mail notification:

- Click on **Setup** option at the top and then select the **Notifications Methods** on the left and you will get the following page:

- Enter the SMTP server and other properties required in your environment and click on **Apply**. If you want to make sure that you have entered the correct properties, click on **Test Mail Server** and you should get a test e-mail from Enterprise Manager.

Setting up e-mail preferences for admin user

In a typical enterprise there is more than one administrator sharing the same Enterprise Manager to manage their systems. Each administrator may have separate access and profiles. If you want to use Enterprise Manager to send e-mails to the right administrators you have to set e-mail preferences for the admin user.

Click on **Preferences** on the top and enter the e-mail address assigned for the admin account as shown next. You may have more than one e-mail address for an admin user.

Setting the notification rules

You do not want to get paged for every event and you want to customize when you want to get alerted. You have to set notification rules so let us learn how to do that:

- Click on **Rules** on the left and you will get the screen with all the notification rules as shown:

- We want to create a new notification rule for the alerts on WebLogic Server. Click on **Create** button and enter as details.

Change the target type to WebLogic Managed server and add the managed targets if you want the rule for specific WebLogic Server instances as follows:

Preferences

Create Notification Rule

| General | Availability | Metrics | Policies | Jobs | Actions |

* Name New WebLogicServer

Description

☑ Make Public
Allow other administrators to subscribe to this rule.

* Target Type Oracle WebLogic Managed Server ▼

⦿ Apply rule to all Oracle WebLogic Managed Server targets
◯ Apply rule to specified Oracle WebLogic Managed Server targets or groups containing Oracle WebLogic Managed Server targets

| General | Availability | Metrics | Policies | Jobs | Actions |

- Click on the **Availability** Tab and select the options when you want to be notified. For example you want to be notified when the Server goes down or the metric error is raised.

ORACLE Enterprise Manager 10g
Grid Control

Setup Preferences Help Lo

Home Targets Deployments Alerts Compliance Jobs Repor

Preferences

Create Notification Rule

Cancel

| General | Availability | Metrics | Policies | Jobs | Actions |

Select the availability states for which you would like to receive notifications. You will receive notifications when there is a transition from another state to the selected state.

☐ Up
☑ Down

Corrective Actions on Target Down
☐ Problem ☑ Succeeded
☐ Agent Unreachable
Agent and/or host may be down, or there are network problems between the Oracle Management Server and agent.
☐ Agent Unreachable Resolved
The agent is now reachable and monitoring targets. For non-agent targets, the target's current status will be included in the notification message.
☑ Metric Error Detected
An error occurred during the evaluation of target status.
☐ Metric Error Resolved
The error detected during the evaluation of target status was resolved.
☐ Blackout Started
☐ Blackout Ended

Additional Alert Criteria
Select additional criteria to have the rule apply to availability alerts that have been open for a certain time and have not been acknowledged. These additional criteria apply to Target Down, Agent Unreachable, Bla
Started and Metric Error Start availability alerts.

Additional alert selection criteria is not set. Add

| General | Availability | Metrics | Policies | Jobs | Actions |

Cancel

Click on **Metrics** tab and click on **Add** metrics and select the metrics you are interested in.

Be sure to select the severity states — **Critical/Warning/Clear** — for which you want to be notified.

After you confirm the metrics, you will see the list of metrics that you have selected for notification. Optionally, you can select a policy violation for notification. You can also select a job as the notification method. Once you confirm the notification rule, it will be created!

If an alert occurs it will come directly to your inbox. So, if you set up an e-mail account on your Blackberry or iPhone, you will always be on top of the issues.

Enterprise Manager also allows you to set up a notification schedule and blackouts. You may remember from our discussion earlier, that blackout is a time when you do not want to get notified when an alert is raised. For example, you take your WebLogic Servers down during the weekends and you probably do not want to cause unnecessary panic during that period by false alerts. We leave you to explore those as an exercise!

Jobs and corrective action

Many enterprise systems and applications require batch jobs. For example, you may have a requirement to restart your WebLogic Servers every Sunday at mid-night or restart your WLST script that initializes some data for your application. Many customers use cron jobs to automate such jobs. Enterprise Manager provides capabilities to schedule one time or recurring jobs.

Let us discus how you can schedule a WebLogic Server control job to schedule a job to restart WebLogic Server.

You can schedule the Job from the **Administration** tab from the Domain, Cluster, or Server homepage as shown in the following figure. This page provides a list of jobs submitted for the domain/cluster.

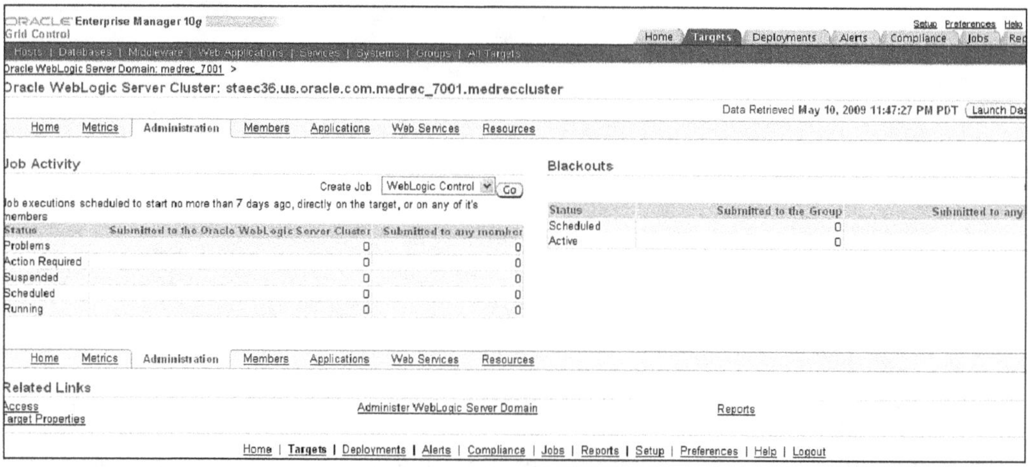

We have to enter the schedule, credentials, job type, and so on for a job. You have to enter a name for the job to uniquely identify the job. Note that these are stored in the repository database.

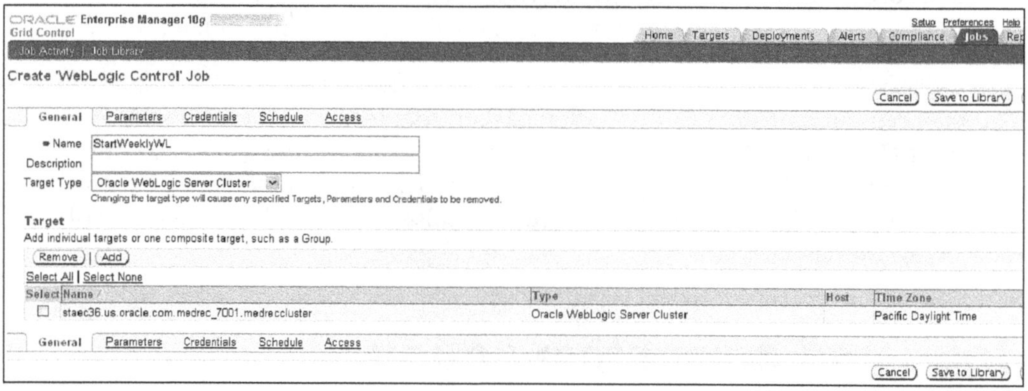

You have to select the parameters to specify whether to start/stop or restart the cluster/server.

You have to select the parameters to specify whether to start, stop, or restart the cluster/server.

You have to enter the schedule for the job and then submit the job.

```
Create 'WebLogic Control' Job


   General    Parameters    Credentials    Schedule    Access

  Type    ○ One Time (Immediately)  ○ One Time (Later)  ⊙ Repeating
             Frequency Type  [ Weekly      ▼ ]
              Days of Week    □ Monday □ Tuesday □ Wednesday □ Thursday □ Friday □ Saturday □ Sunday
                Time Zone    [ Each target's timezone                    ▼ ]
                Start Date   [ May 10, 2009    ] ▦
                Start Time   [ 12  ] : [ 00 ]  ⊙ AM ○ PM
             Grace Period    ⊙ Indefinite
                             ○ End After     [        ]  Hours     [        ]  Minutes
              Repeat Until   ⊙ Indefinite
                             ○ Specified Date
                                 Date    [                    ] ▦
                                         (example: May 11, 2009)
                                 Time    [      ] : [      ]  ⊙ AM ○ PM
```

After you schedule the job, the job will run as per the schedule. You can monitor the job and see the history of the job. You may get an e-mail if the job fails.

Corrective action job

Earlier in this chapter, we discussed alert notifications. Let's assume that you are a very proactive administrator and want to fix it automatically when a problem happens. For example, when the active number of JDBC connections reaches a certain threshold, you want to reset it by running a WLST script. This is the kind of job that automatically gets invoked in response to an alert notification, is called a *corrective action* job.

Add the corrective action by selecting the advanced setting for the metric as shown in the following screenshot:

```
Edit Advanced Settings: Status


  Corrective Actions
  Critical  <none>  ( Add )
       ☑  Allow only one corrective action for this metric to run at any given time

  Advanced Threshold Settings
        Critical Threshold  Down
  Number of Occurrences  [1     ]
      Collection Schedule  Every 1 Minute



  ☑ TIP Empty Thresholds will disable alerts for that metric.

```

You can either use the WebLogic Server Control Job or create your own job that runs a WLST script and that can be used as a corrective action.

Configuration management

In the last chapter, we learned about configuration management and how Enterprise Manager helps to manage configurations for IT resources of your enterprise. The configuration management features offered by Enterprise Manager help to reduce manual and error prone tasks; thereby freeing WebLogic administrators to focus on more proactive maintenance activities. Many administrators use ad-hoc processes such as spreadsheets to track assets in their IT environment, and that leads to several issues and administrators have no way to enforce policies.

Asset tracking

Enterprise Manager helps you to automate the asset tracking by collecting WebLogic Server configuration files at regular intervals and stores them in the **Configuration Management Database (CMDB)** as a part of the repository database. This helps you to track any changes in your WebLogic configurations by allowing you to compare two different versions of configurations for the same server or two different servers. It also allows you to compare configuration files between two servers in two completely different domains. For example, you can compare the configuration between your **UAT (User Acceptance Test)** environment and your production environment.

Enterprise Manager collects the following configuration details for WebLogic Servers:

- Ports, resource usage, and tuning settings
- Deployed applications and their associated modules
- Java DataBase Connectivity (JDBC) data sources and connection pools
- Virtual hosts Java Message Service (JMS) resources
- Configuration of startup/shutdown classes, JOLT connection pools and Work Managers
- Configuration files (for example, `config.xml`, `*-jdbc.xml`, `*-jms.xml`, applications)

You can access the configuration management features by accessing the **Administration** link from your admin server or managed server homepage. If you want to examine the current configuration of your WebLogic Server, you can access the **Last Collected Configuration** link, and you will see a similar page:

You can access the **Applications**, **JDBC Resources**, **Virtual Hosts**, and **JMS Resources** by navigating to the respective links. The startup/shutdown, jolt connection pool, work manager settings can be accessed by selecting the **Miscellaneous** link. You can view the configuration files by navigating to the **Configuration Files** link.

> The configuration files are stored in the administration server for your WebLogic Server, and hence these are collected only for the admin server. The agent has to be locally present in the admin server host for the `config` file collection.

If you want to view the history of your configuration changes, then you can navigate by going to history. You can view and search for any configuration changes. You will see the changes, as shown in the following screenshot:

You can further drill down to view the actual changes by clicking on the history records. For example, when we click on the three changes that occurred for our server, we see the following:

You can save a gold version of your WebLogic Server configurations in the software library. This can help you track any configuration changes that may cause issues in your production environment due to configuration drift. As we discussed earlier, Enterprise Manager allows you to compare different versions of saved configurations or configurations between two entirely different servers. We leave those as exercises for you!

Policy management

In the last chapter, we briefly discussed about policies. Policies are best practices that you follow in your organizations. Proactive assessment of key compliance areas such as security and configuration helps identify vulnerabilities; and indicates where best practices are not being followed. Oracle Enterprise Manager ships with the following out-of-the-box policies for Oracle WebLogic Server and also enables administrators to define their own specific policies and groups.

- Server Domain Administration Port is enabled
- Server Performance Pack is enabled
- Managed Server Production Mode is enabled

Enterprise Manager tracks these policies and alerts when these are violated. You can view these violations in WebLogic Server Homepage and have notifications similar to metric alerts.

Let us discuss how to enforce your own policy. Let us assume that your organization does not allow the use of default port 7001 in any production WebLogic Server. We will demonstrate by creating a custom policy.

1. You can create custom policies by navigating to the compliance option and then selecting the library. You will see all policies (both out of box and user defined policy). You can select add to create a new custom policy and then select the target type as Oracle WebLogic Server and enter the severity type, for example, **Critical**, **Warning,** or **Informational** and category for example **Security**, as shown in the following screenshot:

2. The policy engine actually verifies by executing a SQL statement. You have to enter the SQL statement for your custom policy. Refer to the *Enterprise Manager Extensibility Guide* on the management view that you can use for the SQL Query. You can validate the SQL statement by clicking on the validate button as shown in the following screenshot:

You have to enter the **Non-Compliant** and **Compliant** messages for the policy. The non-compliant message is used when a policy violation alert is used.

After you have successfully entered an SQL Query you have to enter the violation condition. The violation condition can be based on a threshold value or a where clause.

The column name that you entered in the select clause is used for comparison for a violation. You have to enter the violation condition and default value. For example, we are checking if the port number is equal to 7001 in the following diagram. You can change the value when enforcing the policy with a WebLogic Server target.

3. In the next step, you can test the policy against a target. You can select a target and then run the test and you will see the violation if it occurs as in the following figure:

Edit Policy: Review

Cancel | Back | Step 6 of 6 | Finish

Name **CannotUseDefaultPort7001**	Category **Security**
Target Type **Oracle WebLogic Managed Server**	Number of Key Columns **1**
Severity **Critical**	Evaluation Schedule **Evaluation Upon Upload**
Description	
Details Link	
Impact of Violation	
Recommendation	
Non-Compliant Message **Policy CannotUseDefaultPort7001 is non-compliant.**	
Compliant Message **Policy CannotUseDefaultPort7001 is compliant.**	

SQL Query SELECT target_guid, to_number(value) port
FROM esm_collection_latest WHERE property='port'

Threshold

Column Name	Data Type	Comparison Operator	Threshold Value
PORT	Number	=	7001

Cancel | Back | Step 6 of 6 | Finish

4. Select a WebLogic Server where you want to test the policy.

Details   SQL Query   Violation Condition   **Test**   Evaluation Schedule   Review

Edit Policy: Test

Run a test evaluation against a single test target. Test results will be rendered below.
(OPTIONAL) Click Next to skip test.

Cancel | Back | Step 4 of 6 | Next

* Target sta00224.us.oracle.com.webcenter_: (Run Test)

Results

General

Severity	✕ **Critical**
Compliance Score (%)	**100**
Importance	**Normal**
Category	**Security**
Description	

Violations

Date Tested
(No Policy Violations)

Cancel | Back | Step 4 of 6 | Next

5. Finally you can review the policy and confirm and create the policy. The policy will be created and shown in the list. You can search by the target type or name. Another way to create a policy is to export an existing policy and make changes for a new policy and import it to Enterprise Manager.

Here is an example of a XML policy that you can import to create a new user defined policy.

```xml
<?xml version = '1.0' encoding = 'UTF-8'?>
<UserDefinedPolicy oms_version="10.2.0.5.0" xmlns="http://www.
oracle.com/DataCenter/ConfigStd">
    <PolicyName>CannotUseDefaultPort7001</PolicyName>
    <TargetType>weblogic_j2eeserver</TargetType>
    <SqlSource>SELECT target_guid, value
FROM esm_collection_latest WHERE property='port' </SqlSource>
    <PolicyTest>
        <ThresholdCriteria>
            <ColumnName>VALUE</ColumnName>
            <TestOperator>EQ</TestOperator>
            <ThresholdValue>7001</ThresholdValue>
            <ThresholdType>String</ThresholdType>
        </ThresholdCriteria>
    </PolicyTest>
    <KeyColumns>1</KeyColumns>
    <Severity>Informational</Severity>
    <Category>Capacity</Category>
    <ViolationMessage>Policy CannotUseDefaultPort7001 is non-
compliant.</ViolationMessage>
    <ClearViolationMessage>Policy CannotUseDefaultPort7001 is
compliant.</ClearViolationMessage>
    <EvaluationScheduleInfo>
        <FixedInterval unit="hour">24.0</FixedInterval>
    </EvaluationScheduleInfo>
</UserDefinedPolicy>
```

Enforcing a custom policy

Now that we have created a user defined policy, we will see how to enforce this policy from a WebLogic Server. To enforce a policy you have to select the metric and policy settings from a WebLogic Server and then go to the policy settings. You have to select add policy from library and find the policy that you added earlier as shown in the following figure:

EM will evaluate the policy as per the collection interval specified, and if the violation occurs then you will see the violation in the WebLogic Server Homepage.

Service level management

We introduced the concept of service level management in the last chapter. Service Level Management will let administrators be proactive and ensure that applications meet the performance and availability criteria agreed with your business/ user community.

Think of a service as an entity that provides a business service or functionality. For example, an application allowing the creation of an order or the searching and viewing of an existing order. Some simpler forms of services are business functions that are supported by protocols such as HTTP, SOAP, or SMTP.

You can use Enterprise Manager to define your services, based on applications deployed on WebLogic Server. These services could be web application invoked through browser or web services invoked though SOAP.

Before we get into it, let us review some of the basic terminologies that we will use while creating a service and using the service level management feature.

- *Availability* is a condition that determines whether the service is considered to be accessible by the users or not. For example, the components hosting the service e.g. Weblogic Server or database may be down.

- *Service Test* is a functional test defined by an IT administrator against the service to determine whether or not the service is available and meeting the performance standard.

- *System* is a group of underlying components, such as hosts, WebLogic Server, databases, and on which the service runs.

- *Beacon* is a functionality built into Oracle Management Agent that is used to pre-record transactions or service tests. The beacons may be geographically located across different locations to perform the service test

- *Service Level* is an operational or contractual objective between the customer and IT for service availability and performance.

Enterprise Manager allows the creation of services based either on availability of underlying components or based on service tests. For example, you can create a generic service for a system component that is a collection of WebLogic Server and the underlying database. If either the database or WebLogic Server is down, then the service is deemed unavailable.

The second type of service is based on a service test. For example, you are running the MedRec application or web service. You can create a service test for your application. In this section we will discuss a service based on a service test. There could be several types of services such as Generic Service, Aggregate Service, Forms or Web Application based service. From a WebLogic Server perspective, we will primarily be interested in a Generic Service or Web application service.

Creating a system

A service depends upon a system. Hence before we create a service, let us create a system. Think about the classic MedRec application offering several services e.g. the creation of a new patient record is a service. Assume that your application is based on an Oracle database and WebLogic Server, then you should create a system with the WebLogic Server, database and underlying host machine. Note that the Enterprise Manager automatically creates a system with these components when you create a service for your application, if both Oracle database and WebLogic Server are being monitored in the same instance by Enterprise Manager.

You can manually create a service by selecting the system option from the targets menu item and then selecting the component that you want to add to your system. For example, the following figure shows a system named **WebLogicAndDatabaseSystem** that includes two WebLogic Servers, database and the underlying host machine.

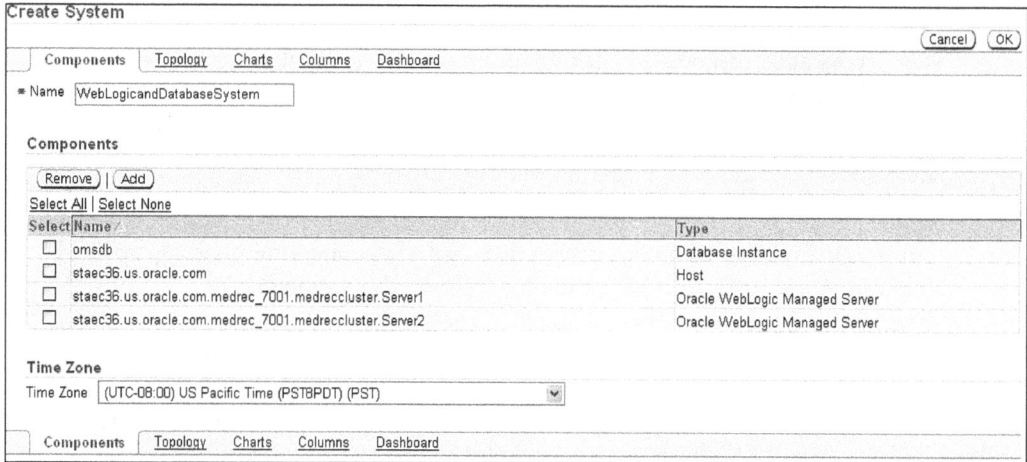

You can view the system in the topology viewer or launch a dashboard report for your management. A system is useful when you want to monitor the complete application infrastructure as a single system. You will get all alerts, security violations, service alerts, and so on, aggregated at the system level. The following screenshot shows the homepage for the MedRec system that we are going to use for creating a service.

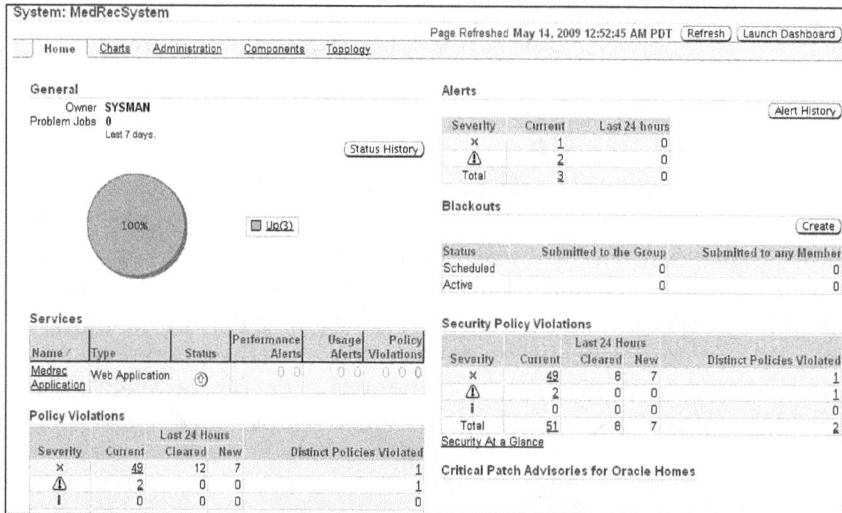

Creating a service

We discussed earlier in this chapter that a service can be based on a service test or the availability of components. You can create a generic service based on the MedRec system that we created earlier. The problem with the services based on system availability is that the actual performance of the service is not measured and the service availability is based on the availability (up/down status) of the components that constitute the system. However, a service that is based on a service availability test has at least one service test defined, that is automatically invoked by a beacon at regular intervals and Enterprise Manager measures the perceived performance. You can locate beacons in different geographical locations based on where your user communities are and that will help you to measure performance based on different locations.

To create a service based on a web application such as the MedRec application you have to select a web application, and then add a new web application as shown in the following diagram:

You have to enter the right details, such as your system and **Homepage URL** for your application and then select the availability, based on the service test as shown in the following figure:

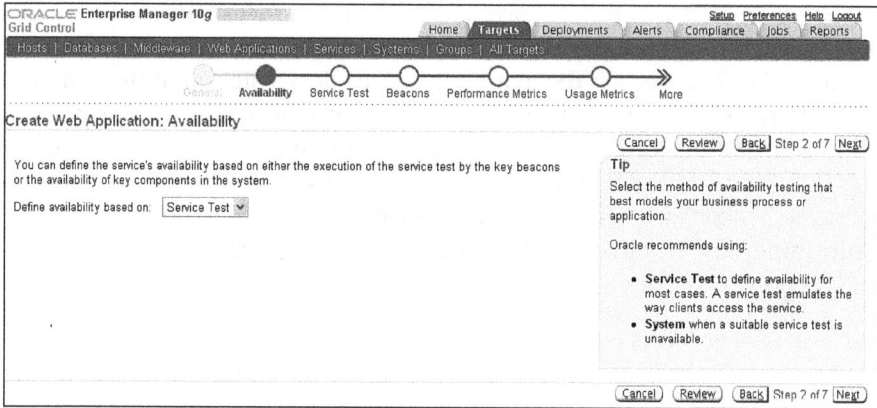

Then we have to enter the service tests that we want to perform. You can add one or more tests based on the synthetic transaction that is performed by the users of the system. For example, we want to add a test to check login into the MedRec system as a patient or as an administrator.

> You can perform these tests based on a basic single URL or a transaction that you can record. Note that you have to use Internet Explorer to record a transaction.

For simplicity we are just using **Basic Single URL**, as shown in the following figure:

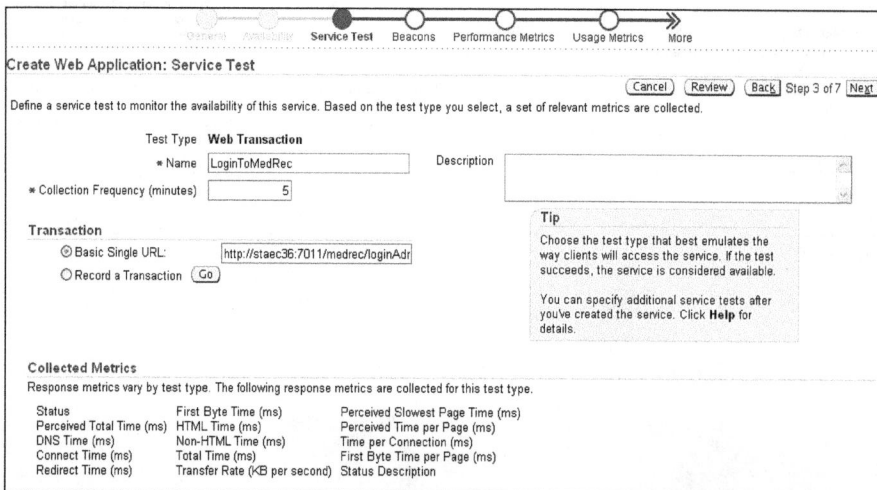

After that, you have to select the beacons that you want to use to invoke the service tests. As we discussed earlier, beacons are nothing but Oracle Management Agents.

> In a production environment you want to locate beacons in the same geographical location where users are located. For example, if you have users based in North America, Europe, and Japan, then you would want to create at least three beacons in these locations so that you can test the service performance from these user's perspectives.

You can verify the test at this stage to make sure that you have entered the correct URL for the web application. You can add one or more beacons if you have agent installed on multiple locations. It is always a good idea to select multiple beacons for your service test.

After you add the service tests, you can specify the performance metrics for the test. The performance metrics could be based on tests such as the warning and critical threshold for the perceived page performance. There are several other metrics for the service test such as DNS Time, Connect Time, Redirect Time, HTML Time, Non-HTML Time, and so on. You can also define some performance metrics based on your system. For example, you can add some performance metrics based on JMX Metrics exposed by WebLogic Server, such as **Average Response Time** or **Invocations** from your WebLogic Server.

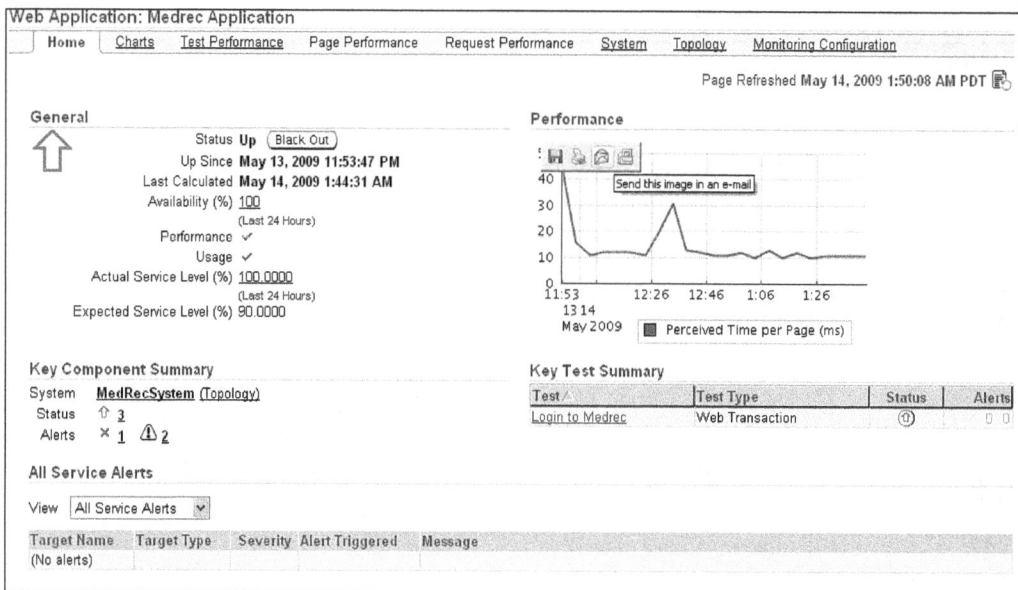

You can add some usage metrics based on JMX Metrics exposed by WebLogic Server. Finally, you can review the service and create the service. You can view the service by going to service homepage. You can view the status of the service, its performance, availability of the underlying components, service alerts, alerts for the system components, and a summary of the tests.

You can change the service rule based on your requirements. For example, you probably do not care about the performance aspects of your application during the weekends or you want to set blackout for service alerts for official holidays.

Edit Service Level Rule

Service Level is a measure of service quality.Service Level is calculated as percentage of time during business hours a service meets specified availability and performance criteria. The actual Service Level will be calculated for different time periods, but the same criteria will apply for all these time periods. (Cancel) (OK)

Expected Service Level

Specify the percentage of time during business hours that you expect your service to meet the availability and performance criteria described below.

Expected Service Level [90.0]

Actual Service Level

Business Hours

Days ☑ Monday ☑ Tuesday ☑ Wednesday
☑ Thursday ☑ Friday ☐ Saturday
☐ Sunday

Start Time [00 ▼] : [00 ▼] End Time [24 ▼] : [00 ▼]

Service Time Zone (UTC-08:00) US Pacific Time (PST)

Availability Criteria

For Service Level calculations, specify the availability states during which the Service will be considered UP.

☑ Up ☐ Under Blackout

☑ Unknown (Pending, Agent Unreachable, Metric Error)

Performance Criteria

Optionally select performance metrics that will be evaluated when computing Service Level. A critical alert on any of the selected metrics will count as a Service Level violation.

Available Performance Metrics   Selected Performance Metrics

⊘ Move
⊘⊘ Move All
⊘ Remove

Perceived Time per Page (ms)
Status

Once you create the service tests, the beacon will automatically wake up and invoke the service tests at regular intervals. There are several out-of-the-box reports such as Service Dash boards and Service Test Summaries that you can use to publish information to your stake holders. The service level management feature will keep your services up and running and proactively monitor the services before there are user complaints about service level violation. It is worth noting that Enterprise Manager allows you to creating SOAP Tests for Web services and automatically creates a service when a SOAP Test for a web service is created.

Role based access control

You may have a large enterprise where you use Enterprise Manager to monitor your complete infrastructure such as databases, application servers, packaged applications, and so on. There are Administrators for each of the target types. As an Administrator you are responsible for only WebLogic Server Domains and you want to view/monitor only those targets from Grid Control. How do you do that?

It's simple—Enterprise Manager provides Role Based Access Control. Instead of using the default sysman user, it is recommended that you create users for each of the administrators and grant appropriate privileges. You have to create a user that has access to only the targets you are interested in. Let me assume that you want to create a user named **WebLogic** that has access to only a few WebLogic servers and let us walk you through how to achieve this.

Creating an EM user and assign targets

Logon as a super administrator and let us create a user named **robtheadmin**.

1. You can create a user by selecting **Setup** menu and then selecting **Create User** as in the following screenshot:

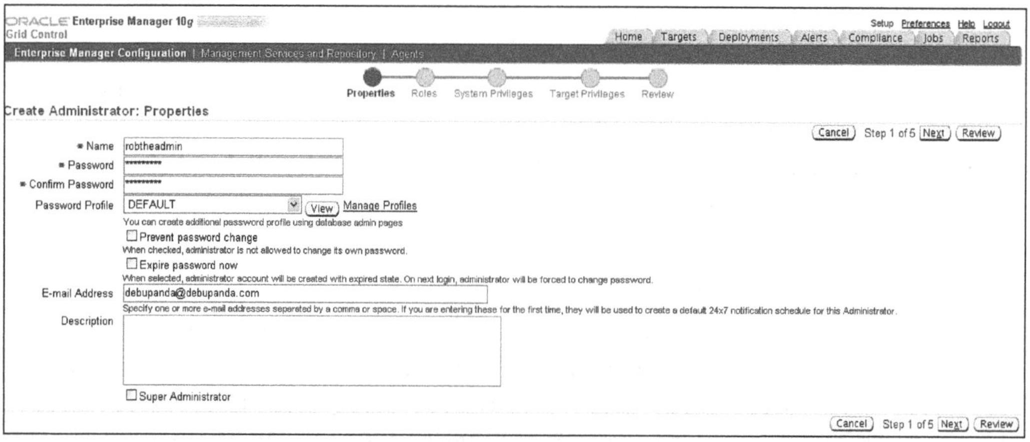

2. Then assign the appropriate roles such as **PUBLIC** or any new roles that you have defined. You can add system privileges such as **Add Any Target**, **View Any Target**, and so on if you need to assign.

3. In the next step, you can select that the targets the users should have access to. You can assign specific privileges to the target, for example **Operator**, **Full**, or **View**, as shown in the following screenshot:

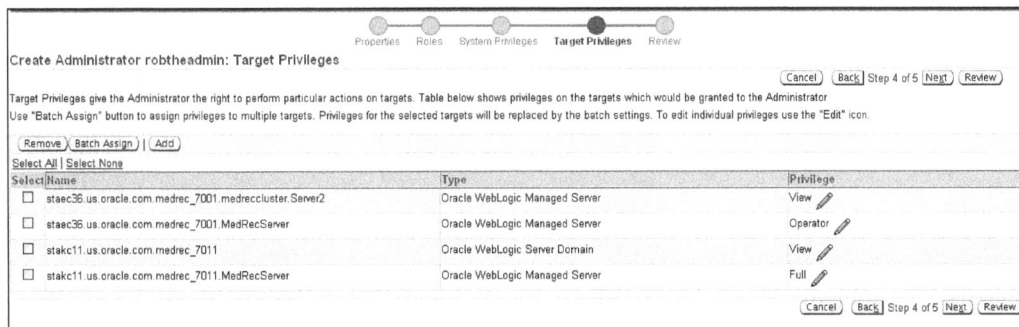

After you create the user **robtheadmin**, the user will have appropriate privileges.

After you logon as **robtheadmin** user, you will see that the homepage for WebLogic users shows only the WebLogic Servers that assigned privileges on.

Summary

We discussed all of the aspects of managing Oracle WebLogic Server. You learned how to add a WebLogic Server into Oracle Enterprise Manager. Enterprise Manager supports both real time and historical performance monitoring of WebLogic Server and you can use historical data for performance trending and capacity planning. The configuration management aspect of WebLogic Server can help you to track changes and compare configurations between different servers and also enforce policies. You can use service level management aspect of Enterprise Manager to create services and measure service performance. Finally, we discussed how to use the role based access control feature of Enterprise Manager.

In the next chapter, we will discuss managing Oracle Application Server. Enterprise Manager supports some interesting functionalities such as provisioning and patching of Oracle Application Server. See you at the next stop!

5
Managing Oracle Application Server

In the last chapter, we learned how to manage multiple domains of WebLogic Server using Enterprise Manager Grid Control. In this chapter, we'll learn how to manage multiple Oracle Application Server installations using Enterprise Manager.

Oracle Application Server (OAS) is a J2EE compliant application server for Java applications. The OAS product stack comprises of many components. On a broad level, Oracle product stack can be categorized in different product categories. Major product categories for OAS are as follows:

- **Core**: It provides the core stack to run enterprise java applications. Components included in this category are OC4J (J2EE container), OHS (Oracle HTTP Server), and WebCache.
- **Identity management**: This category provides support for Identity management services like single-sign-on, authentication, and authorization. Besides OC4J, this category contains components like OID (Oracle LDAP server), **DAS (Distributed Authentication System)**, and so on
- **SOA suite**: This category contains products that provide the integration platform for Service Oriented Architecture. Besides OC4J this category contains components like BPEL process manager, Enterprise Service Bus, and so on.
- **Content Management**: This category contains products like Portal, Reports, and Discoverer.

In this chapter, we'll learn about monitoring and management of core Oracle Application Server components. Monitoring and management of SOA Suite and Identity Suite are covered in more detail in Chapters 6 and 8 respectively. But as we saw that all other suites contain components from core suite, knowing about core suite management will be very helpful in understanding the management of other suites.

We'll start with the target model and discovery process for Oracle Application Server. After that we'll look at the tasks that an Oracle Application Server Administrator needs to perform; we'll show how Enterprise Manager can make those tasks easier. We'll also provide some recommendations, best practices on performing those tasks through Enterprise Manager.

Discovery and Target Model

To discover Oracle Application Server, Enterprise Manager Agent needs to be installed on the same host as the application server. There are two scenarios for the application server's discovery:

- The agent is installed after the installation of the application server: in this scenario, nothing needs to be done for the application server's discovery besides installing the agent, the agent discovers the existing application server during installation. In Chapter 2, *Installing Enterprise Manager Grid Control*, we learned how to install a new agent. During the installation of an agent, the user is prompted to provide details of Oracle Management Server; using those details, the agent uploads details about the newly discovered application server targets.

- The application server is installed after agent installation: in this scenario, you will need to trigger the discovery process from Enterprise Manager Console to discover the application servers that got installed after agent installation. For this scenario, click on targets in the top menu bar and select **Middleware**. On this page, you will see all the middleware targets and the option to discover new middleware targets.

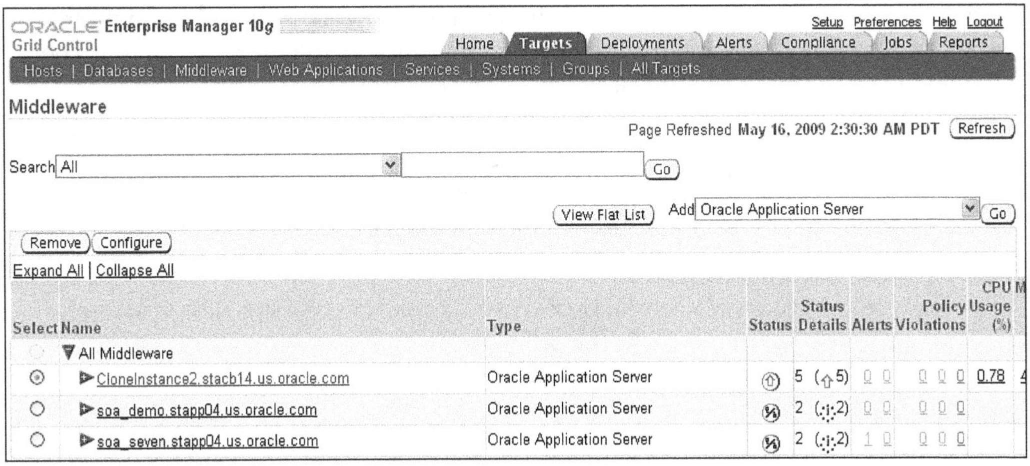

From this page select **Oracle Application Server** from the drop-down list on the right-hand side and click on **Go**, on the following page you will be asked to provide the host name where the agent is running. Clicking on the icon next to the text box will open another browser window and, using that, you can select a host. Select the host where you want to discover the new application server.

The following screenshot shows such a screen, after the host is selected:

On this screen click on **Continue**, you will be shown a processing page and after a few seconds you will be shown all the application servers that got discovered. The following screenshot shows such a page:

ORACLE Enterprise Manager 10*g*
Grid Control
Home | Targets | Deployments | Alerts | Complia
Hosts | Databases | **Middleware** | Web Applications | Services | Systems | Groups | All Targets

Discover Application Servers: Results

The following targets were successfully discovered by the Agent. By clicking the OK button, all the Oracle Application Server targets and their member targets will be added to monitor automatically.

Name	Type
sourceinstance.staec34.us.oracle.com	Oracle Application Server

(Cancel) (OK)

Home | **Targets** | Deployments | Alerts | Compliance | Jobs | Reports | Setup | Preferences | Help | Logou

Copyright © 1996, 2009, Oracle and/or its affiliates. All rights reserved.
Oracle is a registered trademark of Oracle Corporation and/or its affiliates.
Other names may be trademarks of their respective owners.

Once you click on **OK** for confirmation of the new application server target and all member targets like OC4J, the HTTP server will be added to the repository and a confirmation screen will be displayed as shown next:

ORACLE Enterprise Manager 10*g*
Grid Control
Home | Targets | Deployments | Alerts | Compliance
Hosts | Databases | **Middleware** | Web Applications | Services | Systems | Groups | All Targets

Confirmation

Targets are added successfully.

(OK)

Home | **Targets** | Deployments | Alerts | Compliance | Jobs | Reports | Setup | Preferences | Help | Logout

Copyright © 1996, 2009, Oracle and/or its affiliates. All rights reserved.
Oracle is a registered trademark of Oracle Corporation and/or its affiliates.
Other names may be trademarks of their respective owners.
About Oracle Enterprise Manager

In case a new component is created after discovery of the application server, you can use the same flow to discover the new component target.

> On UNIX servers the user-ID with which you install agent, and the user-ID with which you have installed Oracle Application Server, should belong to the same UNIX user group. This is to ensure that the agent process has read permissions on all configuration files for Oracle Application Server.

Let's look into the application server target model. In the introduction to this chapter, we saw that the Oracle Application Server product has many components, Enterprise Manager provides out-of-the-box target types for each component type of Application Server stack. Some core target types for Oracle Application Server product are:

- Application Server Farm: Application Server Farm is a group of application server instances, we'll use Application Server Farm and Farm interchangeably in this chapter

- Application Server Instance: Application Server Instance is group of components that are running from the same set of binaries

- Application Server Cluster: Application Server Cluster is group of components of the same type and is used for providing High- Availability and load- balancing support, for example cluster of OC4J

- OC4J: J2EE compliant container to run Java applications

- Oracle HTTP Server: HTTP listener for routing traffic to J2EE container

- WebCache: Component for caching HTTP traffic

The Oracle Application Server target model also keeps the associations and hierarchy between various targets, like the association between Application Server Instance and OC4J within the Application Server Instance.

These associations are very helpful when multiple Application Server Farms, Application Server Instances and components, are managed from the same Enterprise Manager. Users can see a hierarchical and topological view of all the application server targets. The following screenshot shows one such view of all of the application server targets:

Select	Name	Type	Status	Status Details	Alerts		Policy Violations			Us
	▼ All Middleware									
◉	▼ 10gAS.hr848.us.oracle.com	Oracle Application Server	⊗	3 (⋮3)	0 0		0 0 0			
○	10gAS.hr848.us.oracle.com_HTTP Server	Oracle HTTP Server	⊗	⋮	1 0		1 1 0			
○	10gAS.hr848.us.oracle.com_home	OC4J	⊗	⋮	0 0		1 0 0			
○	10gAS.hr848.us.oracle.com_PeopleSoft	OC4J	⊗	⋮	0 0		1 0 0			
○	▶ EnterpriseManager0.sta00556.us.oracle.com	Oracle Application Server	⊗	6 (⋮6)	0 0		0 0 0			
○	▶ EnterpriseManager0.stang13.us.oracle.com	Oracle Application Server	⬆	6 (⬇1 ⬆5)	0 0		0 0 0	0		
○	▶ EnterpriseManager0.stbct11.us.oracle.com	Oracle Application Server	⊗	5 (⋮5)	1 0		0 0 0			
○	▶ siebel.admnhost	Oracle Application Server	⬆	2 (⬇2)	1 0		0 0 0			
○	▼ soa_demo.stapp04.us.oracle.com	Oracle Application Server	⬆	2 (⬆2)	0 0		0 0 0			
○	soa_demo.stapp04.us.oracle.com_home	OC4J	⬆	⬆	0 0		0 0 0			
○	soa_demo.stapp04.us.oracle.com_bpel	Oracle BPEL Process Manager	⬆	⬆	0 0		0 0 0			
○	▼ soa_seven.stapp04.us.oracle.com	Oracle Application Server	⬆	2 (⬆2)	0 0		0 0 0		5	
○	soa_seven.stapp04.us.oracle.com_home	OC4J	⬆	⬆	0 0		0 0 0		1	
○	soa_seven.stapp04.us.oracle.com_bpel	Oracle BPEL Process Manager	⬆	⬆	0 0		0 0 0			
○	▼ stapp04.us.oracle.com.servicebus_7021	Oracle WebLogic Server Domain	n/a	1 (⬆1)	0 0		0 0 0			
○	▼ stapp04.us.oracle.com.servicebus_7021.xbusServer	Oracle WebLogic Managed Server	⬆	⬆	0 0		2 0 0		1	
○	stapp04.us.oracle.com.servicebus_7021.xbusServer_osb	Oracle Service Bus	⬆		0 0		0 0 0			
○	stacz61.us.oracle.com.domain_7001.wls_cluster	Oracle WebLogic Server Cluster	⬆	⋮	0 0		0 0 0			

Tasks for Oracle Applications Server Administrator

Let's look at the tasks that need to be performed by an Oracle Application Server Administrator and how the Enterprise Manager features help in performing that task. At the end of each task we'll provide some pointers to explore the features defined.

We'll start with the first task that is installation.

Provisioning

Whenever a new application has to be deployed on a new Application Server or the capacity of an existing application is augmented, the administrator needs to provision Oracle Application Servers. Most of such provisioning activity is repetitive in nature and can be automated. We learned about provisioning a framework and deployment procedures in Chapter 1, *Enterprise Manager Grid Control*.

Enterprise Manager provides out-of-the-box deployment procedures to provision Oracle Application Server. These deployment procedures support following three scenarios for provisioning:

- Provisioning from installable software: This scenario covers first time installation of software. This scenario is more common when building a new system from scratch.

- Gold image creation: After the first installation from installable software, administrator performs some configuration on the software, and applies some patches on the software. The gold image of such a system can be created and saved for subsequent installations.

- Provisioning from reference environment or gold image: This scenario is more common when expanding the capacity of an existing system or building a new system by cloning an existing installation.

The out-of-the-box procedures provided by Enterprise Manager contain a set of steps that install/clone software as per best practices suggested by Oracle. These best practices are actually guidelines and often need some environment specific customizations. Administrators can customize out-of-the-box deployment procedures to achieve such customizations on top of recommended best practices.

> Recommendation: To customize out-of-the-box deployment procedure, create a copy of the deployment procedures and add customizations in the copy. Use the new deployment procedure for provisioning of Oracle Application Server.
>
> Recommendation: Create a gold image for Oracle Application Server and save it in the software library. For all new provisioning of Oracle Application Server, use this gold image. Whenever new patches are applied, build a new gold image.

Enterprise Manager provides deployment procedures for provisioning of Oracle Application Server versions 10.1.2.0.2, 10.1.3, and 10.1.3.1. It also provides deployment procedures for Forms and Reports 9.0.4.

How to use this feature

To find out more on this feature, go to the Enterprise Manager homepage and click on the **Deployments** tab on the top, then on the next page click on **Application Server Provisioning Procedures** and you will see a page from where all the deployment procedures for Oracle Application Server are listed. From this page, you can customize a deployment procedure or schedule a deployment using a deployment procedure. The screenshot below shows this page:

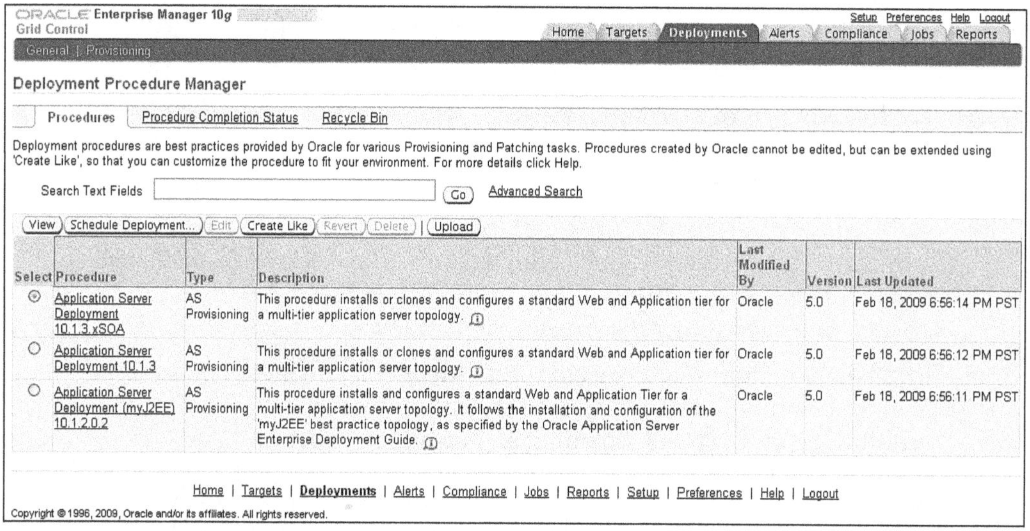

To view all the steps performed by a deployment procedure, select the radio button next to it and click on the **View** button. The following screenshot shows the steps for 10.1.3 deployment procedure:

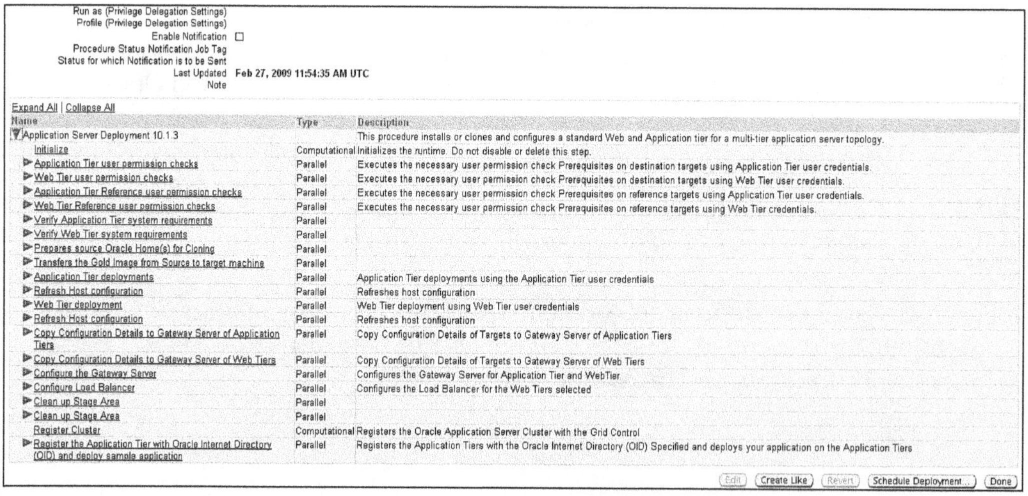

Lets go and try out one of the deployment procedures. We will use a deployment procedure to extend 10.1.3 cluster by cloning an existing server. For this exercise you will need the following:

- A cluster of two 10.1.3 application servers, the application servers and the cluster should be discovered and monitored by Enterprise Manager:

- A host to clone the new application server. This host should meet the pre-requisites for the application server installation. This host should be discovered and monitored as a target from current Enterprise Manager. You will need to install an agent on this host to achieve this.

After this setup, Click on the **Middleware** tab, and you will see a page similar to the one shown next. You will see a cluster and two servers under the cluster.

To start the cloning of the application server, go to the **Application Server Provisioning Procedures** page from the **Deployments** tab. You will see a page, which was shown earlier. From that page, select the radio button next to the **Application Server Deployment 10.1.3** and click on **Schedule deployment**. This will start an interview wizard for the cloning operation. On the first screen, you can select the reference environment or the software library as the source. You will also see an option to save the image in the software library. On this page, select a cluster as the source, and you will see some values getting populated in other fields.

After selecting a cluster, your page will look like the following screenshot:

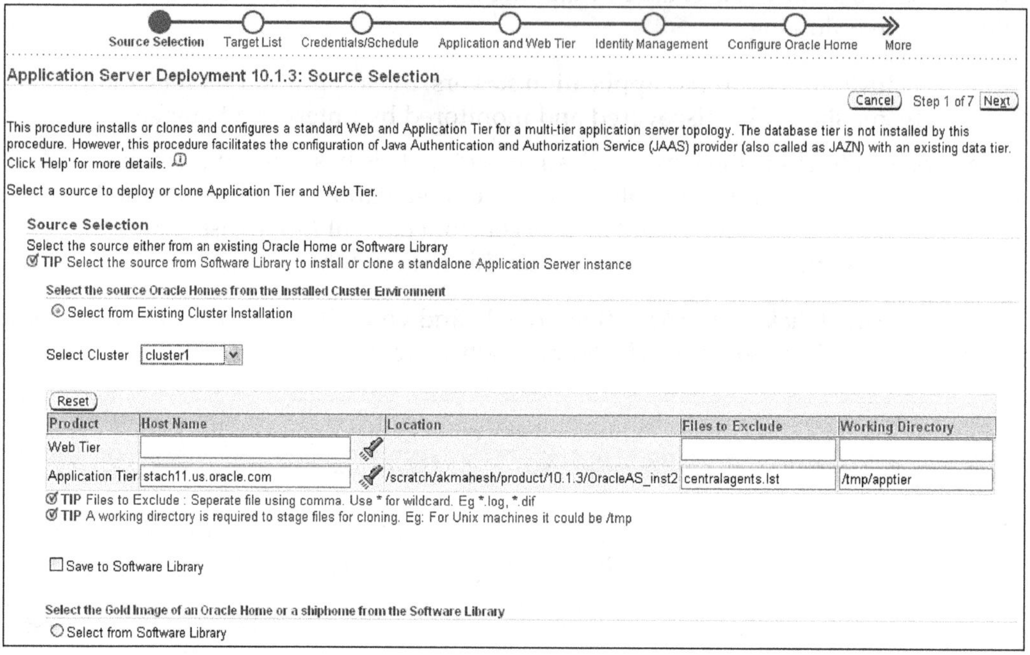

Click **Next** on this page, you will be asked to select the host where you want to clone the new application server. After you have added the host, your page will look like the one shown next:

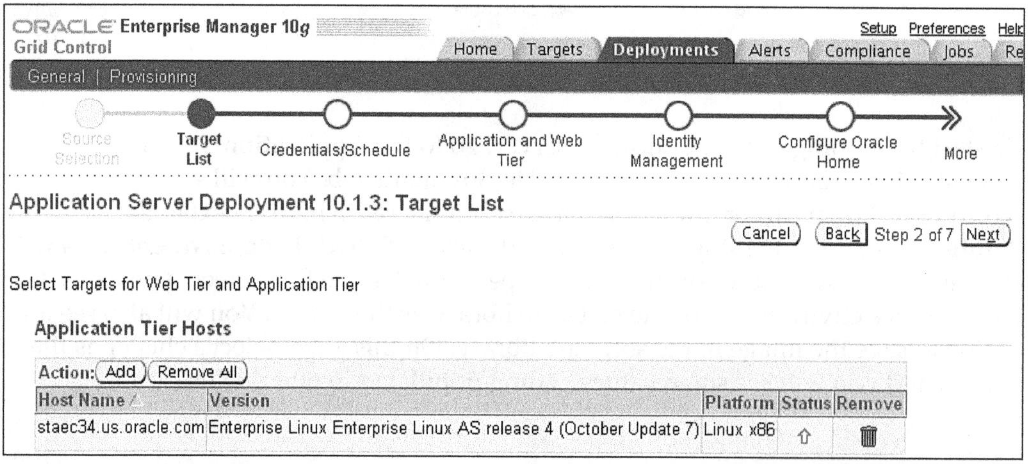

On this page, click on **Next,** and you will be asked to provide the host credentials for the new host where you want to clone the application server, the host credentials for the agent on the new host and the host credentials for the source application server Oracle Home, as shown in the following screenshot:

Source Selection	Target List	**Credentials/Schedule**	Application and Web Tier	Identity Management	Configure Oracle Home	More

Application Server Deployment 10.1.3: Credentials/Schedule

(Cancel) (Back) Step 3 of 7 (Next)

Provide credentials and choose a time to schedule this procedure.

Target Host Credentials

○ Use Preferred Credentials ⊙ Override Preferred Credentials

Host Credentials [Same for all Oracle Homes ▾]

* Username [   ]
* Password [   ]

Agent Home Credentials

○ Use Preferred Credentials ⊙ Override Preferred Credentials

Host Credentials [Same for all Oracle Homes ▾]

* Username [   ]
* Password [   ]

Source Oracle Home Credentials

○ Use Preferred Credentials ⊙ Override Preferred Credentials

Host Credentials [Same for all Oracle Homes ▾]

* Username [   ]
* Password [   ]

Provide credentials and click on **Next**, on the next page you will be asked to provide OC4J credentials for source and to-be cloned server:

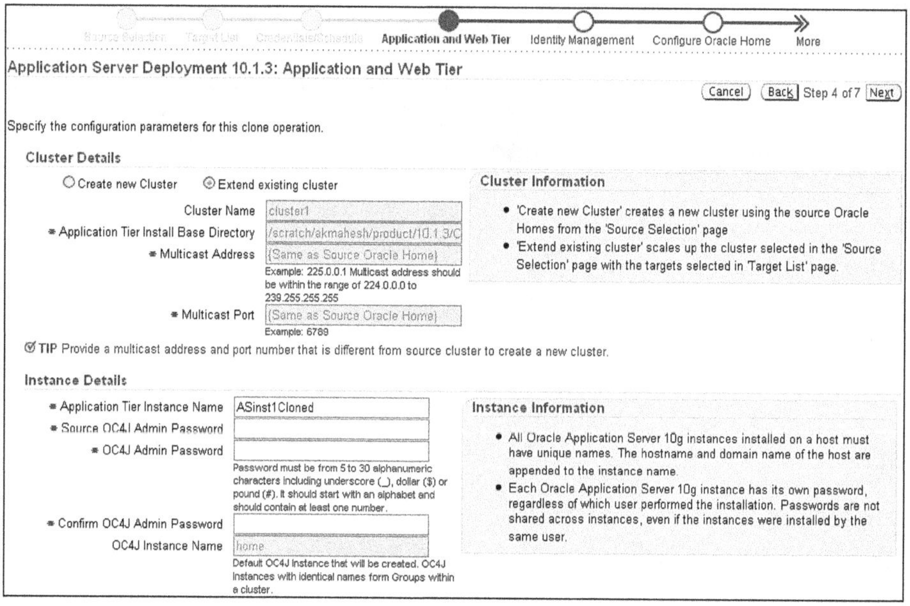

The next two pages you can skip with default values, after that you will be shown a review page, as shown next:

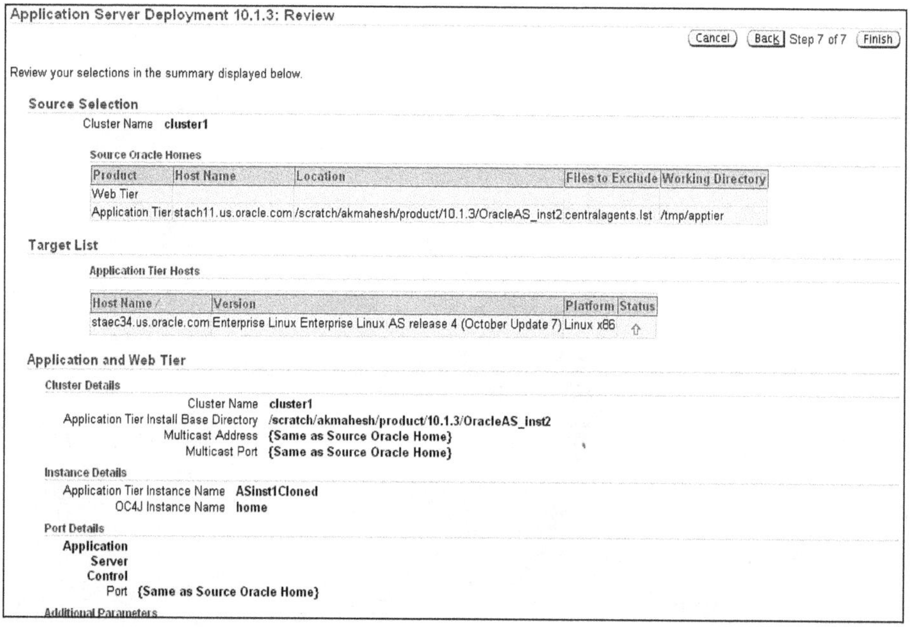

Review the details and click on the Finish button, and you will be shown the page as shown next. This page shows the details of all the deployment procedure runs. On top, you will see the one submitted by you and the name of this run starting with the name of the cluster that we are extending.

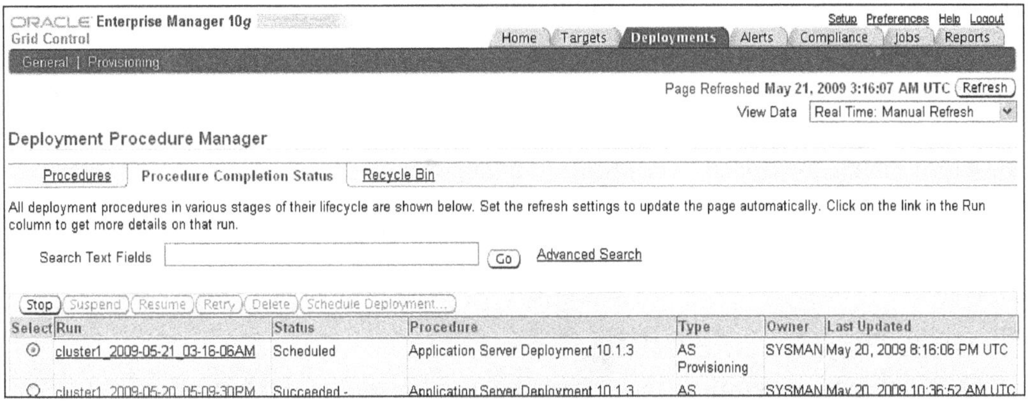

After the completion of the deployment procedure you will see the status shown as completed on this page. Revisit the **Middleware** tab and you will see the new application server instance as shown next:

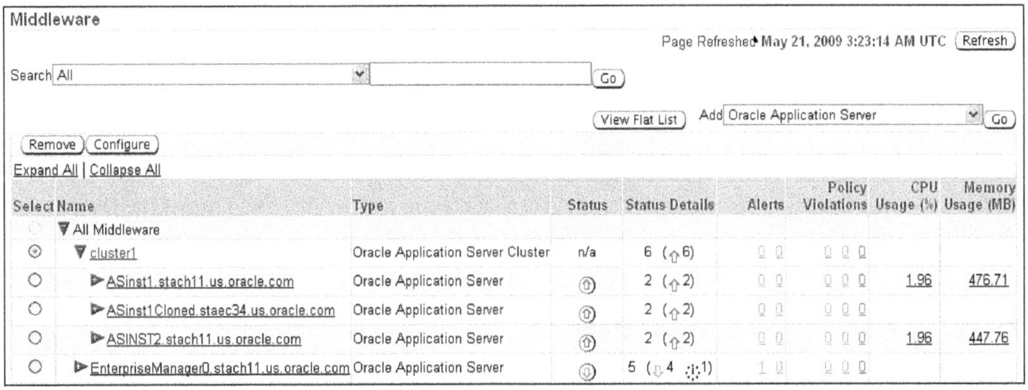

Monitoring

After the provisioning is completed and applications are deployed in the production environment, administrator needs to ensure applications and components in application server stack are working fine. Besides the monitoring, the administrator also needs to proactively look for possible bottlenecks or whether there is the need to add more capacity.

As most of the applications are built with a distributed multi-tier architecture to monitor the applications, the Administrator needs to monitor all the tiers, and all the components on which the application depends.

In the following sections, we'll look at the various monitoring tasks for the application server administrator.

Monitoring availability

When it comes to monitoring, the most important metric is the availability metric. Availability metric defines whether the monitored target is available for serving application requests or not. Enterprise Manager uses status metric of application server targets to monitor availability.

Oracle Application Server components provide status information, and that is collected by Enterprise Manager, and is used to show the status of the component on console. Targets like Oracle Application Server Farm, cluster, and instance, represent a group of Application Server Components and do not have status metric. Status of such targets is shown as the aggregate status of all components.

We learnt in the earlier chapters that Enterprise Manager repository keeps all the historical metric data. Historical status data can be used to find the availability of Oracle Application Server target for a given period of time.

How to use this feature

To see the current availability of a target, go to the target homepage. The following screenshot shows the homepage of an Oracle Application Server Target, where the **Status** of application server and **Components** is displayed. This page also shows the availability of Application Server Target for the last 24 hours:

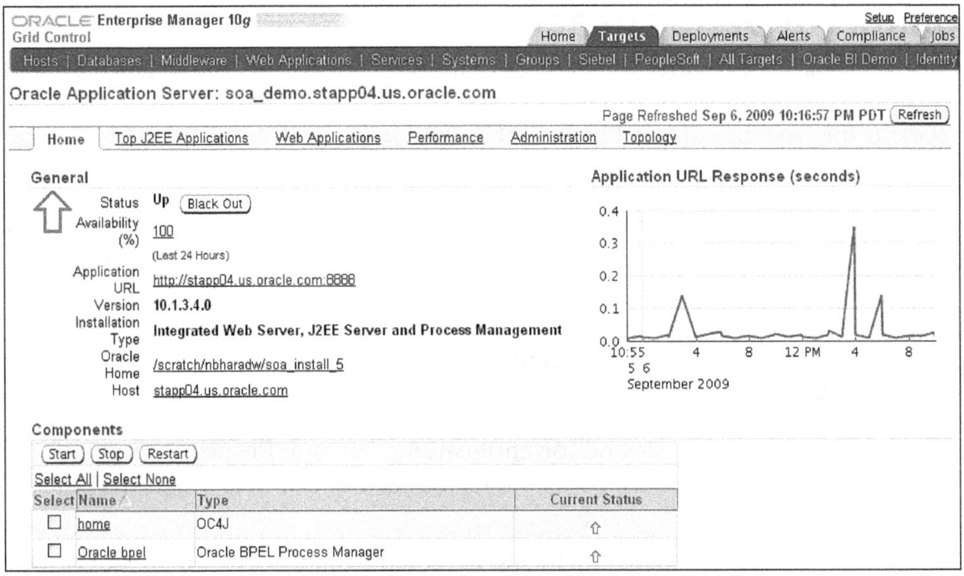

You can click on the **Availability** link and on the next page you can see the availability for an other period of time such as last 7 days or 31 days or some other customized time range.

The following screenshot shows the availability of the OC4J target for the last seven days. You can view the availability for any other duration using the **View Data** drop-down list.

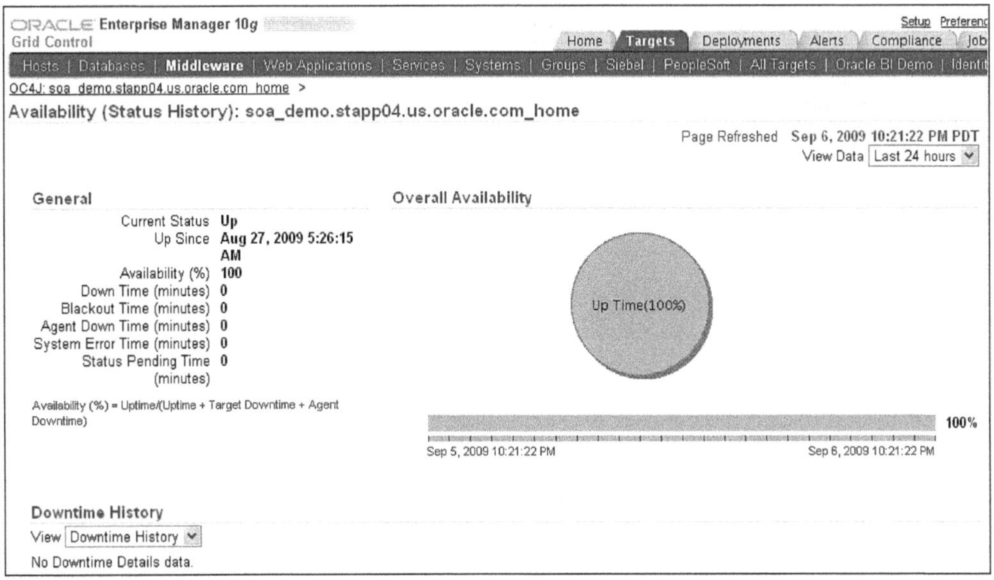

Monitoring performance

Enterprise Manager provides the metrics to monitor the health and performance of the components of the application server stack. The Application server administrator can look at the current data and historical data to perform A trend analysis that can help in identifying possible bottlenecks and capacity enhancement needs.

There are some metrics that are common across the application server components and represent the system resource usage like the CPU usage, and the memory usage by component, and so on. Besides the common resource metrics, there are lots of component specific metrics. Some useful component specific metrics for some core components are given below. For a complete list of metrics for all the application server components please refer to the Enterprise Manager documentation.

- OC4J: Requests per second for application, Average Response time for application, active JDBC connections for each datasource, Requests per second for each webservice
- Forms: Number of forms sessions, Total memory used by all forms sessions
- Reports: Average response time to process a request, Number of failed jobs
- Oracle HTTP Server: Request throughput, Average Response time, and Average Response size

How to use this feature

To use this feature, go to the target homepage, for most common metrics you will see some performance tabs on the homepage. The following screenshot shows the **Performance** tab for the OC4J target. From this page you can see the links for other performance pages like top servlets, top jsps, and so on.

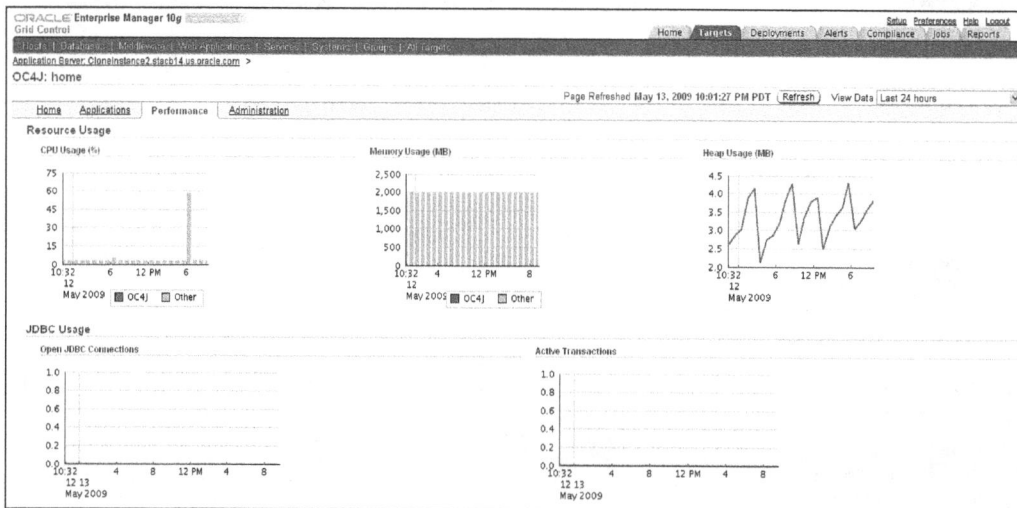

If you don't find a metric on the **Performance** tab and from links in the performance tab, don't loose your heart. Go to the homepage and click on the **All Metrics** link, you will find all of the metrics for the target there. You can find the current, as well as the historical data for all the metrics.

Applications performance monitoring

Other than monitoring the performance and health of individual Oracle Application Server components, the system administrator needs to monitor the health and performance of the application that is using multiple Oracle Application Server components. Most frequently, multi-tiered applications depend on multiple Application Server components and some non-Application Server components. To effectively monitor an application, the administrator needs to monitor a few things that are listed in the following sections.

Monitoring of Application Infrastructure

By Application Infrastructure, we mean all of the components that provide runtime support for an application. The administrator should monitor all such components collectively, as performance/availability issues on one of the components can affect application performance/ availability. For example, a J2EE application runs on OC4J, persists data in an Oracle database, and traffic to the application is routed through an HTTP server. If the HTTP server goes down, then for all practical purposes, the application is also down.

Enterprise Manager provides a construct **system** to group related targets. Enterprise Manager also provides a construct **service**, this service can be used to define and monitor the Service Level Agreements for a system.

To monitor an application, administrator can define a system that groups all the related targets and can define service for this system. Using this, a service administrator can monitor the availability of application infrastructure. A system and service can be created manually by adding all the related targets to a system.

It sounds like a lot of work, but Enterprise Manager provides support for creating a system and service automatically. Enterprise Manager introspects the application configuration to find out all the related targets for the application, and creates a system and service. For example, if there is an application that runs on a cluster of OC4Js and persists data in two databases, and traffic is routed to this application through an HTTP server, Enterprise Manager can look at the application configuration and build a system that groups the OC4Js, HTTP server and databases.

How to use this feature

Go to one of the OC4J homepages and click on the **Applications** tab; under **Active Applications** you will see all the applications. To create a system for an application, select the application and click on the **Create Service** button, on the next page you will be asked to provide a service name. The following screenshot shows this page.

On this page provide a service name and click on **OK**, it will create a service with the name you provided and a system by the same name with `_system` appended to it.

The following screenshot shows the homepage of a service, where it shows the availability of service that represents the application infrastructure. Under the **Key Component Service**, you can see the status of all of the components behind this service, you can also see alerts for all of the components in one place.

Monitoring end-user experience

Most of the time, the application issues are first reported by the users of the applications and at that time, it is very difficult to know the sequence of events that led to the issues.

The administrator can find such issues proactively and can get the correct sequence of events that led to the issue, if they can record typical user actions and replay it every fixed interval, and record the outcome of those actions.

Enterprise Manager provides a construct **test** that can be used to record user actions and it can be repeated from different **beacons**. Beacon is just a regular Enterprise Manager Agent that is converted to act as a beacon. You can put one beacon in each of the geographical locations where your user community resides and schedule the tests to be executed.

How to use this feature

From the Enterprise Manager homepage, click on the **Services** tab. From the next page, click on the service that you created in the previous section. It will take you to the service page, which you saw in the earlier exercise. On the service page select the **Monitoring Configuration** tab, the following screenshot shows the page that appears on doing so:

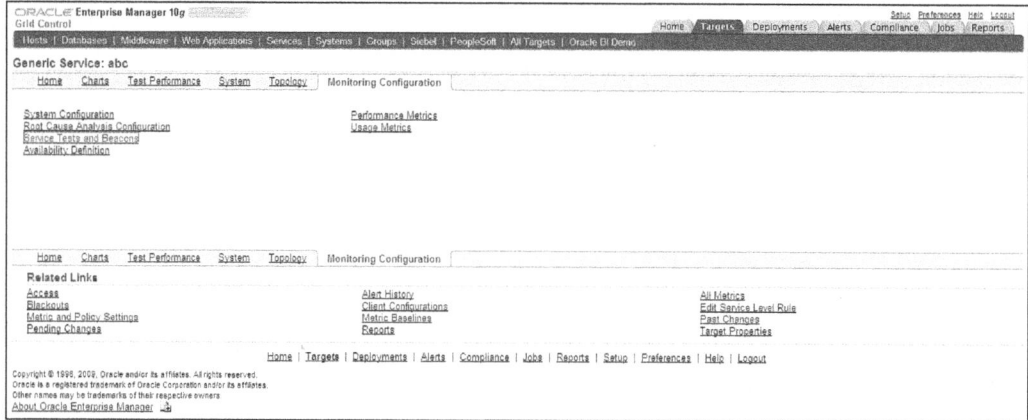

On the previous page, click on the **Service Tests and Beacons** link. From the next page, you can add various test types. For this exercise, select **Web Transaction,** and click on **Add**. You will see the page as shown in the following screenshot:

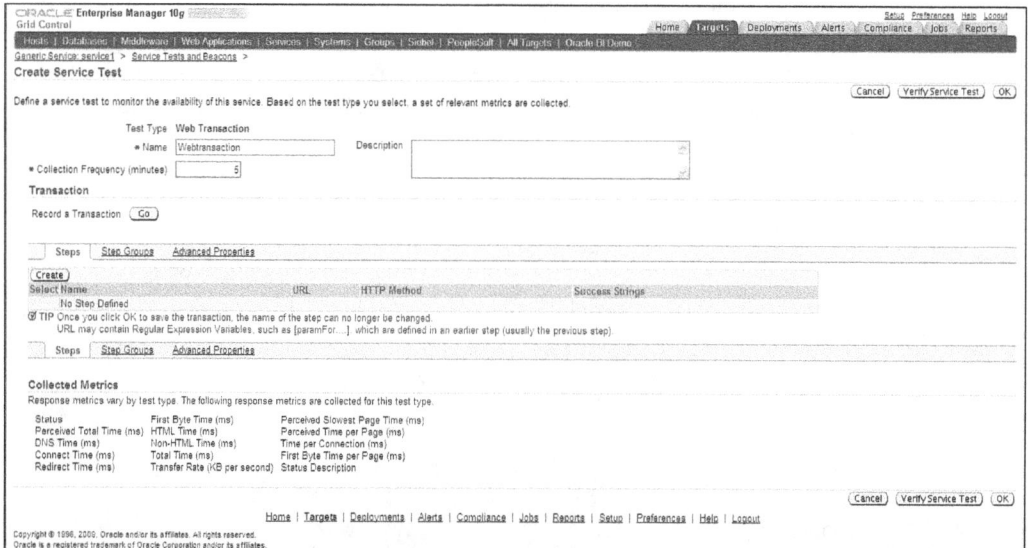

On this page, click on the **GO** button, next to **Record a Transaction**. The page that appears is shown in the following screenshot:

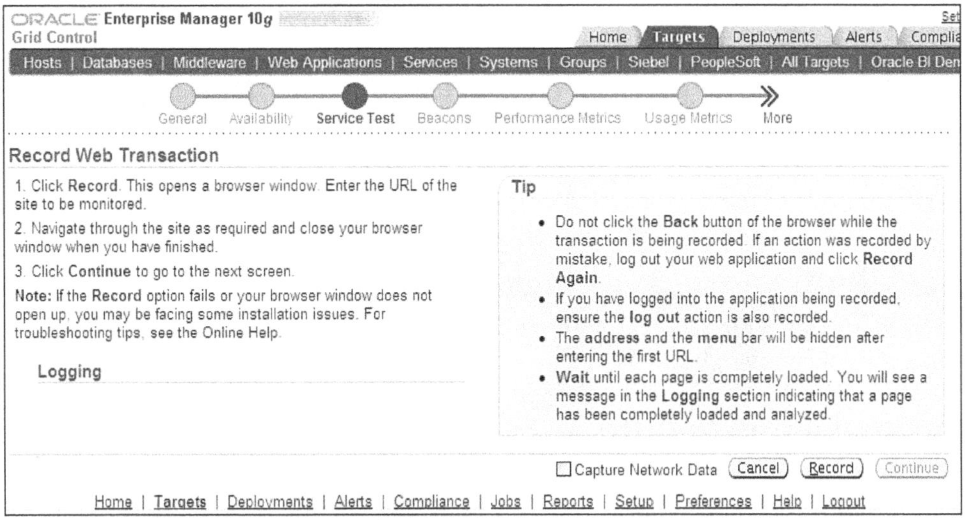

When you click on **Record** on this page, a new browser window will be opened, whatever web transaction you perform in this window will be recorded with Enterprise Manager. You can go to some of your application pages. After you have finished recording the transaction, close the new browser window, and click on the **OK** button in the main browser window. Your test is created and the test will be repeated at a fixed interval (the default value of the interval is every 5 minutes).

For every execution of this test, a status metric is generated and you can monitor the status of the test from the service homepage, as shown in the following screenshot:

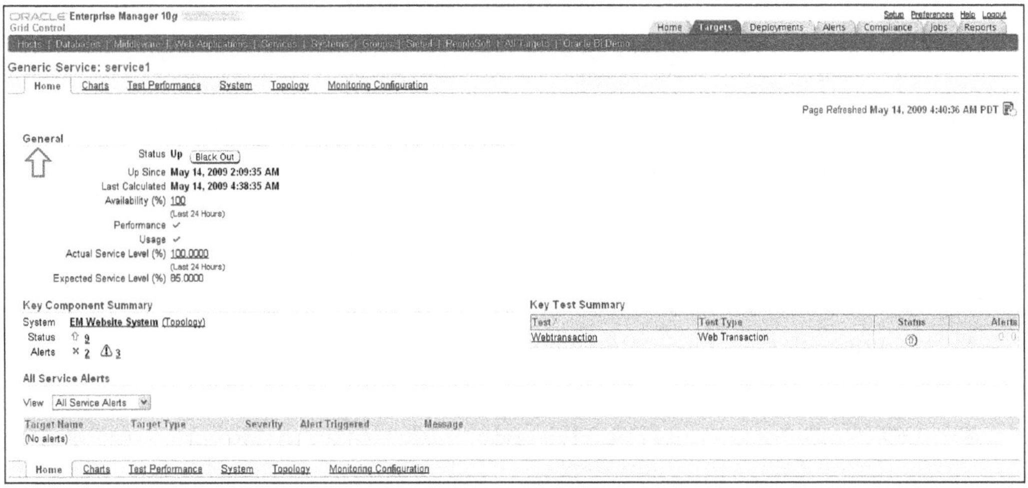

Using this service page, you can monitor all of the components on which an application depends, and you can monitor application availability as seen by the real user.

Thresholds and notifications for metrics

We learned in Chapter 3 that for each metric, you could set warning and critical thresholds. As an administrator, you will need to define these thresholds for various metrics. Enterprise Manager Console provides an interface, using which, you could set up the warning and critical thresholds.

You would like to be notified of some of the critical alerts; to achieve this, you need to define for which metrics you want to receive the notification, and what the notification mechanism is.

How to use this feature

To define the thresholds for a target, go to the target homepage and click on **Metrics and Policy Settings**. From this page you can update the thresholds for each metric.

To set up notifications methods, go to the Enterprise Manager homepage, and click on the **Setup** link in the top-right corner, on the subsequent page click on the **Notification Methods** link. From this page, you can configure your notification methods.

To define on what metrics you want to receive notifications, click on the **Preferences** link on the Enterprise Manager homepage. On the next page, you can see the **Notification Rules** link and using this, you can configure for which metrics you want to receive notifications and what the notification mechanism is.

Configuration management

Once the Application Server targets are installed and the monitoring setup is completed, the next important task for Oracle Application Server Administrator is Configuration management.

Enterprise Manager collects lots of important configuration parameters for Oracle Application Server targets. For example, some important configuration parameters that are collected for OC4J target are:

- Memory related: starting heap size, maximum heap size, and so on
- Network related: port range for AJP/HTTP/RMI
- JDBC Resources: name, JNDI Location, JDBC driver, maximum connection, minimum connection, and so on

Enterprise Manager also collects the configuration files for Oracle Application Server targets. Some of the important configuration files collected for an HTTP Server target are:

- `httpd.conf`
- `mod_oc4j.conf`
- `ssl.conf`
- `mime.types`

With this data you can perform tasks discussed in the next sections.

Configuration change tracking

Enterprise Manager provides the configuration change tracking feature, using this, you can see the complete configuration change history for the Application Server target. You can use this information in various ways, to identify any unauthorized configuration changes, or to co-relate performance changes with configuration changes.

How to use this feature

From any OC4J homepage click on **Administration** tab, from that tab click on the **Last Collected Configuration** link; you will see the last collected configuration for that OC4J target. You can see configuration categorized in different tabs. The following screenshot shows such a page:

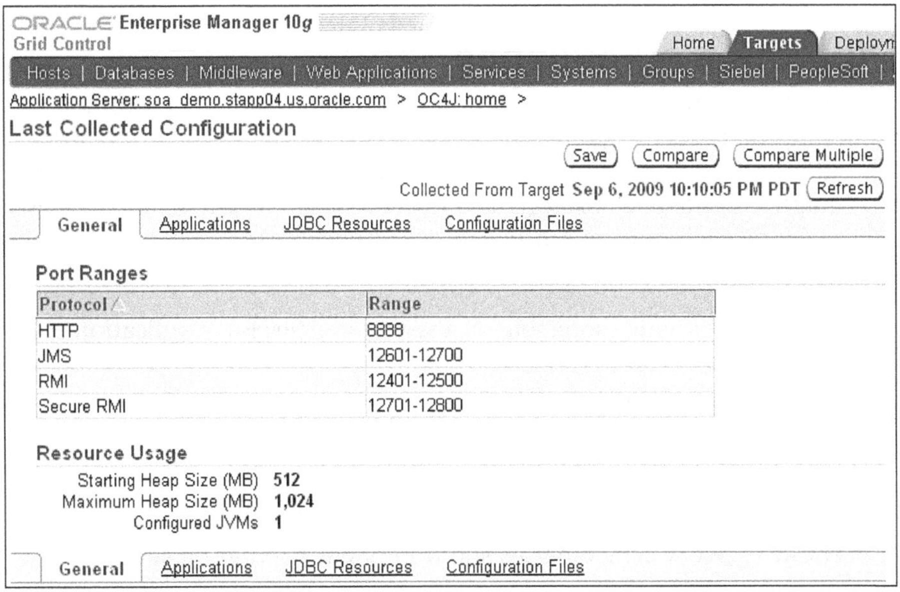

From this page you can go to configuration change history by clicking the **Configuration History** link. The following screenshot shows one such page:

This page allows you the flexibility of seeing all of the configuration changes or the configuration changes for a certain time window, you can use **Change Discovered after/before** fields to define such a window. The number under **History Records** shows the changes for that target. You can click the number link and on the next page, you will see the exact change made to the target configuration.

Configuration compliance

For every product there are some configuration guidelines by the product vendor, besides that every organization has it's own configuration guidelines. The Administrator needs to find out which targets don't conform to the guidelines. We learnt in Chapter 3, *Enterprise Manager Key Concepts and Subsystems*, that policy is a construct to define such rules or guidelines, and policies can be evaluated against a target to check for conformance.

Enterprise Manager provides some out-of-the-box policies for Application Server targets and some of them are:

- HTTP Server: HostNameLookup should be set to 'off'
- HTTP Server: Directory indexing should be disabled
- OC4J: Datasource passwords should not be in clear text
- WebCache: WebCache binaries should not have setuid bit set

Besides these policies, you can also define new policies. All the policies are saved in the policy library, you can decide on what policies should be enforced.

How to use this feature

From the Enterprise Manager homepage, select the **Compliance** tab. On the **Compliance** tab you can see the policy violation for all the targets under the violations sub-tab. You can filter violations by a particular target or target type. The following screenshot shows all of the violations for OC4J targets in a datacenter. It shows the name of OC4J, the policy that is violated, category of policy, most recent violation and for how long the policy is violated. It also shows the compliance score for a target that reflects the percentage of policies that a given target conforms to. From the **Library** sub-tab, you can see the library of all policies, and from the **Associations** tab, you can find out which policy is enforced on which target.

All such violations of policies can also be sent out as notifications. In the previous section, you learnt how to set notification rules for the metric alerts, the same page can be used to define notification rules for the policy violations.

Configuration comparison

We learnt in Chapter 3, *Enterprise Manager Key Concepts and Subsystems*, that configuration comparison is a great tool for troubleshooting. It's very common that something works in one environment and doesn't work in another environment. To troubleshoot such cases, administrators compare configuration of one environment with an other.

Enterprise Manager provides a great interface to do configuration comparison for Application Server targets, where you can see the summarized view of comparison and can drill down to individual configuration parameters. It also provides a file level comparison of the Application Server target configuration files.

How to use this feature

From any OC4J homepage click on the **Administration** tab, from that tab click on the **Last Collected Configuration Link**; you will see the last collected configuration for that OC4J target. From that page click on the **Compare** button and you will see a page, where you can select another target of the same type for comparison. The following screenshot shows one such page:

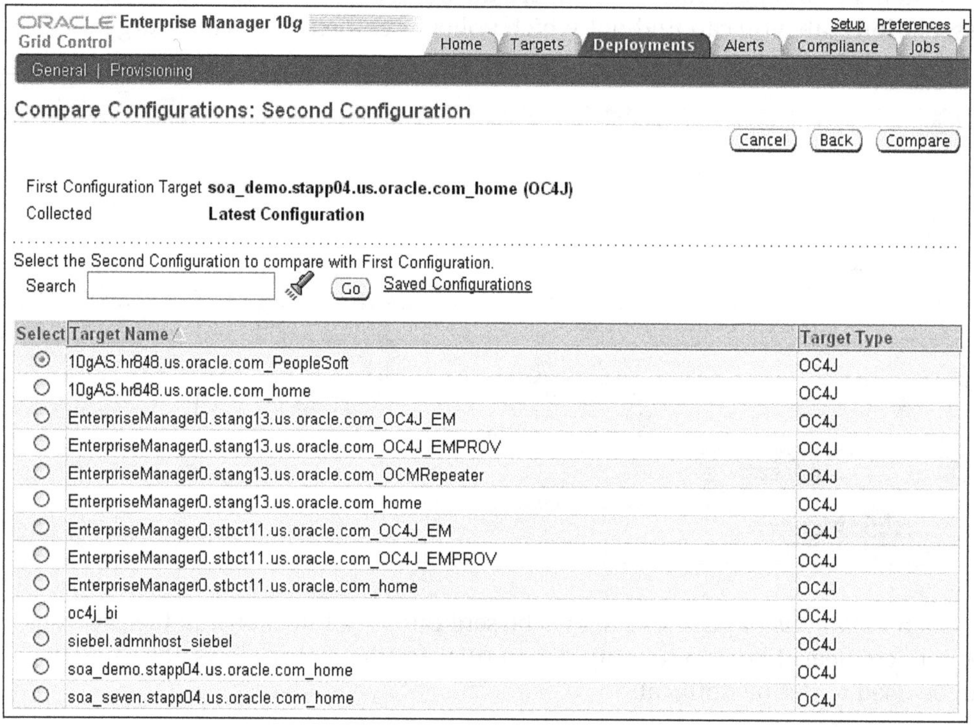

Select one target for comparison, and click on the **Compare** button. You will see a comparison page, as shown in the following screenshot:

You can see the summary of the comparison, which shows that there is a difference in the General configuration, applications are different, and some configuration files were updated. You can go to the respective tab to see the exact configuration comparison. We'll leave that as an exercise for you.

Under **Configuration Files** tab, you can see the file level comparison for the configuration files. The following screenshot shows one such view:

Patching

Patching is one of the routine tasks for the Oracle Application Server Administrators, ensuring all of the application servers are up-to-date with the latest patches is a tedious job.

The administrator needs to know the versions and current patches applied for all Application Servers. Using this information, the administrator can download all the required patches and can apply such patches on the application servers. The administrator also needs to check for new patches with regularity, which is a time-consuming process.

Enterprise Manager has an automated patching solution for Oracle Application Servers, where Enterprise Manager keeps on checking and downloading all required patches from "Oracle My Support" site. In Chapter 1, *Enterprise Manager Grid Control*, we learnt that Enterprise Manager keeps the inventory of all of the software and patches. This inventory information is used by Enterprise Manager to download only the needed patches.

Enterprise Manager also provides the deployment procedures to patch Oracle Application Server.

How to use the feature

The first step is to configure Enterprise Manager for getting patch advisory and patches from My Oracle Support site. Patch advisory is a list of suggested patches for all Oracle Products that is published by Oracle periodically. Using this configuration, Enterprise Manager can connect to My Oracle Support site and download the required data. For that configuration, click on the **Setup** link on the Enterprise Manager homepage, on the next page click on **Patching Setup**. On this page, you will need to provide the credentials for My Oracle Support account. Enterprise Manager uses these credentials to authenticate for My Oracle Support and download patches. The following screenshot shows the page where you can configure these credentials:

After this setup, Enterprise Manager can periodically connect to My Oracle Support site and download the latest patch advisory. The patch advisory has a list of recommended patches for all Oracle products, going through the whole list and finding out which patches your datacenter needs, could be time consuming and you could miss out on some of the patches. Enterprise Manager evaluates patch advisory with the inventory of Oracle products in the datacenter and finds out what Oracle products need to be patched.

These details are listed on the Enterprise Manager homepage; the following screenshot shows this data. You can see those details under the **Critical Patch Advisories for Oracle Homes** section. In this illustration, you see that **15 Oracle Homes** need to be patched.

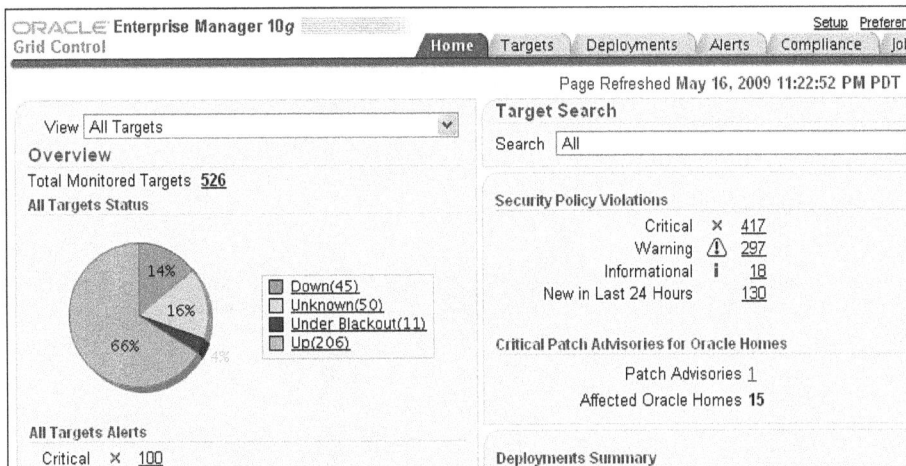

So, now we know that 15 Oracle Homes need to be patched, but you need to find which 15 Oracle Homes and what the Oracle Products are running on those Oracle Homes. To find this out, you need to click on the link next to the Patch advisories and you will see the page as shown next:

Patch Advisories

(Show Remedies)

Select	Advisory ▽		Impact	Abstract		Affected Hosts	Distinct Affected Homes
⊙	Critical Patch Update April 2009		Security	Oracle Critical Security Update		10	15

Patchsets to Apply

Patchset	Product	Release	Platform	Advisory	Homes
No patchsets found					

Interim Patches to Apply

Patch ▽	Product	Interim Patch Applicable on	Platform	Advisory	Homes
8333655	Oracle Database	11.1.0.6.0	Microsoft Windows (32-bit)	Critical Patch Update April 2009	2
8307237	Oracle Database	10.2.0.4	Microsoft Windows (32-bit)	Critical Patch Update April 2009	1
8298240	Oracle Fusion Middleware	10.1.3.3.0	Linux x86	Critical Patch Update April 2009	1
8298240	Oracle Fusion Middleware	10.1.3.3.0	Microsoft Windows (32-bit)	Critical Patch Update April 2009	3
8298235	Oracle Fusion Middleware	10.1.2.3	Linux x86	Critical Patch Update April 2009	3
8298235	Oracle Fusion Middleware	10.1.2.3	Microsoft Windows (32-bit)	Critical Patch Update April 2009	1
8290534	Oracle Database	10.1.0.5	Linux x86	Critical Patch Update April 2009	2
8290506	Oracle Database	10.2.0.4	Linux x86	Critical Patch Update April 2009	1
8290402	Oracle Database	11.1.0.6.0	Linux x86	Critical Patch Update April 2009	1

Patch Advisories	Affected Homes	Remedies

This page shows a filtered view of the detailed patch advisory, it shows only the patches applicable to the products that you have in your datacenter. It also shows the number of Oracle Homes where these patches need to be applied. The right-most column in the table provides the link to Oracle Home, where a particular patch needs to be applied. Once you click on that link you will see a page as shown next:

Critical Patch Advisories for Oracle Homes >

Critical Patch: 8298240

The following homes have been identifed as homes in your configuration that may need to be updated with this patch. Please review the ReadMe, and select all homes from the list below that you have determined will need to be patched.   (View ReadMe)

For advanced features like multiple patch application, patch flow customization, sudo and PAM support use the " Deployment Procedures " functionality. For details on Deployment Procedures, consult the relevant documentation

Status	
Downloaded	
Created On	
Last Referenced On	
Type	**Patch**
Description	
Product	**Oracle Fusion Middleware**
Release	**10.1.3.3.0**
Platform	**Microsoft Windows (32-bit)**
Language	**American English**
Manually Posted	

Affected Oracle Homes

(Patch)

Select All | Select None

Select	Oracle Home	Host
☑	D:\10.1.3.1\OracleAS_1(oracleas1) ⓘ	emgc-amp41.us.oracle.com
☑	C:\AS(oracleas1) ⓘ	emgc-bi.us.oracle.com
☑	D:\10.1.3.1\OracleAS_1(oracleas1) ⓘ	emgc-amp3.us.oracle.com

ⓘ The Oracle Home version does not satisfy the Patch pre-requisite version. You must upgrade the Oracle Home to the Patch pre-requisite version before applying the Patch.

(View ReadMe)

Home | Targets | **Deployments** | Alerts | Compliance | Jobs | Reports | Setup | Preferences | Help | Logout

On this page, you see which Oracle Homes need to be patched and the host where these Oracle Homes are installed. You will see many blanks on this page such as **Status**, **Downloaded**, **Created On**, and so on, because so far we have downloaded only patch advisories and not the actual patches.

At this point you know about all the patches that you need to apply to stay up-to-date with the recommendations from Oracle. You also know the Oracle Homes and hosts where these patches are applied. It's time to apply the patches.

Enterprise Manager provides a deployment procedure to apply the patches on Oracle Application Servers, using this, you can apply one or more patches on one or more application server targets. In the next few steps, we'll see how to use that deployment procedure.

To use the Application Server deployment procedure, click on the **Deployments** tab on the Enterprise Manager homepage. From the **Deployments** tab, click on the link, **Patching through Deployment Procedures**, this takes you to a page that lists various deployment procedures. The following screenshot shows such a page:

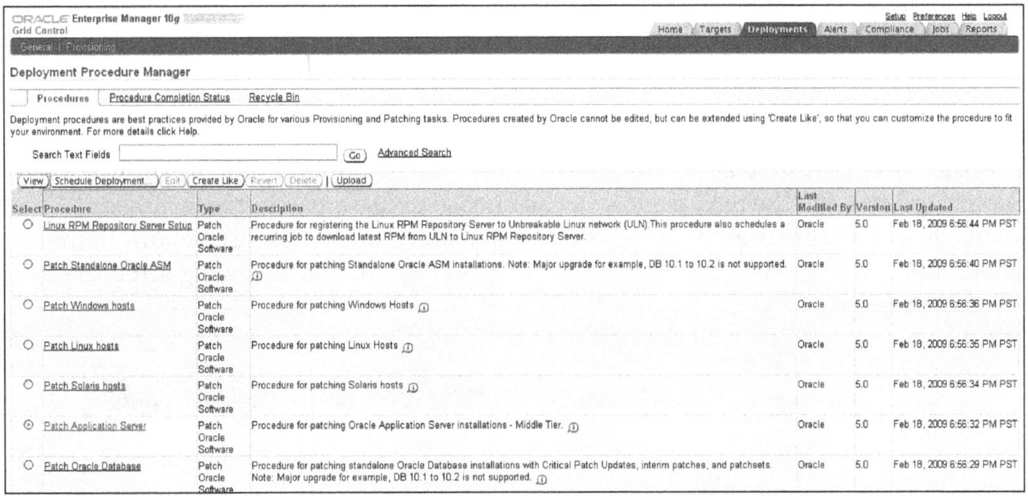

From this page, select the radio button next to **Patch Application Server** and click on the **Schedule Deployment** button on the top of the table. You will see a page as shown next:

On this page you need to provide the staging location where this patch will be staged. The patch will be applied from this staging location. You will need to select the patches you want to apply, to do so click on the **Add** button under Application Server updates. On the next page, you can choose to use a patch that is already available in the software library or choose a patch from My Oracle Support. In this illustration, we'll go with the My Oracle Support option. The following screenshot shows this page:

On this page, you can enter the details to search the patches that you want to apply. For this illustration we used a patch number that we got from the patch advisory, Oracle Fusion Middleware as product family, Oracle Application Server as Product and Linux X86 as platform. Once you click on the **GO** button, Enterprise Manager will search My Oracle Support to get more details on patches that meet search parameters. In this case, the search returns with only one patch. The following screenshot shows the page after performing a search on My Oracle Support:

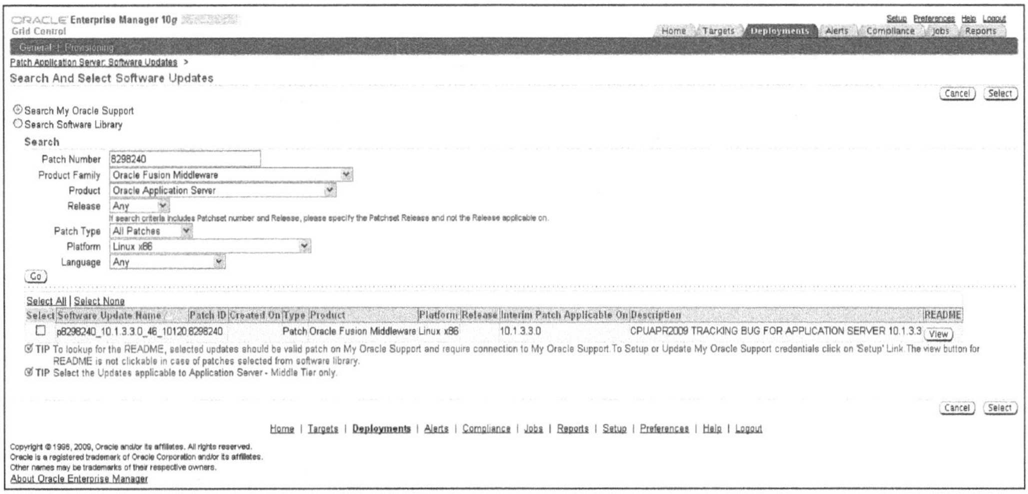

Once you have made the choice through the **Select** check box, you can click on the **Select** button. You will be taken back to the first page of the deployment procedure, and your screen will look like the figure shown next:

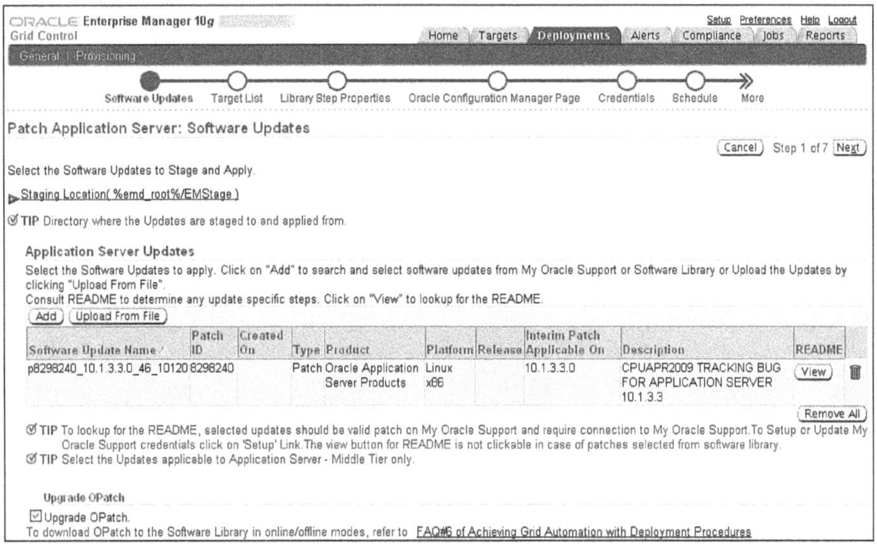

There are a few more things to see before we go to the next step, this page provides an option to upgrade the Opatch. Opatch is a tool provided by Oracle to apply the patches. Enterprise Manager can also upgrade the Opatch as part of patching, if required. You can also choose to blackout the target during patching to avoid unnecessary alerts if the target has to be stopped during patching.

Once you click on **Next,** you will see **Step 2** of this flow where you can add the targets that you want to apply the patches to. The following screenshot shows that page:

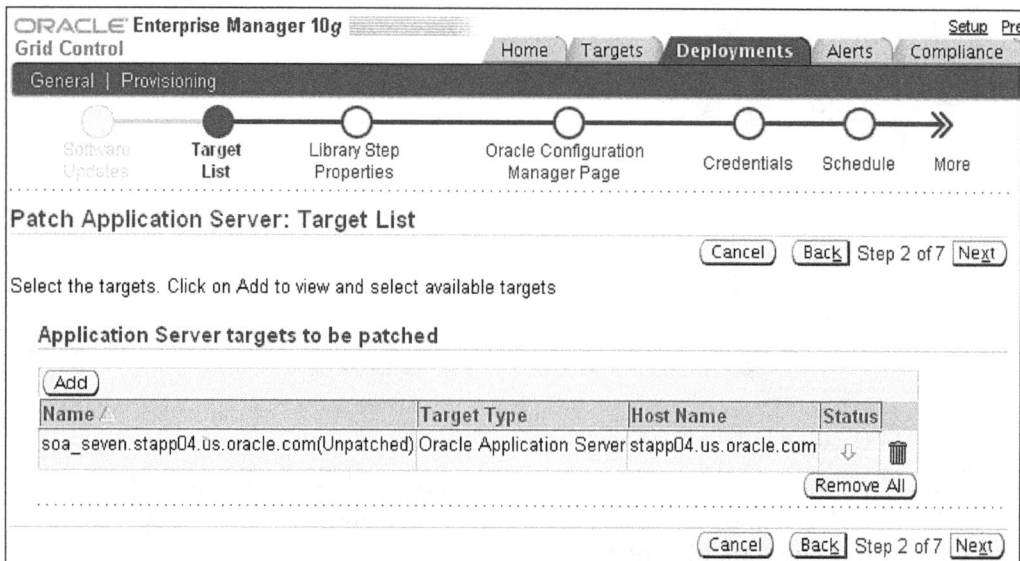

On the next few pages, you will be prompted to provide some more details, like host credentials for the hosts where product to be patched are running. You will also be asked to provide a unique name for this patching operation—using that, you can track the status of the operation later on. Once you go through these steps this patching operation will be scheduled, where Enterprise Manager will download the patch from My Oracle Support and will apply that patch on a selected target.

You can keep track of the patching operation from the **Deployments** tab by clicking on **Procedure Completion Status**. On this page, you will see the status of all deployment procedures. The following screenshot shows one such page:

Once the deployment procedure shows success status on the previous screen, your patches are applied to the selected application server.

Summary

In this chapter, we learned how to manage Oracle Application Server targets using Enterprise Manager. The key takeaways from this chapter are:

- Enterprise Manager supports management of multiple farms and application server instances

- Enterprise Manager provides provisioning support for Oracle Application Servers

- Provisioning support for Application Server includes initial provisioning and provisioning from a referenced environment

- Using Enterprise Manager, you can monitor the availability and performance of application server components

- To monitor an application, you need to monitor all the Application Server components that provide runtime support for application

- You can monitor applications using the web transaction test

- You can use configuration collections of Oracle Application Server for change tracking and configuration compliance

- Enterprise Manager provides patching automation for Oracle Application Server

In this chapter, we covered the management and monitoring of Oracle Application Server. In the next chapter, we will learn about management of Forms and Reports Server and Applications. See you at the next stop!

6
Managing Forms and Reports Services and Applications

Oracle Forms and Reports are components of Oracle Developer Suite and are very popular tools used to build enterprise applications. These were primarily used to build client-server applications. However, Forms Services and Report Services components of Oracle Application Servers allowed users to deploy Oracle Forms and Reports in the web and therefore, Oracle Forms and Reports became very widely deployed applications in many organizations. Also, many packaged applications such as Oracle eBusiness Suite use Oracle Forms and Reports. In the previous chapter we learnt about the management of Oracle Application Server.

In this chapter, we will learn about the management of Oracle Forms and Reports Services and Forms applications from Grid Control. We will discuss the following:

- Architecture of Oracle Forms and Reports Server
- Monitoring of Forms Server, Reports Server, and Forms applications
- Cloning and provisioning of Oracle Forms and Reports Server.

Architecture of Oracle Forms and Reports Services

Oracle Forms and Reports Services run on a middle-tier instance of Oracle Application Server. Forms Servlets and Reports Servlets are actually Java servlet applications that run inside an OC4J container, and facilitate communication between the client browser and the Forms/Reports process that run in the middletier server. The following figure depicts the architecture for Forms Services:

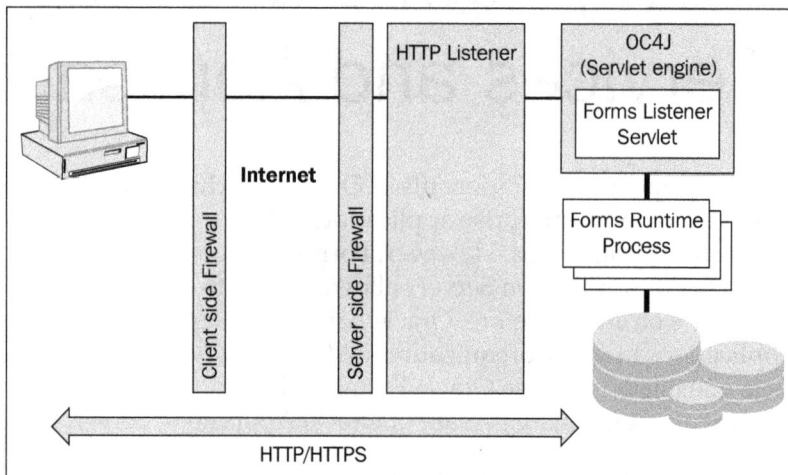

The Forms Listener services acts as broker between client browser and Forms Runtime Process where Forms applications are deployed. The Forms Server manages the application logic and connections to the database on behalf of the client.

The Reports Services have a similar architecture. You may have both Forms and Reports Services deployed as a part of the same middle-tier instance.

You can use Oracle Application Server Control to manage Oracle Forms and Reports Services. Note that you need Oracle Management Agent to manage Oracle Forms and Reports Services with Oracle Application Server Control. You can use Oracle Enterprise Manager Grid Control to manage your Oracle Forms and Reports Services. This will help you to monitor your entire application infrastructure from a single management console. You will get several additional benefits such as historical metrics for your server, service level management for Forms applications, and deployment automation for your application server environment.

Monitoring of Oracle Forms and Reports Services

Proactive monitoring of Forms and Reports Services are key aspects of ensuring availability for Forms and Reports applications. In this section, we will learn about discovery and monitoring of Forms and Reports Services.

Discovery of Oracle Forms and Reports Server

In the last chapter, we discussed the discovery of Oracle Application Server. We learnt about the Oracle Application Server discovery process. If Oracle Forms and Reports Services are installed with a middle-tier instance of Oracle Application Server then those are automatically discovered by Enterprise Manager Grid Control. The following screenshot shows the homepage of an Oracle Application Server instance that has Forms and Reports Services running. You can monitor the health of Forms and Reports Services and OC4J instances where these services are running. Also you may use Oracle HTTP Server or Web cache running infront Forms Servers and you can monitor all of them together. This helps you to diagnose if your Forms and Reports applications are running slowly or not responding.

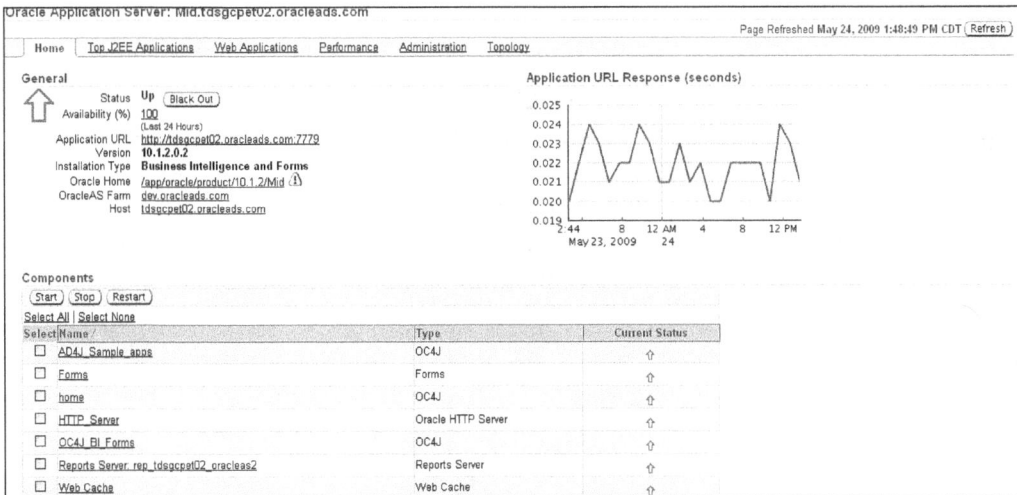

Managing Forms Server

You can find out the **Status** of Forms Service from the Forms Server homepage in Grid Control. You can get a historical view of the availability of the Oracle Forms Server. If you want to make any configuration changes to your Forms Server then you can access the **Oracle Application Server Control** from the Forms homepage, as shown in the following figure.

You can also take the benefits of EM Job system to recycle Forms Server or application server. For example, should you want to recycle your Forms Server every weekend then you can do that.

Setting the metric thresholds

Similar to the other targets such as Oracle Application Server and Oracle WebLogic Server, you can implement a proactive monitoring for Forms Server through setting the metric thresholds and getting notified when an alert is raised. You can set **Warning Threshold** and **Critical Threshold** for several metrics such as **Status**, **Total CPU(%)** usage, **Total Memory(%)** usage, **Total number of users**, and so on, as shown in the following screenshot:

Metric	Comparison Operator	Warning Threshold	Critical Threshold	Corrective Actions	Collection Schedule	Details
Response Time (ms)	>	500	1000	None	Every 1 Minute	⬚⬚
Status			Down	None	Every 1 Minute	⬚⬚
Total CPU (%)	>			None	Every 1 Minute	⬚⬚
Total CPU (%)	>			None	Every 1 Minute	⬚⬚
Total Memory (%)	>	80	90	None	Every 1 Minute	⬚⬚
Total Memory (%)	>	80	90	None	Every 1 Minute	⬚⬚
Total number of users	>			None	Every 1 Minute	⬚⬚
Total Private Memory (%)	>	80	90	None	Every 1 Minute	⬚⬚
Total Shared Memory (%)	>	80	90	None	Every 1 Minute	⬚⬚

For example, you can set a threshold that states that you want to get a warning alert when the number of users reaches 50, and get a critical alert when the number of concurrent users reaches 75. If you want to set up a notification mechanism, such as an email, then you can do so. You can refer to our discussions on setting up notifications mechanisms in Chapter 4, *Managing Oracle WebLogic Server*, and those same steps apply here.

Managing Reports Server

You can monitor the health of Reports Server and Report Jobs from Enterprise Manager Grid Control. You get the benefits such as historical performance data and proactive monitoring from Grid Control. As we have discussed earlier, Grid Control does not provide any support for making configuration changes for Reports Server. The following screenshot shows the homepage for the Reports Server.

You can get both the real time and historical view of the performance data for the Reports Server and Reports Jobs submitted/running on the Reports Server. For example, you can get metrics such as CPU and memory usage for the Reports Server and average response time, and so on. The historical metrics enables you to perform a trend analysis for your Reports Server and plan for future growth. Similarly, Grid Control provides you both real time and historical data about the job load, completed job, and potential run-away jobs, as shown in the following screenshot. This helps you to take the appropriate action.

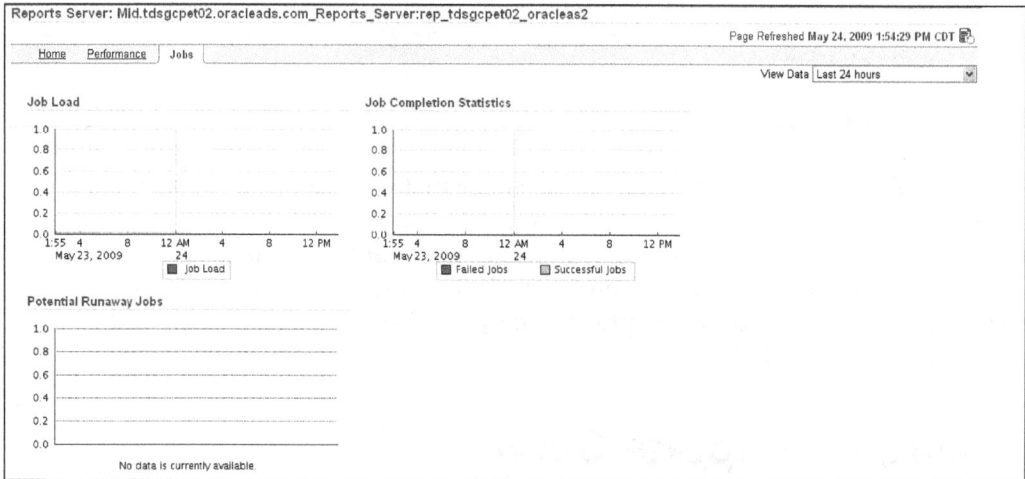

Setting the metric thresholds

You can set the metric thresholds for a few critical metrics that you want to proactively monitor. One of the key metrics is monitoring the failed Reports. You do not want your user communities to be upset with the failed Reports. The failure of Report Jobs could be due to problems in the Reports Server, the host, or the underlying database, and you would want to be notified before it becomes a real problem. Grid Control allows you to set a threshold for a failed job ratio and an alert is raised as soon as the threshold is raised. For example, we have set the **Warning Threshold** and **Critical Threshold** as **25**% and **33**% respectively in the following screenshot.

However, you may want this to be lower in your environment.

Monitoring Forms applications

The most interesting feature of Forms Management using Grid Control is to perform Service Level Management for Forms applications. You can create/model Forms application target in Grid Control and use that to monitor your Forms application. For example, you have built a custom application such as an HR, Finance, or Customer Service and deployed that to the web. You can use Grid Control to monitor the performance of Forms application. You may remember our discussion in Chapter 4, *Managing Oracle WebLogic Server*, where we created a web application for a custom Java application. You can use a similar approach to define, monitor, and playback a specific flow of your Forms application, where each flow is recorded as a single Forms transaction. Simply put, a Forms transaction consists of a set of user actions within a single application when using Forms, for example, querying an employee record. Grid Control allows you to record multiple Forms transactions by using the playback recorder that automatically records the Forms actions.

There are two aspects to Forms transaction monitoring and end-user performance. The Forms transaction monitoring helps you to track down the performance of a specific Forms transaction and verify whether you are meeting the **Service Level Agreement (SLA)** for the transaction.

However, the end-user monitoring feature allows you to measure the response time data, as experienced by end-users while they are performing a Forms operation. Grid Control helps you to measure the total response time, server time, and the database time for Forms operations such as Commit, Query, Runform, Callform, Newform, and Openform. This can help you to identify bottlenecks in your application. Grid Control also helps you to define a watch list for the most important Forms actions for your application and monitor and view the response metrics of those critical operations.

> The end-user performance monitoring requires the Forms application to be front-ended with Oracle HTTP Server, Oracle Web cache, and Apache HTTP Server. If you want to really monitor the real user performance, Oracle Real User Experience Insight Product is recommended.

To enable Forms transactions monitoring you have to perform the following system:

- Configure your Windows client
- Configure SSL certificate for your Enterprise Manager
- Enable Forms transaction recording in your Forms Server
- Build a system or redundancy group that includes the Forms Server, Oracle HTTP Server, Web cache, and OC4J system that is used for your Form application
- Create a Forms application
- Create one or more Forms transactions
- Associate one or more beacons for performing the service test

> The Forms transaction monitoring and end user performance monitoring only works in specific versions of Oracle Forms, please check the certification list of the Grid Control documentation for your version.

Configure your Windows client

You will probably use a Windows client such as a laptop or a desktop that you use for accessing Grid Control. You will probably use this client to record the Forms transaction. This client needs to be configured with proper Java permissions to record and playback the Forms transaction. You have to ensure that your user home directory has a `.java.policy` file with permissions to access Forms application running on each Oracle Application Server. The following should be the contents of `.java.policy` file:

```
grant codeBase " http://formsServerHost:port/forms/java/*»
{permission java.security.SecurityPermission
                                    «putProviderProperty.SunJSSE»;
};
```

If you are using Forms application as a part of Oracle eBusiness suite then the contents of the `.java.policy` file should look as follows:

```
grant codeBase "http://appsHost:appsPort/OA_JAVA/oracle/apps/fnd/
jar/*"
{
  permission java.security.SecurityPermission
                                    "putProviderProperty.SunJSSE";
};
```

Ensure that you replace the URL with the correct host and port name for your application.

Configure SSL certificate

You have correctly configured the SSL certificate if you are using any of the following:

- If you are using a secured Grid Control to record the Forms transaction, then you have to ensure that the certificate used by Grid Control is trusted by Oracle Jinitiator or Java Plug-In that you use to run Forms application
- If you use secured Forms application, then you have to ensure that the certificate used by the Forms application is added to the Oracle Management Agent that plays back the Forms transaction.

Refer to the *Oracle Enterprise Manager Grid Control Advanced Configuration Guide* for detailed instructions on how to perform these steps.

Creating a Forms System

As we discussed earlier, you have to create a Forms System target that contains the Oracle Web Cache or Oracle HTTP Server/Apache HTTP Server targets, Forms Server as shown in the following screenshot. We have also learnt about system modeling in Chapter 4, *Managing Oracle WebLogic Server*.

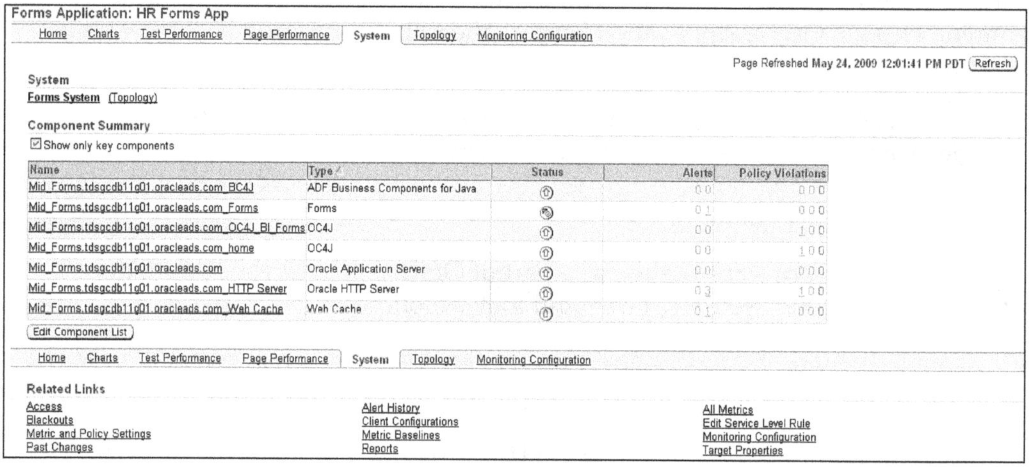

You must include these components as of part of your Forms application or as part of a key Redundancy Group. The Redundancy Group for HTTP Server is referred to as the HTTP Server HA Group.

Creating Forms application

Creation of Forms application is similar to web application. You can create a Forms application Target by going to **Services** page and selecting **Forms Target** from the **Add** drop-down list, as shown in the following screenshot.

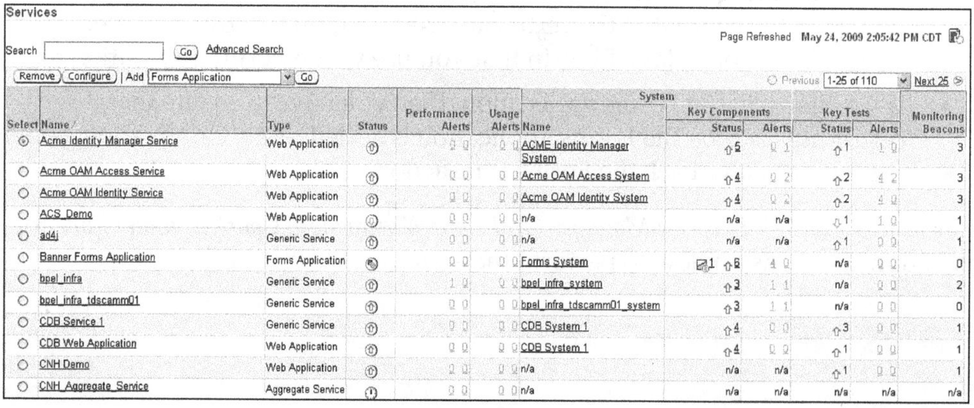

Then, you provide a unique name for the Forms application. If you are planning to use the Forms application monitoring from Grid Control extensively, then you should select a good user-friendly name.

Then you can select the availability, either based on the system or the service test. In the next step we will record a service test for Forms monitoring.

> You have to use Internet Explorer to record a service test. The transaction recorder will be downloaded automatically from the OMS on your first attempt to record a transaction. The recorder requires some Microsoft libraries to be installed on your computer and it will be downloaded automatically. You must have Internet access to download these libraries from the Microsoft website.

Recording of a Forms transaction is similar to a web transaction that we learnt about in Chapter 4, *Managing Oracle WebLogic Server*. You have to enter the test name and collection frequency before you start recording a transaction. Note that collection frequency is the frequency at which the beacon wakes up to perform the Forms test.

You have to click on **Go** and then enter the URL for the Forms Server. It will launch JInitiator or Java plug-in and then the Forms will be loaded. You have to login to the application and perform the steps that you want to record. After you close the window the data will be captured. After you have successfully recorded the transaction, you have to select the beacons, performance metrics, and usage metrics. We leave those as an exercise.

There are a few things that you have to make sure for Form Server recorder. You have to ensure that you have specified the correct **Forms Server URL**.

If you are using a Single Sign-on Server or Oracle Applications Login, make sure that you change the login type and enter the correct login URL. You can specify some **Advanced Properties** such as **Forms Module Path**. This parameter specifies the absolute path of the location of the Forms binaries on the server host. This is typically useful when you record a transaction against one Forms Server and then playback the same against another server.

Connection Type	HTTP or HTTPS
Recording Description	Forms Version : MENU_ITEM_SELECTED, Execute Query, WINDOW1 Menu item "Execute Query" selected in Window "WINDOW1".

▼ Credentials

Login URL	
Login Type	Forms Login
* Username	scott
* Password	••••••

▼ Advanced Properties

Database Connect String	dev
Forms SID	
Forms Module Path	
Configuration	**Name** **Value** =

Collected Metrics

Response metrics vary by test type. The following response metrics are collected for this test type.

Status	Slowest Time (ms)
Total Time (ms)	Network Latency (ms)
Login Time (ms)	Database Time (ms)
Forms Time (ms)	Server Time (ms)
Average Time Per Message (ms)	Status Description

> In order for Forms Transaction Recording to work successfully you have to enable Forms Transaction monitoring. You can do so by accessing the **Monitoring Configuration** link from the Forms Server **Home** page and selecting **Enable Transaction Monitoring**.

Once you have successfully created the service test and selected the beacon, the service test will be executed, and you can monitor the performance of your application. You can enforce the correct service level rule and if you get a service level violation, then an alert will be raised. You can create several reports such as Service Dash Board report for reporting purposes. We leave that as an exercise for you.

Forms and Reports provisioning

In Chapter 5, *Managing Oracle Application Server,* we learnt about the provisioning of Oracle Application Server. The Grid Control deployment procedures help you to clone a test environment to production or vice versa. This greatly automates a lot of manual and error prone tasks. Grid Control provides Forms and Reports Provisioning Deployment Procedure that supports cloning and configuration of Oracle Application Server Forms and Reports Services installations.

Note that Forms and Reports Services install type allows you to install and configure Forms and Reports Services without having to install and configure all of Oracle Application Server 10*g*. If you use Oracle Application Server Forms and Reports Services installed as a part of Oracle Infrastructure, then you cannot use this deployment procedure. Grid Control supports cloning of Oracle Forms and Reports Services either from a reference install or from a gold image.

> Only a limited number of platforms and versions are certified for provisioning Forms and Reports Services. Check the certification matrix with Oracle support to verify whether your platform/version is certified. Also, you have to make sure that both the source and target hosts are managed by Oracle Management Agent 10.2.0.4 or higher.

Also, you have to remember that the Forms and Reports Provisioning Deployment Procedure does not support cloning of Oracle Application Server Web Cache to machines with virtual host names.

You have to perform the following tasks to clone Oracle Forms and Reports Services software:

* Select the Deployment procedures from the Deployment procedure Manager section by navigating to **Deployments** tab and then selecting the **Forms and Reports Provisioning** Deployment procedure, as shown in the following screenshot:

Select	Procedure	Type	Description	Last Modified By	Version	Last Updated
○	Live Migration	Virtualization	Perform live migration of a particular virtual machine or live migrate all virtual machines in a particular virtual server.	Oracle	1.0	Mar 6, 2009 7:25:36 PM CST
○	Oracle Database Replay Client Provisioning	Database Provisioning	This procedure installs or clones a database replay client on the selected hosts. It follows the best practices specified by the Oracle Database Installation Guide. ⓘ	Oracle	5.0	Feb 18, 2009 6:56:47 PM CST
○	Oracle Database Provisioning	Database Provisioning	This procedure installs or clones a single instance database home and configures a database on the selected hosts. It follows the best practices specified by the Oracle Database Installation Guide. ⓘ	Oracle	5.0	Feb 18, 2009 6:56:38 PM CST
○	Application Server Deployment (myJ2EE) 10.1.2.0.2	AS Provisioning	This procedure installs and configures a standard Web and Application Tier for a multi-tier application server topology. It follows the installation and configuration of the 'myJ2EE' best practice topology, as specified by the Oracle Application Server Enterprise Deployment Guide. ⓘ	Oracle	5.0	Feb 18, 2009 6:56:11 PM CST
◉	Forms and Reports Provisioning	Forms and Reports Provisioning	This procedure clones forms and reports instance on selected hosts. It follows the best practices specified by the Forms and Reports Installation Guide. Refer to online help for updated information on certification, supported methods for provisioning and related information ⓘ	Oracle	4.0	Apr 25, 2007 5:15:23 AM CDT

- Select the **Forms and Reports Provisioning** deployment procedure you want to run, and click on **Schedule Deployment...**.

- You can select the source from which to clone and the destination host machines on which to clone Forms and Reports Services, and schedule the deployment operation.

- You can review the page and the click Finish to schedule the deployment.

Grid Control will copy the binaries and configurations to your new hosts and provision new servers in the new hosts. Also Grid Control will automatically discover the newly installed Forms and Reports Servers for monitoring purpose.

Summary

Oracle Forms and Reports are a very popular framework to build enterprise applications on. Oracle Forms and Reports Server run on top of Oracle Application Server. Forms and Reports Services are automatically discovered when Oracle Application Server is discovered. Grid Control allows monitoring of Forms and Reports Server and Forms applications. You can use Forms Transactions and beacons to manage the service level for Forms applications. Grid Control also helps automation of Forms and Reports Server by providing a deployment procedure.

In the next chapter, we'll be learning about the management and monitoring of BPEL Process Manager, that is used for orchestration of services of Service Oriented Architecture. We'll also learn how Enterprise Manager helps in monitoring the business processes that are executed using BPEL Process Manager.

7
SOA Management—BPEL Management

The **Service Oriented Architecture (SOA)** is fast becoming the preferred choice for implementing new business systems or integrating existing business systems. Most of the middleware vendors provide some platform or product suite for implementing cost effective Service Oriented Architectures. These product suites are also used for flexible and faster integration of disparate systems hence some times these are referred to as integration suites.

Oracle Application Server SOA suite is one of the leading integration platforms in the market. SOA suite contains many components. In this chapter, we'll focus on the management of a core component of SOA suite and that is BPEL process.

In this book, we'll use the term BPEL PM for Oracle BPEL process manager.

In this chapter, we will cover the:

- Introduction of BPEL process manager. We'll introduce you to BPEL PM, typical usage, and deployment.
- Discovery of BPEL process manager. BPEL PM can run on all major J2EE containers like OC4J, WebLogic, and WebSphere. We'll cover the discovery of BPEL PM on all major J2EE containers.
- Monitoring of BPEL Process Manager and BPEL processes.
- Configuration management for BPEL process manager. Besides the configuration management of BPEL PM, we'll also provide an overview of configuration management for business processes implemented as BPEL executables.

- Lifecycle management for BPEL process manager. We will also cover provisioning of business process implemented as BPEL executables. Provisioning and patching for BPEL PM running on OC4J.

- Best practices for the management of BPEL PM.

Introducing BPEL Process Manager

Business Process Execution Language (**BPEL**) is fast becoming the standard for business process orchestration. Using BPEL, one can define interactions between various web-services. Most of the major software vendors like Oracle, IBM, and Microsoft support BPEL standard and have products compliant to BPEL standards.

BPEL process manager is a product from Oracle that is a container for the execution of BPEL executables. Users can deploy the BPEL definitions on a BPEL process manager, and the BPEL process manager takes care of runtime tasks like scheduling, load balancing, failover, persistence, and so on.

In this book, we will use the term BPEL process for business process definition defined using BPEL constructs, and BPEL PM for BPEL process manager.

BPEL PM is a Java based product that can run on top of a J2EE container. BPEL PM is certified to run on top of OC4J, WebLogic, and WebSphere J2EE containers. BPEL PM also needs a database for storing the state of each BPEL process invocation. This database is generally referred to as dehydration store. BPEL PM uses Oracle database as dehydration store. Just like any other J2EE application, traffic is routed to BPEL PM through the HTTP gateway or load balancer.

The following screenshot shows one sample deployment of BPEL PM where BPEL PM is deployed on a cluster of OC4Js and the dehydration store is running on top of Oracle RAC database. Traffic to BPEL PM is routed through Load balancer.

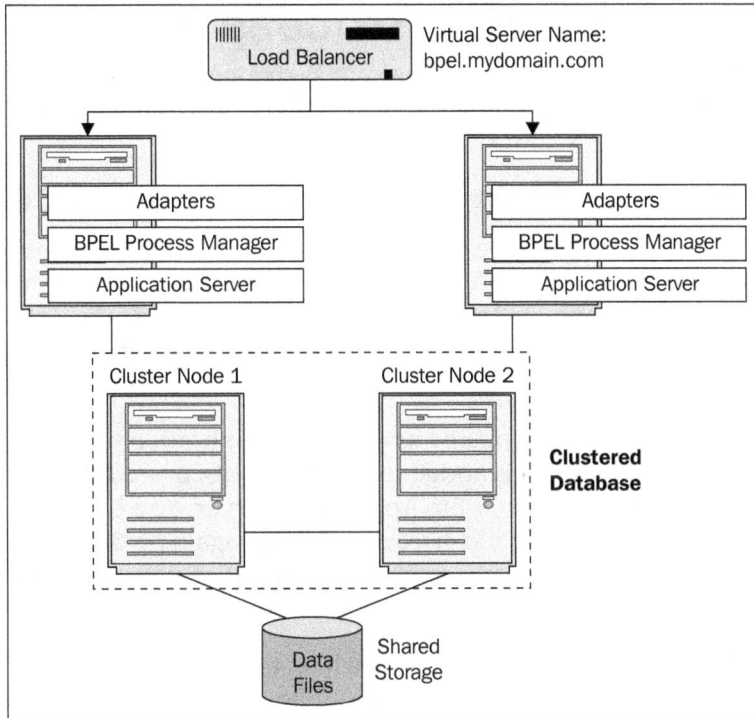

Supported versions

Enterprise Manager provides BPEL PM management from release 10.2.0.3 onwards. The following is the support Matrix for Enterprise Manager for different versions of BPEL PM on different J2EE containers:

EM Version	BPEL PM 10.1.3.3/4 + OC4J 10.1.3.3/4	BPEL PM 10.1.3.3/4 + WebLogic 9.2	BPEL PM 10.1.3.3/4 + WebSphere 6.1	BPEL PM 10.1.3.1 + OC4J 10.1.3.1	BPEL PM 10.1.2 + OC4J 10.1.2
10.2.0.5	Yes	Yes	Yes	Yes	Yes
10.2.0.4	Yes	Yes	Yes	Yes	No
10.2.0.3	No	No	No	Yes	No

You can see that in every release after 10.2.0.3, more certifications are added to Enterprise Manager. Besides more certifications, many new features were also added in 10.2.0.4 and 10.2.0.5 releases. In this book, we'll be explaining the features available for 10.2.0.5.

Discovery of BPEL Process Manager

BPEL PM can run on top of OC4J, WebLogic, or WebSphere J2EE containers. The discovery process is different for BPEL PM on different J2EE containers.

BPEL Process Manager running on OC4J

We learned in Chapter 5, *Managing Oracle Application Server*, that Oracle Application Server and components of Oracle Application Server like OC4J are automatically discovered as part of agent installation. In case Application Server is installed after the agent installation, you will need to discover application server by triggering the discovery process from the console.

BPEL PM on OC4J also gets discovered as part of an application server and OC4J discovery. In case the BPEL PM is added to an already discovered Application server, you will need to re-discover the Application Server. You can re-discovery an application server by starting the discovery process again on that host. You may want to quickly revisit the discovery section for application server in Chapter 5, *Managing Oracle Application Server*.

Once the BPEL PM is discovered, you will see it on the **Middleware** tab along with other application server components. The following screenshot shows the **Middleware** tab where BPEL PM is listed along with other components:

At this point, a BPEL target is discovered and some basic metrics like status and so on are getting collected. But to get more advanced metrics, you will need to go through two more steps. We will discuss those steps in the following sections.

Monitoring configuration

In this step, we'll provide some credentials to Enterprise Manager. Using those credentials, Enterprise Manager can mine the data in the dehydration store, or can make **Remote Method Invocation** (**RMI**) calls to BPEL PM during runtime to collect some very useful metrics.

To do this configuration, go to BPEL PM homepage by clicking on the BPEL PM link on the **Middleware** tab. Once on the homepage, click on the **Monitoring Configuration** link. This will take you to the page, as shown next:

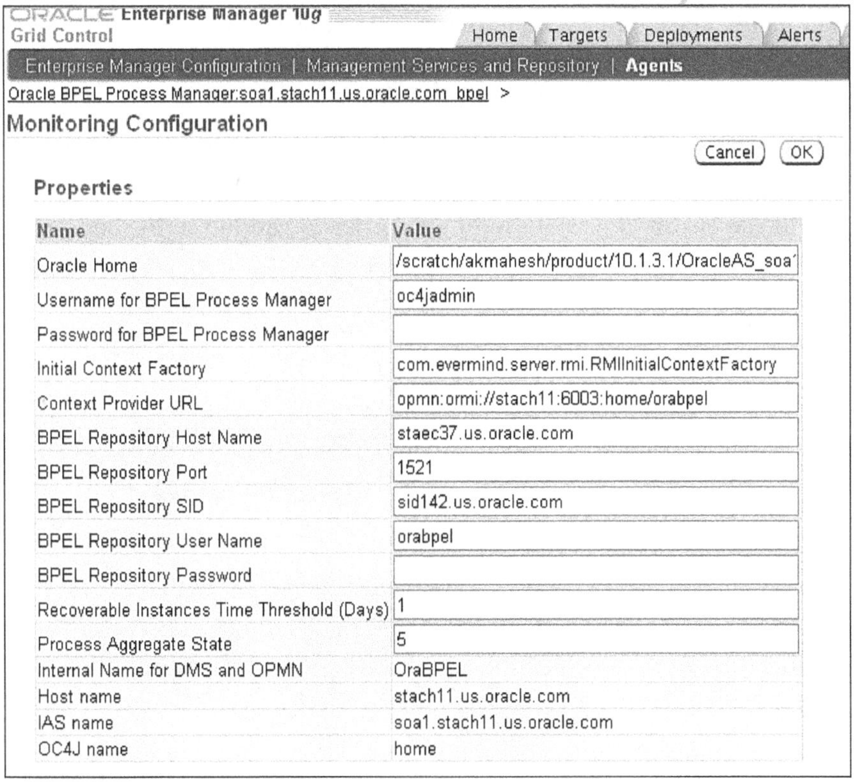

On this page you need to provide:

- Username and password for BPEL PM: Provide the credentials that you use for login on to the BPEL Console. By default, **Username** is pre-populated to **oc4jadmin**.

- BPEL repository host, port, SID, username, and password: All of these fields except password are pre-populated. Enterprise Manager gets values for these fields by looking into the BPEL PM configuration, please make sure that those values are captured correctly.

Once you have provided these values, click on the **OK** button to save these values. After this configuration you will need to do some more steps on agent side.

Agent configuration

To get finer details the agent needs to make RMI calls to a BPEL runtime, for that, some JAR files are needed in the agent class path, these JAR files are in Oracle Home of BPEL server, we just need to make entries in agent class path. To do so:

1. Log on to the BPEL server host, go to the Oracle Home for the agent and open file `sysman/config/emd.properties`.

2. In this file ensure the following JAR entries are added in the beginning of `CLASSPATH` property:

   a. `$BPEL_SERVER_ORACLE_HOME/opmn/lib/optic.jar`

   b. `$BPEL_SERVER_ORACLE_HOME/bpel/lib/orabpel.jar`

   c. `$BPEL_SERVER_ORACLE_HOME/bpel/lib/orabpel-common.jar`

   d. `$BPEL_SERVER_ORACLE_HOME/bpel/lib/orabpel-thirdparty.jar`

   e. `$BPEL_SERVER_ORACLE_HOME/j2ee/home/oc4jclient.jar`

   f. `$BPEL_SERVER_ORACLE_HOME/j2ee/home/j2ee_1.3.01.jar`

3. Replace `BPEL_SERVER_ORACLE_HOME` with the actual path of `Oracle Home` where BPEL Process Manager is installed.

4. Restart the agent, to restart the agent use `emctl` command in the `bin` directory of agent `Oracle Home`.

At this point, configuration for the advanced metrics is over. To check if everything is fine, please visit the **Processes** tab on BPEL PM homepage. You should see the BPEL process deployed on your BPEL PM. If you don't see the BPEL processes, click on the **Refresh** button and you will see the BPEL processes, as shown in the following screenshot:

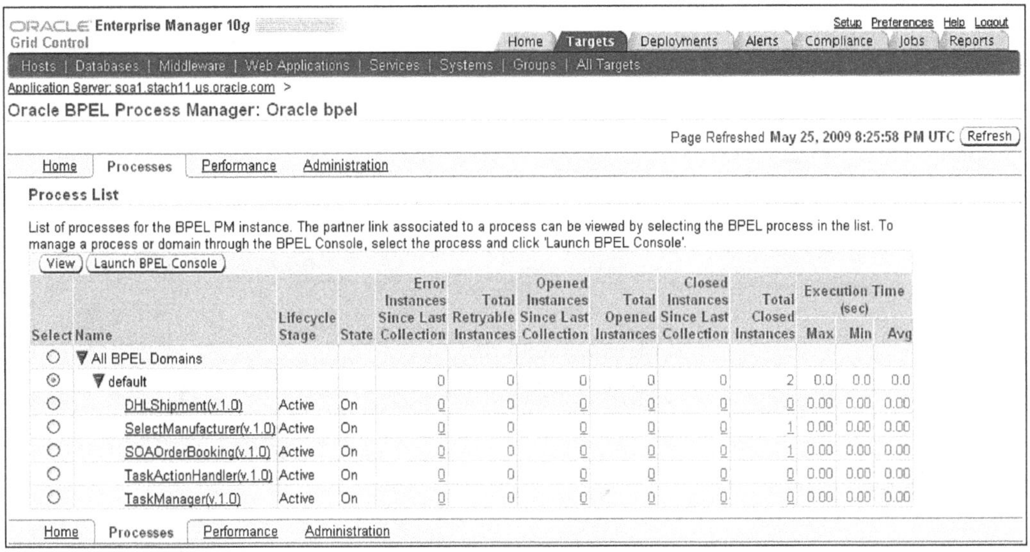

Congratulations!! At this point you have configured your BPEL PM target on OC4J for advanced metrics.

BPEL Process Manager running on WebLogic

Before discovering BPEL PM running on WebLogic Server, the WebLogic Server and the corresponding domain should be discovered and monitored by Enterprise Manager.

The starting point for BPEL PM discovery is the agent homepage for the agent through which the WebLogic domain is monitored. From this agent homepage, under **Monitored Targets** section, select **Oracle BPEL Process Manager** from the drop-down and click on **Go**. The following screenshot shows the agent page where you can see the option to add BPEL PM:

Once you click on **Go,** a three-step wizard will be launched and you will have to provide details at each step:

1. Select the WebLogic Server where BPEL PM is running. If you select a WebLogic Server where BPEL PM is not running, it will be suggested that you select a new server.

2. Provide Oracle Home where BPEL PM is installed and Application Server Home where WebLogic Server is installed.

3. Host credential where BPEL PM is running.

At the end of the wizard BPEL PM running on WebLogic will be discovered.

Monitoring Configuration

After the discovery, you will have to provide credentials to Enterprise Manager for the dehydration store and BPEL PM. This step is the same as it was in the case of BPEL PM on OC4J, therefore, you can refer to the section, *Monitoring configuration* for BPEL PM on OC4J.

BPEL Process Manager running on WebSphere

The discovery of BPEL PM running on WebSphere is very similar to the discovery of BPEL PM running on WebLogic. The WebSphere server where BPEL PM is running should be discovered and monitored by Enterprise Manager. The starting point of discovery is the same, that is the agent homepage.

The only difference is in the second step of the previous section where you will need to provide one additional parameter. This parameter is the location of the BPEL PM application on the host on which WebSphere is running.

Monitoring BPEL PM and BPEL processes

In the previous sections, we learnt how to discover BPEL PM and BPEL processes. We saw that the discovery process is different for BPEL PM running on different J2EE containers. The good news is that the monitoring aspect is the same, irrespective of the underlying J2EE container.

Monitoring BPEL PM

We know that BPEL PM runs on top of a J2EE container, uses Oracle database as a dehydration store, and that traffic to BPEL PM is routed through some HTTP gateways. To effectively monitor BPEL PM, we need to monitor all related components along with BPEL PM. Performance and availability of any related component can affect the performance and availability of BPEL PM. Collectively, we refer to BPEL PM and related components such as the BPEL eco system.

We learnt in Chapter 5, *Managing Oracle Application Server,* about **System** and **Service** constructs. Using system construct, we can group all such related targets as one system. To monitor the system we can also define a "service" that is based on the system. Using this service, we can monitor the collective availability and performance of all such related targets in one place. If required, we can use this service to define the Service Level Agreements for availability and performance of the BPEL eco system. We refer to this service as "BPEL Infrastructure Service" – it represents the entire infrastructure needed to run BPEL PM.

Creation of the system and service sounds like lot of work, but Enterprise Manager provides an easy way to create system service for BPEL eco system. To use this feature, go to the BPEL PM homepage, there you will see an option to create the system and service. The following screenshot shows the **Create BPEL Infrastructure Service** button:

General		
Status	**Up** (Black Out)	
Up Since	**Unavailable**	
Availability (%)	99	
	(Last 24 Hours)	
Oracle Home	/scratch/akmahesh/product/10.1.3.1/OracleAS_soa1	
Host	stach11.us.oracle.com	

BPEL Server Throughput

```
1.0
0.8
0.6
0.4
0.2
0.0
  1:18    4      8     12
   May 25, 2009
```

■ Closed Instances
■ Error Instances
■ Opened Instance

System And Service

(Create BPEL Infrastructure Service)

System	Status	Alerts	Policy Violations	Service
No items found				

Alerts

Metric	Severity	Message	Alert Triggered	Last Value	Last Checked
No Alerts found.					

Once you click on the **Create BPEL Infrastructure Service** button, you will be asked to provide a name for the service. Once you provide the name and submit the page, Enterprise Manager will create a service by the name provided by you and a system by the same name with _system appended to it, and you will be redirected to BPEL PM. The following screenshot shows one such page where we created a service by the name mybpelservice and system by the name mybpelservice_system:

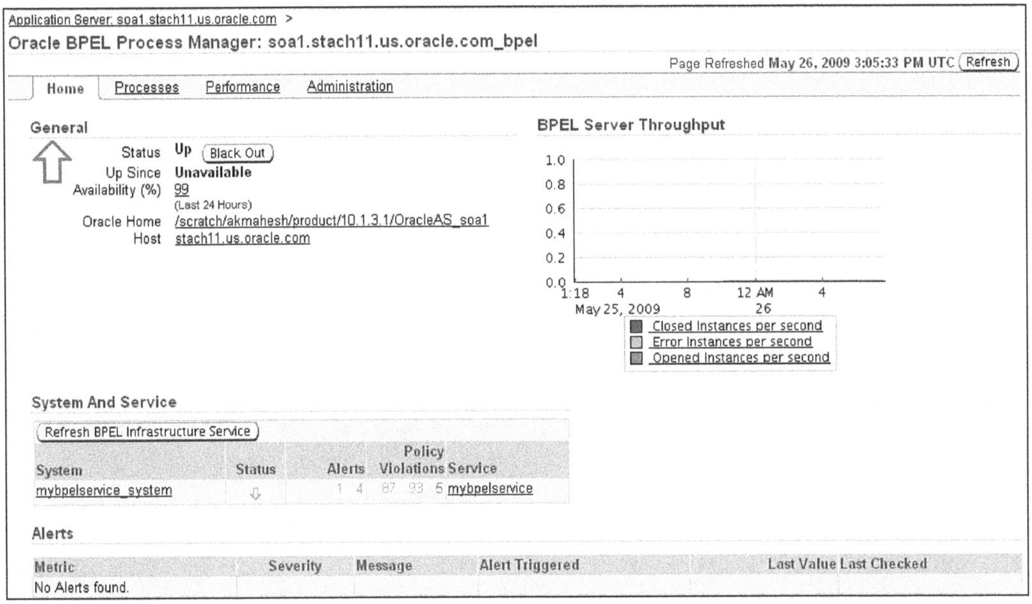

On this page you will see the **Create BPEL Infrastructure Service** button is changed to **Refresh BPEL Infrastructure Service**. In case there are some membership changes in the BPEL eco system, you can click on this button and the system definition also gets refreshed to reflect the current BPEL ecosystem.

Once you click on the link listed under **Service** on the previous image, you will see the homepage for the service, where you can see the service **Status**, overall service **Availability, Expected Service Levels**, and so on. The following screenshot shows the service homepage:

```
Generic Service: mybpelservice
┌──────┬───────┬──────────────────┬────────┬──────────┬────────────────────────┐
│ Home │ Charts│ Test Performance │ System │ Topology │ Monitoring Configuration│
└──────┴───────┴──────────────────┴────────┴──────────┴────────────────────────┘
                                        Page Refreshed May 26, 2009 3:14:34 PM GMT

General
⇧          Status  Up  ( Black Out )
        Up Since  May 26, 2009 8:13:30 AM
   Last Calculated May 26, 2009 8:13:30 AM
   Availability (%)  0
                    (Last 24 Hours)
     Performance  ✓
          Usage  ✓
 Actual Service Level (%)  4.4290
                    (Last 24 Hours)
 Expected Service Level (%)  85.0000

Key Component Summary                       Key Test Summary
System   mybpelservice_system (Topology)   │ Test          │ Test Type │ Status │ Alerts │
Status   ⇧ 7                               │ No Test Defined.                              │
Alerts   ✗ 0   ⚠ 4

All Service Alerts

View  [ All Service Alerts ▼ ]

│ Target │ Target │ Alert │
```

There are some more tabs on this page that contain more details about the service:

- The **Charts** tab displays the performance charts
- The **Test Performance** tab displays the performance of tests defined on the service
- The **System** tab shows all the components for the underlying system
- The **Topology** tab displays the topological view of the underlying system

We will leave it to you to explore the other tabs on the service homepage. We have covered some of the service features in other chapters such as 4 and 5. From this page you can click on the **System** link to see all the components in the system.

Monitoring BPEL Processes

In the previous section, we learned about monitoring the BPEL ecosystem. In this section, we'll learn how we can monitor BPEL processes. At a very basic level, each BPEL process defines the flow and sequence of web services that need to be called to achieve a business operation. For example, an imaginary "Expense Report" BPEL process defines the flow of submissions, approvals, and payments. In this scenario, whenever a user submits an Expense report, one web service call is made to inform his manager, after approval by the manager, another web service call is made to the payment gateway. These web service calls are encapsulated as partner links. At a very basic level, partner links defines what web service needs to be called, what method in web service needs to be called and with what parameters.

Often these partner links represent services from another department or another business entity altogether.

For basic monitoring of BPEL processes there are a lot of good metrics collected by Enterprise Manager. For the advanced monitoring, Enterprise Manager provides a monitoring model for BPEL processes.

BPEL process metrics

Enterprise Manager captures various metrics related to each BPEL process. Some of the important metrics are:

- Total number of instances — opened, closed, retryable
- New instances — opened, closed
- Average, minimum, and maximum time taken by instance

The following screenshot shows one such page where you can see important metrics for all the BPEL processes. You can click on these metrics and see historical views.

To see the details of one particular BPEL process click on any of the processes listed in the previous screenshot and you will see a page as shown next:

On this page, you will see the details about BPEL process such as:

- State, Lifecycle Stage show the current state and lifecycle stage of BPEL process; state can be up or down, and lifecycle can have the value of active or retire.

- Version number and deployment date for BPEL process.

- Total number of Error instances and Retryable instances.

- Throughput and Response metrics. Throughput metrics include incoming, error and closed instances. Response metrics include maximum, minimum, and average time for instances.

- Partner link details and respective WSDL locations.

Monitoring model for BPEL processes

The availability and performance of BPEL process is dependent on two things:

- BPEL ecosystem: If BPEL ecosystem is down, then the process will also be down. This dependency is more on an IT infrastructure.

- Partner links: Generally BPEL process has multiple partner links where each partner link represents a call to a web service. Availability and performance of BPEL process also depends on the availability and performance of partner links. For example, lets assume that there is an "Employee Expense report BPEL process", and for all approved expenses it makes a web service call to the payment gateway for payments to the credit card company. In this imaginary scenario, if the web service for the payment gateway goes down, all of the expense reports will not be paid and that BPEL process will be considered down.

In case you didn't realize, your job as a BPEL Administrator just got more complex. So far you were asked to monitor all the components of the BPEL eco system — now you have to monitor all partner links as well and many of them may be running outside your data centre.

The good news is that Enterprise Manager provides a model to manage this complexity. Before we go into the details of this model, lets revisit the concept of test and beacon.

In earlier chapters (4 and 5), we saw that we can record user actions and repeat those actions periodically to proactively monitor end user experience. These user actions are saved as tests and are executed from beacons. For monitoring of partner links we can use the SOAP test, where we can make a web service call to partner link every fixed interval and can find out its availability.

The monitoring model that Enterprise Manager provides for BPEL process monitoring includes three services:

- BPEL Infrastructure service: We learnt about this in the previous section, how this service represents all the components in BPEL ecosystem.

- Availability service: This service represents all the availability tests for a BPEL process; it could include SOAP tests, Web transactions, and so on.

- Aggregate service: This service is just an aggregate of the previous two services. Using this service you can monitor all the required metrics in one place. You can see the performance of your IT infrastructure as well as the performance of partner links in one place.

Again it may sound very complex to create or maintain this model, let's follow the listed steps to see how Enterprise Manager makes it easy:

1. Go to the **Processes** tab on a BPEL target homepage, click on one of the services and you will see a page that shows details of BPEL process. On this page you will see the option to **Create Service**, click on that to create an Aggregate service. The following screenshot shows the page that you will see after you have clicked on **Create Service**. You can see that the Infrastructure service is a part of this aggregated service.

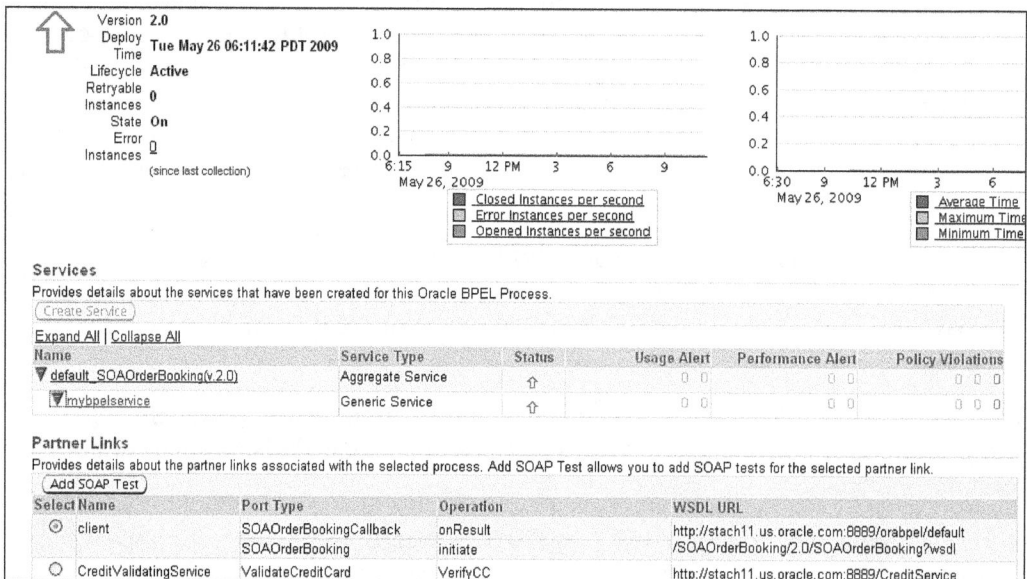

2. From the Partner links section, select a partner link by clicking on the radio button next to it ,and click on **Add SOAP Test**, you will see the page as shown next. Please note that this page is dynamic, Enterprise Manager parses the WSDL and based on the WSDL definition, the data input fields may vary. You may need to talk to your application administrator or owner to fill in those details.

ORACLE Enterprise Manager 10g
Grid Control

Setup Preferences Help Logout

Home Targets Deployments Alerts Compliance Jobs Reports

Hosts | Databases | Middleware | Web Applications | Services | Systems | Groups | All Targets

Application Server: soa1.stach11.us.oracle.com > Oracle BPEL Process Manager: soa1.stach11.us.oracle.com_bpel > Oracle BPEL Process: SOAOrderBooking(v.2.0) >

Create SOAP Test

Cancel   Continue

Enterprise Manager Grid Control automatically creates a service for the SOAP test that is being added to the selected partner link. The name provided for this service is auto-generated and non-editable. The name provided for the SOAP Test is also auto-generated, but it is editable. If you want to change the name of the SOAP Test, then modify the default name.

Service Name **SOAOrderBooking(v.2.0)_availability**
* SOAP Test Name client_test
* Collection Frequency (minutes) 15
Port Types SOAOrderBookingPort

Operations

Select one operation from the following list. These operations are supported and are exposed by the web service.
⊕ initiate [void initiate(SOAOrderBookingProcessRequest)]

Input Parameters
Enter values for input parameters for the selected operation. You can also enter the pregenerated SOAP Envelope by selecting XML Source option.
⊕ HTML Form ○ XML Source

Parameter 1

SOAOrderBookingProcessRequest

PurchaseOrder

ID (String)
CustID (String)

ShipTo

Address

State (String)
Country (String)
Street (String)

3. Click OK on this page. On the next page you will be asked to select some beacons. The following screenshot shows that page:

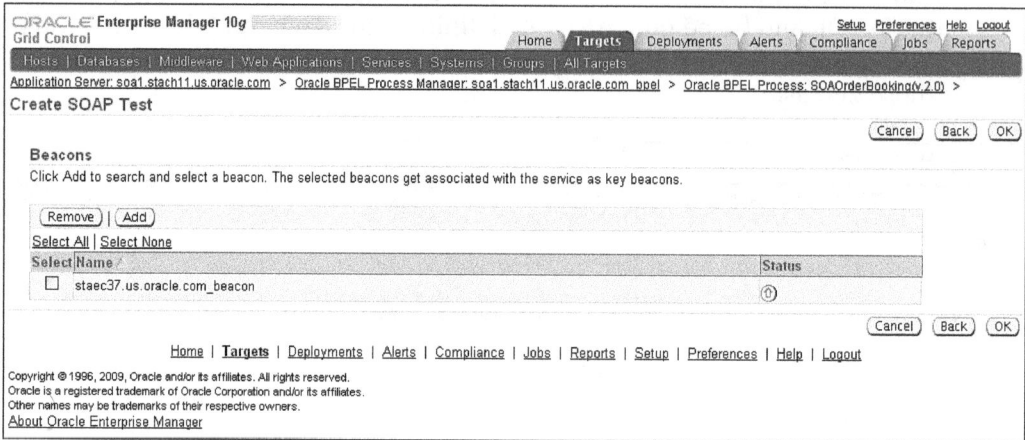

ORACLE Enterprise Manager 10g
Grid Control
Setup Preferences Help Logout
Home **Targets** Deployments Alerts Compliance Jobs Reports
Hosts | Databases | Middleware | Web Applications | Services | Systems | Groups | All Targets

Application Server: soa1.stach11.us.oracle.com > Oracle BPEL Process Manager: soa1.stach11.us.oracle.com_bpel > Oracle BPEL Process: SOAOrderBooking(v.2.0) >
Create SOAP Test

Cancel Back OK

Beacons
Click Add to search and select a beacon. The selected beacons get associated with the service as key beacons.

Remove Add

Select All | Select None

Select	Name	Status
☐	staec37.us.oracle.com_beacon	(i)

Cancel Back OK

Home | **Targets** | Deployments | Alerts | Compliance | Jobs | Reports | Setup | Preferences | Help | Logout

4. Click OK and you will come back to the BPEL process page. You will notice that a new service is added. The name of this service is `<BPEL process name >_Availability` and under this service you can see a SOAP test added.

You have completed the model of your BPEL process, using this model you can monitor all the dependencies for your BPEL process, that include:

- BPEL ecosystem
- Availability of partner links

> SOAP test invokes the actual web service. If the web service is read-only, then there are no issues. If the web service does some updates to the business systems, then by submitting a SOAP test, you are creating some artificial transactions. Make sure that your application has a way to filter out, or ignore these transactions; these transactions should not be treated as regular business transactions. Generally, each application has some special user-IDs or credit card numbers that are ignored and those user-IDs/credit card numbers are used for such synthetic transactions.
>
> If there is no way to filter out artificial transactions – DO NOT use the SOAP test or any other tests that create artificial transactions.

You can explore the other features of the aggregate service by visiting the aggregate service homepage. You can see availability and service levels for the service and you can drill down to Infrastructure service or individual components.

In case the service is down, you can see the root cause of that. The next screenshot shows one such case, where you can see that one of the SOAP tests is getting errors and that indicates that one partner link is down, and that is the root cause of BPEL process availability issues. It is violating the Service Level Agreements also.

Page Refreshed May 27, 2009 12:21:55 AM PDT

Home | Charts | Topology

General

Status **Down** (Black Out)
Down Since **May 27, 2009 12:13:05 AM**
Last Calculated **May 27, 2009 12:19:07 AM**
Availability (%) 82.8
(Last 24 Hours)
Actual Service Level (%) 80.4572
(Last 24 Hours)
Expected Service Level (%) 85.0000

Possible Causes of Service Failure

Grid Control has performed Root Cause Analysis for this service failure and has identified the following possible causes. Click Root Cause Analysis Details to view details related to this analysis.

Confidence **Medium**   Last Analysis **May 26, 2009 11:14:59 PM**

Timestamp (PST)	Target Name	Target Type	Message
May 27, 2009 12:12:11 AM	SOAOrderBooking(v.2.0)_availability	Generic Service	The following key tests are down: client_test

Root Cause Analysis Details

Subservices

Name	Type	Status	Performance Alerts	Usage Alerts	Policy Violations	System Name	Key Components Status	Alerts
▼ default_SOAOrderBooking(v.2.0)	Aggregate Service	ⓘ	0 0	0 0	0 0 0	n/a	n/a	n/a
SOAOrderBooking(v.2.0)_availability	Generic Service	ⓘ	0 0	0 0	0 0 0	n/a	n/a	n/a
mybpelservice	Generic Service	ⓘ	0 0	0 0	0 0 0	mybpelservice_system	0 Z	0 4

Alerts

View: All Alerts

Target Name	Target Type	Severity	Alert Triggered	Message
SOAOrderBooking(v.2.0)_availability	Generic Service	x	May 27, 2009 12:12:11 AM	The following key tests are down: client_test
default_SOAOrderBooking(v.2.0)	Aggregate Service	x	May 27, 2009 12:13:05 AM	Aggregate service is down; {0} sub-services are down: {1}

Home | Charts | Topology

Configuration management

We saw in the earlier chapters that Enterprise Manager collects configuration snapshots that are useful in keeping track of the configuration changes. Enterprise Manager refreshes the configuration snapshot periodically, and any change in the configuration is also recorded in the repository. You can also use the configuration snapshots to compare the configuration of one target with another target of the same type.

Configuration data collected for BPEL PM includes:

- SOAP URL and SOAP callback URL
- Dehydration store details—host, port, s-id for dehydration store
- Cluster configuration if BPEL PM is part of cluster

- List of the BPEL domains and domain specific configuration parameters like minimum and maximum threads

- BPEL PM configuration files like `collaxa-config.xml`, `jgroups-protocol.xml`, and so on

- List of the BPEL processes deployed, and the artefacts for BPEL processes such as `bpel.xml`, `xsds`, `wsdls`, and so on

To see the latest collected configuration for a BPEL PM target, follow the steps listed next:

1. Go to the **Administration** tab on the target homepage and click on **Last Collected Configuration** link. The next screenshot shows the page:

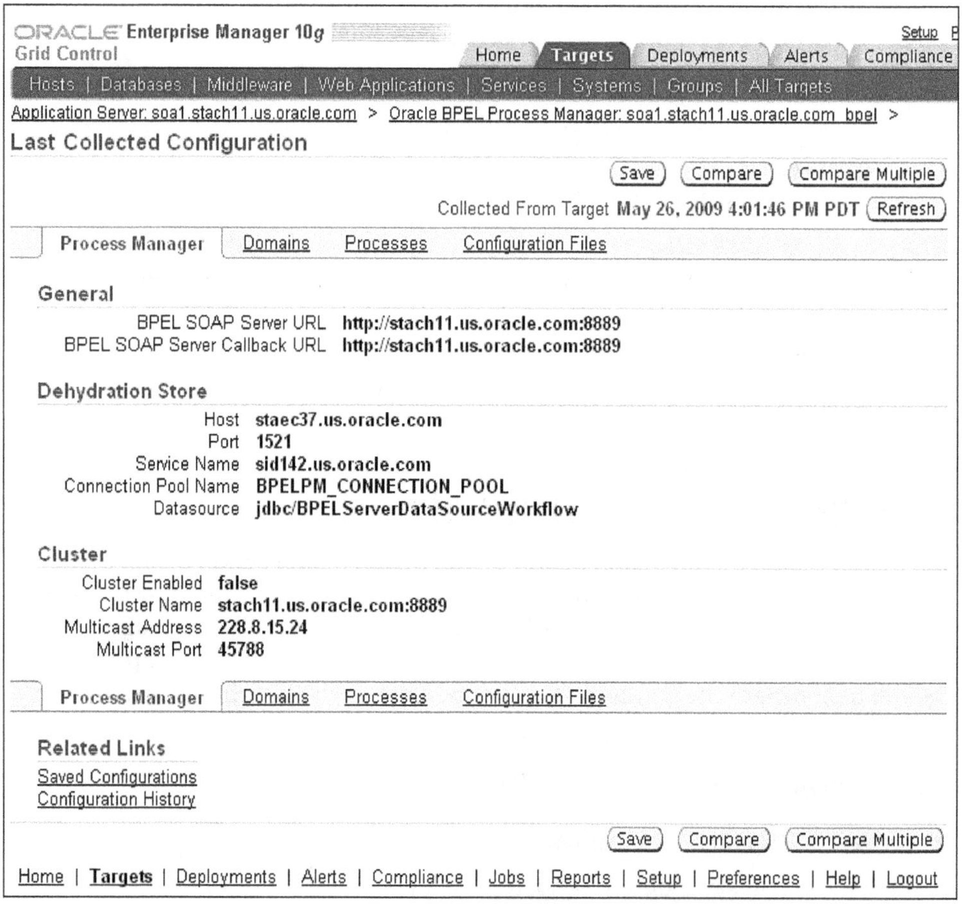

2. Under the **Processes** tab, you will see a list of all BPEL processes. For each process, you will see the list of artefacts, last modification time for the artefact, and size of the artefact. The next screenshot shows one such page:

Collected From Target May 26, 2009 4:01:46 PM PDT (Refresh)		

Process Manager	Domains	Processes	Configuration Files

Expand All | Collapse All

Name	Modification Time	File Size(bytes)
▼ All BPEL Processes		
▼ DHLShipment		
▼ 1.0		
bpel.xml	May 24, 2009 4:58:14 PM PDT	509
DHLShipment.bpel	May 24, 2009 4:58:14 PM PDT	3,988
DHLShipment.wsdl	May 24, 2009 4:58:14 PM PDT	2,299
DHLShipment.xsd	May 24, 2009 4:58:14 PM PDT	638
▼ SelectManufacturer		
▼ 1.0		
bpel.xml	May 24, 2009 4:42:51 PM PDT	684
SelectManufacturer.bpel	May 24, 2009 4:42:51 PM PDT	4,751
SelectManufacturer.wsdl	May 24, 2009 4:42:51 PM PDT	3,588
SelectManufacturerRef.wsdl	May 24, 2009 4:42:51 PM PDT	1,013
▼ SOAOrderBooking		
▼ 1.0		
ApprovalRequired.wsdl	May 24, 2009 4:55:52 PM PDT	5,348
ApprovalRequiredTypes.xsd	May 24, 2009 4:55:52 PM PDT	9,841
bpel.xml	May 24, 2009 4:55:52 PM PDT	3,297
BpelProcess.xsd	May 24, 2009 4:55:52 PM PDT	1,315
common.xsd	May 24, 2009 4:55:52 PM PDT	2,052
CreditValidatingService.wsdl	May 24, 2009 4:55:52 PM PDT	823
CustomerSvc.wsdl	May 24, 2009 4:55:52 PM PDT	823
DBAdapterOutboundHeader.wsdl	May 24, 2009 4:55:52 PM PDT	1,222
DecisionService.wsdl	May 24, 2009 4:55:52 PM PDT	5,339
DecisionService.xsd	May 24, 2009 4:55:52 PM PDT	9,760
DecisionServiceRef.wsdl	May 24, 2009 4:55:52 PM PDT	824
DecisionServiceTypes.xsd	May 24, 2009 4:55:52 PM PDT	9,838
DiscountInformation.xsd	May 24, 2009 4:55:52 PM PDT	445
NotificationService.wsdl	May 24, 2009 4:55:52 PM PDT	11,424
NotificationService.xsd	May 24, 2009 4:55:52 PM PDT	5,971

3. Each artefact is a link. On clicking this link, you can see the content of the artefact that is stored in the Enterprise Manager repository. The following screenshot shows the content of an artefact:

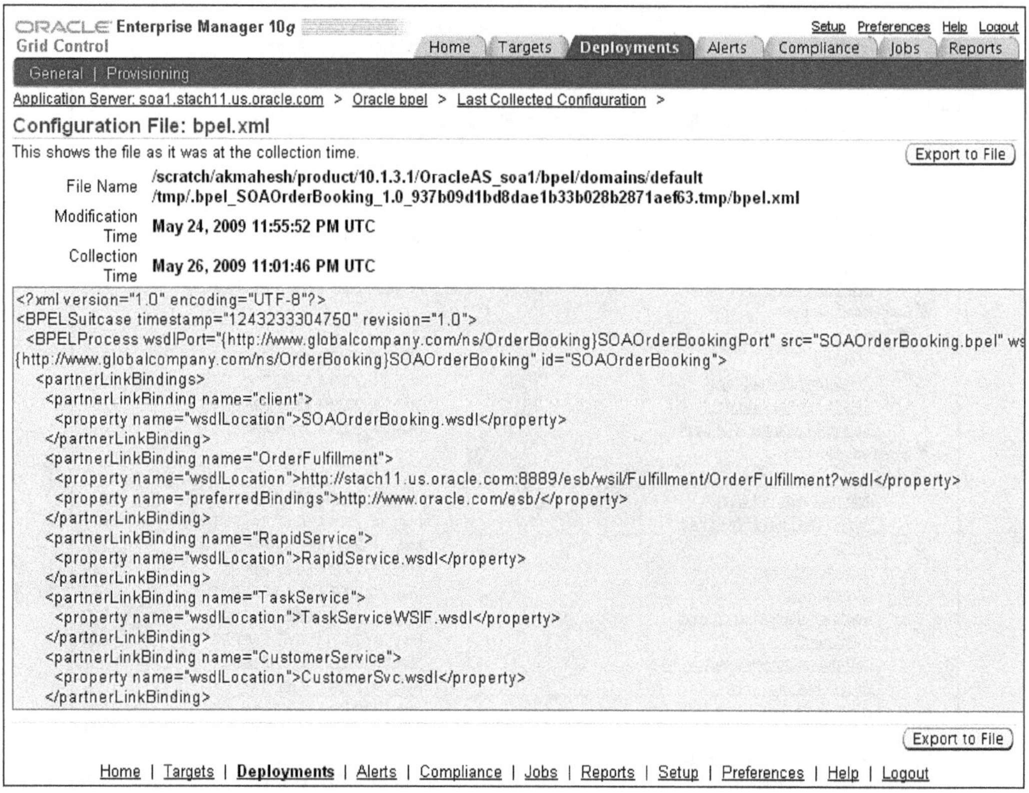

To compare the configuration of a BPEL PM with another BPEL PM, follow the listed steps:

1. Go to the last collected configuration and click on the **Compare** button on the right side, you will be shown a page where you can select another BPEL PM with which you want comparison. The comparison screen will look like the figure shown next. From the **Summary** tab, you can see that there are differences in processes and configuration files.

2. From the **Processes** tab, you can see the difference in processes between two BPEL PMs, the following screenshot shows one such listing:

3. You can drill down further to see exactly what artefact has changed. To do so, click on the icon under the **Results** column, the next page will show the list of artefacts and the artefacts that have changed.

Lifecycle Management for BPEL PM

After the initial setup of BPEL PM, there are some routine lifecycle operations that you need to do as a BPEL administrator. We will discuss those in the following sections.

BPEL suitcase deployment

In a development environment, developers and BPEL process designers deploy BPEL process to BPEL PM directly from the development IDE. This process works fine in the development environment. To deploy the BPEL processes in staging, QA or production environment developers need to package BPEL processes in BPEL suitcases, and system administrators deploy the BPEL suitcases.

Also, there are times when the same BPEL suitcase needs to be deployed in multiple environments, but for each deployment, some customizations are needed. For example, the same BPEL process is deployed in the QA and in the production environment, the BPEL process in QA environment needs to make a call to the partner link of the QA environment and the BPEL process in the production environment needs to make a call to the partner link of the production environment. This can be achieved by applying a deployment plan when deploying a BPEL suitcase. The deployment plan is a simple text file that defines customizations for a given environment. Please refer to the BPEL PM documentation for more details on the format of this document. The following listing shows a snippet of a deployment plan using which the `wsdl` location of a BPEL partner link can be changed during deployment:

```
<partnerLinkBindings>
<partnerLinkBinding name="ReadNewCustomerFileService">
<property name="wsdlLocation">
<replace>ReadNewCustomerFileService.wsdl</replace>
</property>
</partnerLinkBinding>
```

As an administrator, you need to remember which suitcases need to be deployed and which deployment plan needs to be applied, also you may need to deploy the BPEL process during non-office hours.

We learned about the software library in Chapter 3, *Enterprise Manager Key Concepts and Subsystems*, the software library is a central repository to keep any useful artefacts, those artefacts could be the gold image of the Linux server or a BPEL suitcase or a deployment plan. In the next few paragraphs, we'll see how we can store the BPEL suitcase and deployment plan in the software library, once we have them in the software library, how do we deploy them to BPEL PM.

Let's see how to simplify this task by following the listed steps:

1. Upload an artefact in the software library — go to Enterprise Manager homepage and click on the **Deployments** tab, then further click on the **Provisioning** tab. This will show you the listing of artefacts in the software library, it looks similar to the file explorer view in Windows, the following screenshot shows the view of such a listing:

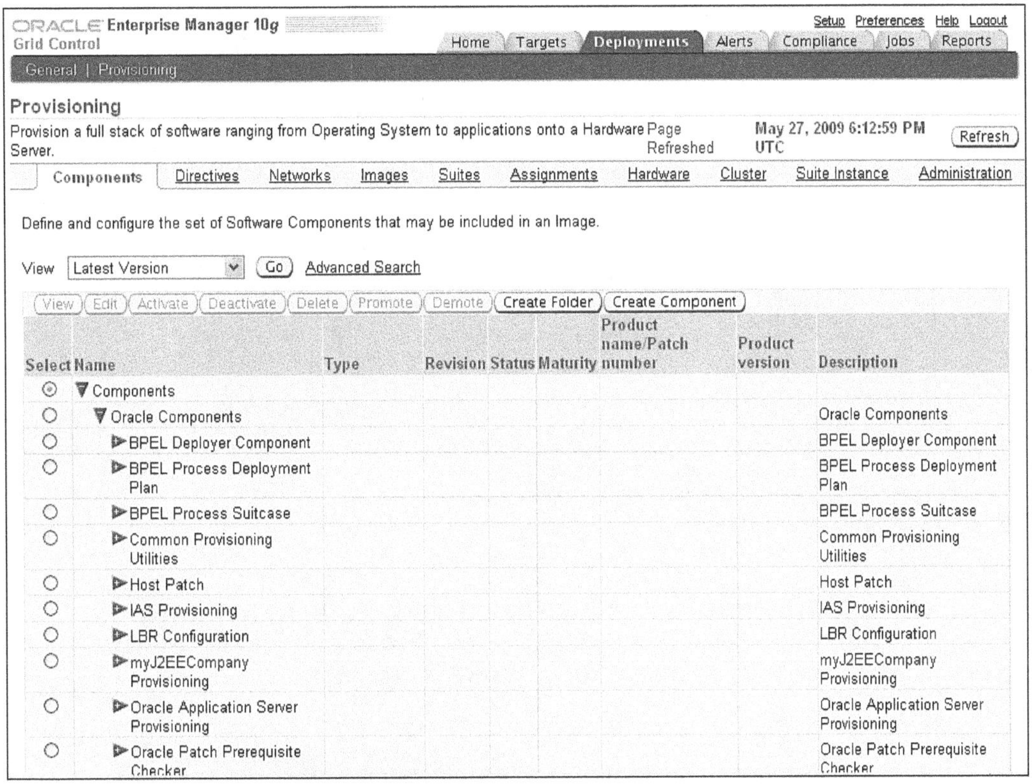

2. From this page you can create/delete new folders and add/delete artefacts in any folder. There are some out-of-the-box folders; **BPEL Process Suitcase** and **BPEL Process Deployment Plan** are two of these. You can load your BPEL suitcases and BPEL deployment plans in corresponding folders. To do so, select a particular folder and click on **Create Component**.

3   On the next screen you select the component type as generic and provide a
name, the following screenshot shows such a screen:

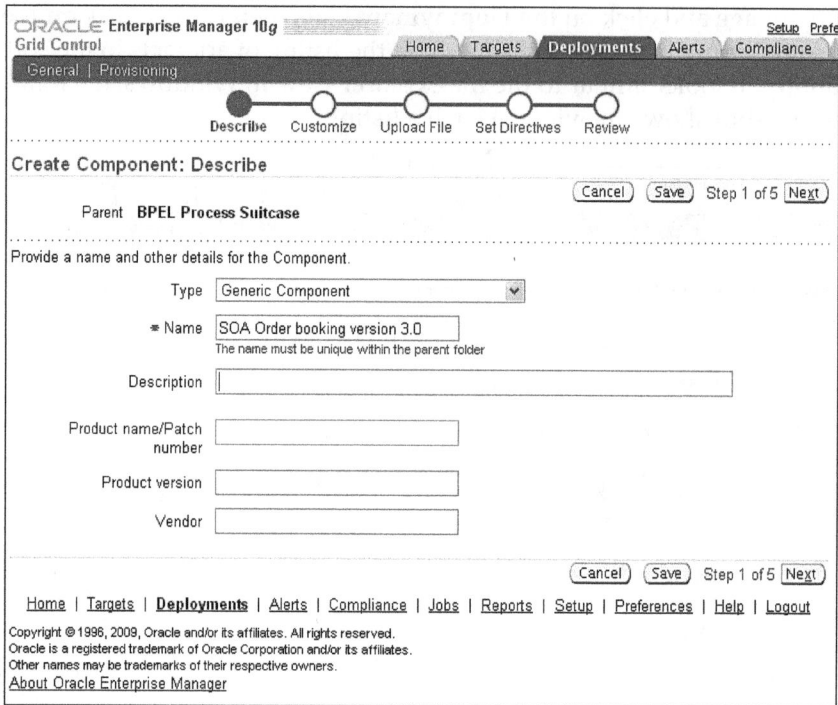

4. The next few screens are very straightforward – you can go through them by
accepting defaults, only on Step 3 do you need to provide the source of your
artefact. The following screenshot shows that screen:

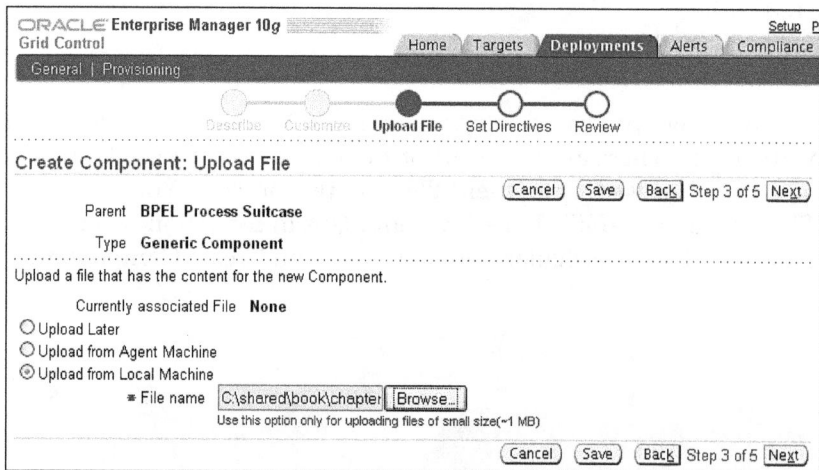

5. On this screen, select **Upload from Local Machine** — that means that you are uploading an artefact from the machine where the browser is running. Complete the rest of the steps and your artefact will be uploaded.

6. Repeat steps 1-5 to upload all BPEL suitcases and deployment plans.

7. To deploy one or more suitcases to one or more BPEL PM, go to the BPEL PM homepage and click on the **Deploy BPEL suitcase** link in the related links section. You will see a page where you can select the BPEL suitcase to be deployed and the deployment plan to be applied.

8. On this page you can also define the order in which BPEL suitcases are deployed; you can use the **Move Up** or **Move Down** button to do so. The following screenshot shows one such page:

9. On the next page you can select the BPEL PM where you want to deploy the suitcases that you selected on the previous screen:

10. In the remaining steps you will be asked to provide the host and BPEL credentials and the schedule for deploying the suitcase. Once you complete the flow and submit the deployment procedure, Enterprise Manager will deploy the suitcase at the scheduled time.

Provisioning and patching of BPEL PM

We saw in Chapter 5, *Managing Oracle Application Server*, that Enterprise Manager provides deployment procedures to provision the Oracle Application Server. Enterprise Manager provides a deployment procedure for cloning of Application server 10.1.3.X, this deployment procedure provides support for provisioning of BPEL PM on OC4J.

In that chapter, we also saw how Enterprise Manager provides support for automating the routine patching needs, the same support is available for Oracle Application Server 10.1.3.X, which includes BPEL PM.

Best practices for BPEL PM management and monitoring

- Monitor the whole BPEL ecosystem, not just the BPEL PM
- Monitor partner link metrics
- Monitor the availability and performance of partner links through tests
- Define the threshold for error metrics
- Keep the gold image of configuration — it will help in troubleshooting
- Keep BPEL suitcases and deployment plans in the software library and use deployment procedures to deploy the BPEL processes
- Use patch automation feature to keep your BPEL PM up-to-date

Summary

In this chapter, we learnt about the complexity of managing BPEL Process Manager. With the help of some exercises, we saw how EM can simplify these complexities. The key takeaways from this chapter before you move on to the next are:

- BPEL Process Manager is used for running business processes defined BPEL, using BPEL constructs
- We need to manage the whole BPEL ecosystem, as the availability and performance of BPEL is dependent on the availability and performance of any related component
- You can do basic monitoring of the BPEL processes using the metrics
- For advanced monitoring you need to monitor the performance of partner links and the BPEL ecosystem. Enterprise Manager provides a model to support that
- You can use configuration management to keep track of BPEL PM configuration changes
- You can use configuration management to compare BPEL PM configuration and BPEL process artefacts, with other BPEL PM
- The software library can be used to keep BPEL suitcases and deployment plans
- Deployment procedures can be used to deploy one or more BPEL suitcases on one or more BPEL PM

We also learned about the monitoring of BPEL PM. BPEL PM is the core component of Oracle SOA Suite. As part of the BEA Systems acquisition in June 2008, Oracle acquired AquaLogic product suite. AquaLogic Service Bus is a core component of AquaLogic product suite, post acquisition it was renamed as Oracle Service Bus. With this acquisition, BPEL PM and Oracle Service Bus became the core of the SOA offering from Oracle. In the next chapter, we will focus on the monitoring of Oracle Service Bus.

8

SOA Management—OSB (aka ALSB) Management

In the last chapter, we learned about the management of BPEL Process Manager component of Oracle SOA Suite. Oracle acquired BEA systems in 2008 and post-acquisition Oracle SOA offerings includes AquaLogic product suite. AquaLogic product suite contains many components. In this chapter, we'll focus on the management of the core component of AquaLogic suite that is Oracle Service Bus (AquaLogic Service Bus before the acquisition).

In this book, we'll use the term **OSB** for **Oracle Service Bus**.

In this chapter, we'll cover:

- Introducing Oracle Service Bus — we'll introduce you to Oracle Service Bus and look at a typical deployment of Oracle Service Bus.

- Discovery of Oracle Service Bus.

- Monitoring of Oracle Service Bus. Besides monitoring of Oracle Service Bus, we'll introduce a model for monitoring services implemented using Oracle Service Bus.

- Configuration ,management for Oracle Service Bus.

- Lifecycle management for Oracle Service Bus – Provisioning of services and projects.

- Best practices for management of Oracle Service Bus.

- Summary of what we have learned.

Introducing Oracle Service Bus (OSB)

In any distributed system, components that run on a distributed platform need to communicate or exchange messages with each other. In SOA based systems, services need to interact or exchange messages with other services also. Oracle Service Bus is a product that provides a platform for interaction and message exchange between services.

Integration of disparate services can be a challenge. There could be a difference in messaging models — some services may support the synchronous model, whereas other services may support the asynchronous model. Some services may support HTTP protocol, whereas other services may support JMS protocol. Oracle Service Bus provides helps in solving many of these challenges by providing the following features:

- Support for different protocols, such as HTTP(s), FTP, JMS, E-mail, Tuxedo, and so on
- Support for different messaging models, such as point-to-point model, publish-subscribe model
- Support for different message formats, such as SOAP, E-mail, JMS, XML, and so on
- Support for different content types such as XML, binary, and so on
- Data transformation using XLST and Xquery — data mapping from one format to another format through declarative constructs

Besides the integration support, OSB provides features that help in managing runtime for the integration of services. Some features are:

- Load balancing: Load balancing is very important when traffic volume between services is very high. Load balancing also helps to achieve high availability.
- Content-based routing: Routing to appropriate service based on content is very valuable in the changing business environment.

OSB provides loosely-coupled bus architecture, where all services and consumers of services can be plugged into, and OSB becomes a central place for defining mediation rules between services and consumers, as shown next:

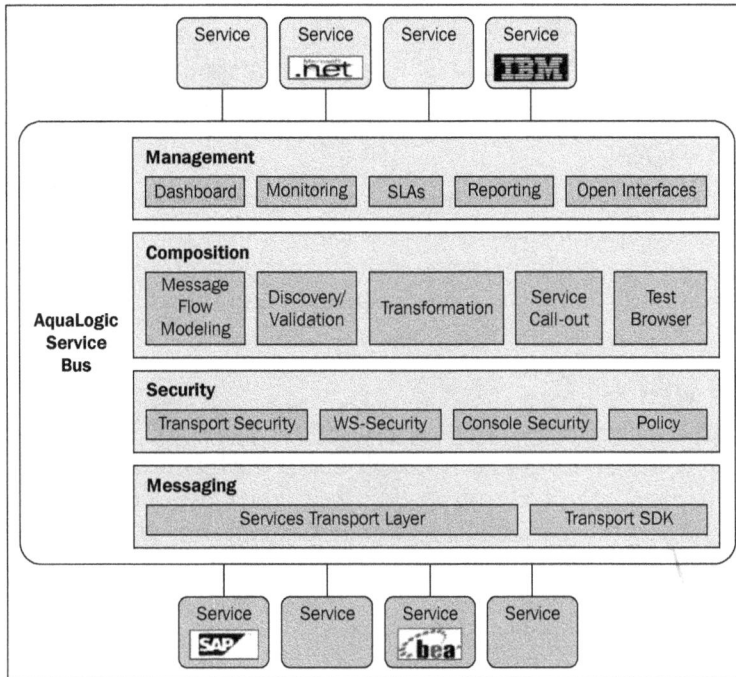

At implementation level, OSB is a set of J2EE applications that run on top of WebLogic J2EE container. It uses various J2EE constructs like Enterprise Java Bean, data source, connectors, and so on. OSB uses a database for storing the reporting data.

OSB can be deployed in a single server model or clustered server model. Generally, in a production environment a clustered model is used, where multiple WebLogic Servers are used for load balancing and high-availability. In such setups, multiple WebLogic Servers are front-ended by a load balancer. The following figure depicts one such clustered deployment.

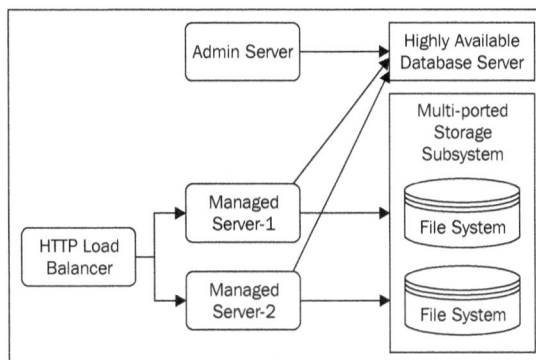

OSB constructs

There are some constructs specific to OSB – let's learn about those constructs.

Proxy service

OSB provides mediation between consumer and provider services. This mediation is loosely coupled where a consumer service makes a call to intermediate service, and the intermediate service performs some transformation and routes it to producer service. This intermediate service is hosted by OSB and called Proxy service.

Business service

Business service is a representation of actual producer service. Business service controls the call to business service, it knows about the business service endpoint. In case of failure in calling producer service, it can retry the operation. In case there are multiple producer services, it knows about the endpoint of each producer service and provides load balancing across those endpoints.

Message flow

Message flow is a set of steps that are executed by the proxy service before it routes to the business service. It includes steps for data transformation, validation, reporting, and so on.

Supported versions

Enterprise Manager provides OSB management from release 10.2.0.5 onwards. The following is the support matrix for EM against different versions of OSB management:

EM Version	OSB 2.6	OSB 2.6.1	OSB 3.0	OSB 10gR3
10.2.0.5	Yes	Yes	Yes	Yes

To manage or monitor OSB from Enterprise Manager 10.2.0.5, some patches are needed on OSB servers. The following table lists the patch number for each supported OSB release:

OSB version	Patch ID
2.6, 2.6.1	B8SZ
3.0	SWGQ
10gR3	7NPS

The SmartUpdate patching tool that comes with WebLogic installation can be used to apply these patches. Before downloading or applying these patches, check Enterprise Manager documentation for any updates on patch Ids.

Discovery of Oracle Service Bus

Oracle Service Bus gets discovered as part of WebLogic domain, managed server discovery. We saw in Chapter 4, *Managing Oracle WebLogic Server*, how Enterprise Manager Agent discovers WebLogic domain and managed servers. Along with domain, cluster and managed server targets, OSB targets are also created and persisted in the Enterprise Manager repository.

Just like WebLogic domain and server targets, OSB can also be discovered and monitored, either by remote agent or local agent. In case you want to use OSB service's provisioning feature you will need to discover/monitor OSB in the local agent mode. In the local agent mode, the agent is installed where the domain admin server is running. In the remote agent mode, the agent can be on any other host on the same network.

After discovery you will see the Oracle Service Bus target on the **Middleware** tab of the EM homepage. The following screenshot shows the OSB target on the **Middleware** tab.

Monitoring OSB and OSB services

Under the BPEL monitoring section, we learnt about the BPEL eco system that
included BPEL PM, dehydration store, database listener, host, and so on, and how
Enterprise Manager provides support for modeling of BPEL eco system as system.
Enterprise Manager provides similar support for managing and monitoring
OSB eco system.

Monitoring OSB

For monitoring OSB, you can go to the OSB homepage, where you can see the
status and availability of OSB. It shows some other details like the host, name of the
WebLogic Server Domain where OSB is installed. It also shows some coarse-grained
historical view of traffic metrics — where it shows message/error/security violation
rates for all the services.

On the **Home** page there is an option to create an infrastructure system and service.
The steps for creating an infrastructure system service is exactly the same as BPEL, so
we will not repeat those steps and will leave it as an exercise. The following screenshot
shows one such homepage after the infrastructure system services are created.

OSB uses **Java Message Service (JMS)** queues for receiving, scheduling, dispatching of messages, it's very important to monitor JMS queues for OSB. From the OSB homepage, click on **JMS Performance**, and you will see the performance of JMS queues used by OSB. The following screenshot shows one such page. You can see the metrics for message inflow and messages pending.

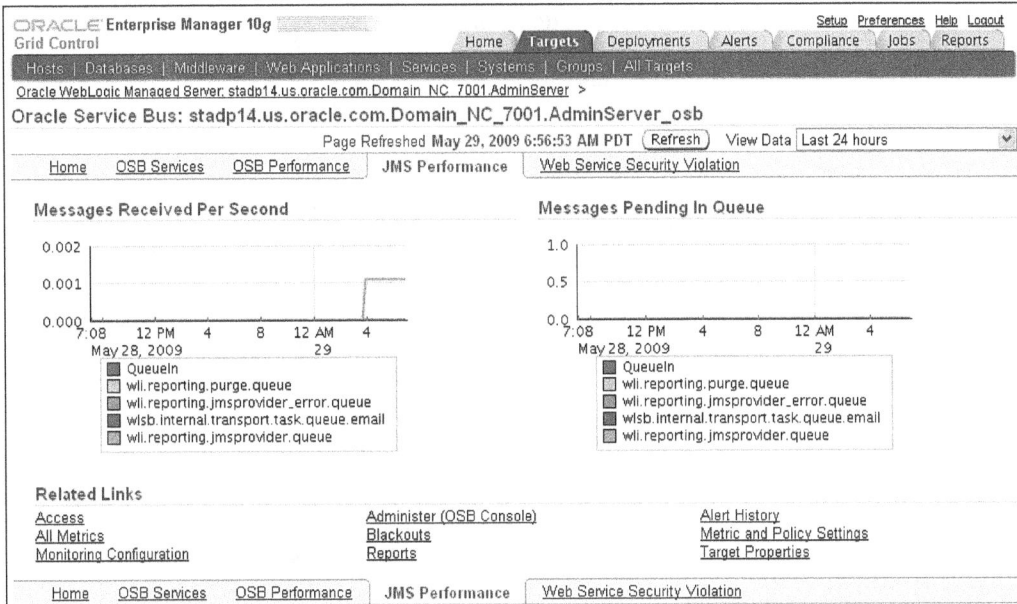

Monitoring OSB services

OSB service monitoring can be divided into two parts—proxy service that receives the requests and business service that dispatches the requests. Proxy service metrics also include the metrics in message flow, where message flow processes the request.

Monitoring proxy services

Performance of proxy services represents the performance seen by consumers of OSB. Besides that, proxy services are hosted by OSB servers. Enterprise Manager collects some very useful metrics for proxy services. These metrics are:

- Status of proxy service
- Throughput metrics at proxy service and endpoint level
- Performance metrics at proxy service level and endpoint level
- Error metrics at service level and end point level
- Security violation at proxy service level

To monitor the performance of message flow, there are some fine-grained metrics available, these metrics include throughput, error rate, and performance at each step in the message flow.

Let's go through the console screens for OSB service monitoring. Go to the **OSB Services** tab from OSB homepage, on that page you will see a listing of all the services that include proxy as well as business services.

You will see every proxy and business services is part of some project. OSB provides a construct project under which different services can be created; project is just a means to categorize different services.

The following screenshot shows such a page where you can see the list of all the projects and services. For each service you see metrics related to throughput, errors, violations, and performance.

			Webservice Security Violation Count Since Last Collection	Error Count Since Last Collection	Message Count Since Last Collection	Average Execution Time (ms)
Select	Name	Path				
○	▼ Services List					
○	▶ REST					
○	▼ MortgageBroker					
○	▼ ProxyService					
○	loanGateway2	MortgageBroker/ProxyServices /loanGateway2	0	2	2	0.00
○	loanGateway3	MortgageBroker/ProxyServices /loanGateway3	0	0	0	0.00
○	loanGateway1	MortgageBroker/ProxyServices /loanGateway1	0	1	1	0.00
○	▼ BusinessService					
○	managerLoanReviewService	MortgageBroker/BusinessServices /managerLoanReviewService	0	0	0	0.00

Collected From May 29, 2009 4:01:23 AM PDT To May 29, 2009 4:06:23 AM PDT (Refresh)

Home | OSB Services | OSB Performance | JMS Performance | Web Service Security Violation

Services List

Provides a list of Oracle Service Bus (OSB) services currently being monitored. To view the references associated with a service, select a business service or proxy service from the list. To manage a service or project through the OSB console, select the service and click 'Launch Console'.

(Launch Console)

Once you click on one of the services, you will see a page where the metrics and other details of proxy service are listed. On this page, you can see the throughput and performance chart for the proxy service. You will also see a section for the EM service model that represents a proxy service. This model is similar to the model that we had for the BPEL process. This mode has three entities:

- Infrastructure service: This service represents all of the components in the OSB eco system.

- Availability service: This service represents all of the availability tests for an OSB proxy service endpoint, it could include SOAP tests, Web transactions etc.

- Aggregate service: This service is just an aggregate of the previous two services. Using this service, you can monitor all of the required metrics in one place. You can see the performance of your IT infrastructure as well as the performance of partner links in one place.

The next screenshot shows such a page where you can see the details of the OSB service:

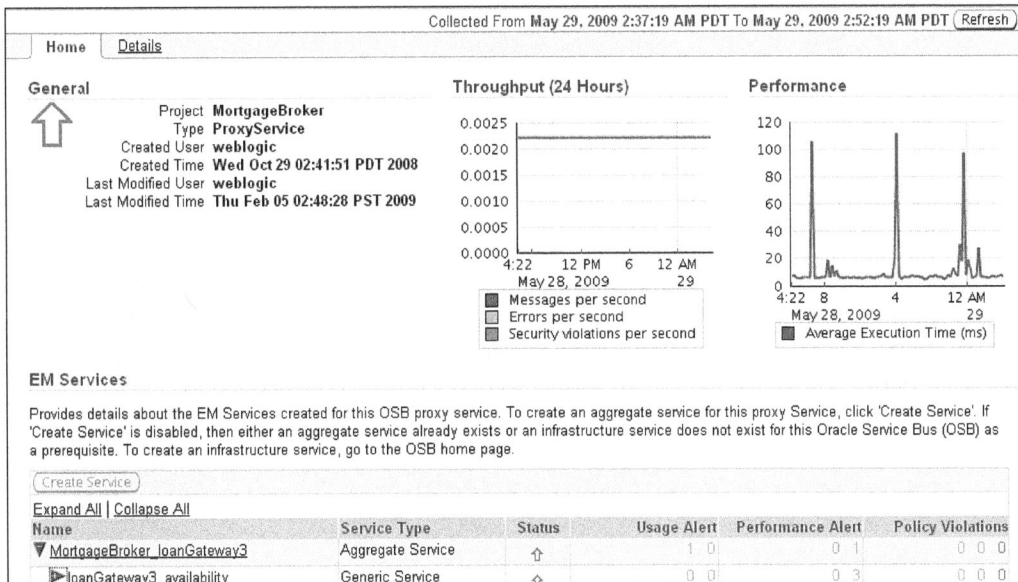

On the same screen, you will see the routing details that show what all business services are getting called from this proxy service. These details are listed under the references section. You will see the status of proxy service endpoint and business service endpoint. Other details available from this page include protocol, endpoint of proxy/business service. The next screenshot shows one such page. From this page, you can add SOAP test for OSB proxy service endpoint and business service end point. These SOAP tests are added to the availability service that we have discussed earlier:

Create Service' is disabled, then either an aggregate service already exists or an infrastructure service does not exist for this Oracle Service Bus (OSB) as a prerequisite. To create an infrastructure service, go to the OSB home page.

(Create Service)

Expand All | Collapse All

Name	Service Type	Status	Usage Alert	Performance Alert	Policy Violations
▼ MortgageBroker_loanGateway3	Aggregate Service	⇧	1 0	0 1	0 0 0
▶ loanGateway3_availability	Generic Service	⇧	0 0	0 3	0 0 0
▼ osb_infra_stapp04	Generic Service	⇧	3 0	0 0	0 0 0

References

Provide details about the routing flow to business services for this service. Additional information such as the load balancing algorithm used, the protocol used, the end point URI exposed, and so on are also shown.

(Add SOAP Test)

Select	Name	Resource Type	Status	Protocol	Load Balancing Algorithm	Weight	End Point URI	Path
○	▼ loanGateway3	ProxyService	⇧	SOAP			http://stapp04.us.oracle.com:7021/loan/gateway3	MortgageBroker/ProxyServices/loanGateway3
○	▼ normalLoanProcessor	BusinessService	⇧	SOAP	round-robin			MortgageBroker/BusinessServices/normalLoanProcessor
○		localhost:7021				10	http://localhost:7021/njws_basic_ejb/NormalSimpleBean	

From the **Details** tab on the same page, you can see the performance and throughput metrics at each individual step in the message flow. For each decision point, transformation, routing, and so on, you can see some useful metrics on this page. The screenshot below shows a listing of steps and metrics for each step.

These metrics include the number of messages processed, number of errors, and average performance time for processing of each message.

Flow Components

Provides information about the flow components for this service.

Expand All | Collapse All

Component Name	Message Count Since Last Collection	Error Count Since Last Collection	Average Execution Time (ms)
▼ Router			
▼ PipelinePairNode1			
▼ PipelinePairNode1_request	10	0	3.20
▼ validate loan application			
validate	2		3.00
▼ <error-handler>			
▼ reply			
▼ ifThenElse	0		0.00
▼ case			
replace	0		0.00
report	0		0.00
▼ default			
replace	0		0.00
log	0		0.00
reply	0		0.00
PipelinePairNode1_response	10	0	0.00
▼ Route to Normal Loan Processing Service	10	0	2.40
route	2		0.50

Monitoring business services

Business service routes the request to services implemented somewhere else. In some cases, these services could be out of your business unit or even organization; in other cases, it could be some service providers for you. For some important services, you might already have some Service Level Agreements defined therefore, for these services it is very important to measure the performance of OSB business services.

Enterprise Manager collects some very useful metrics for business services, which are:

- Status of business service endpoint
- Throughput metrics at business service and endpoint level
- Performance metrics at business service level and endpoint level
- Error metrics at business level and end point level
- Security violation at business service level

The following screenshot shows the page where you can see metrics for business services:

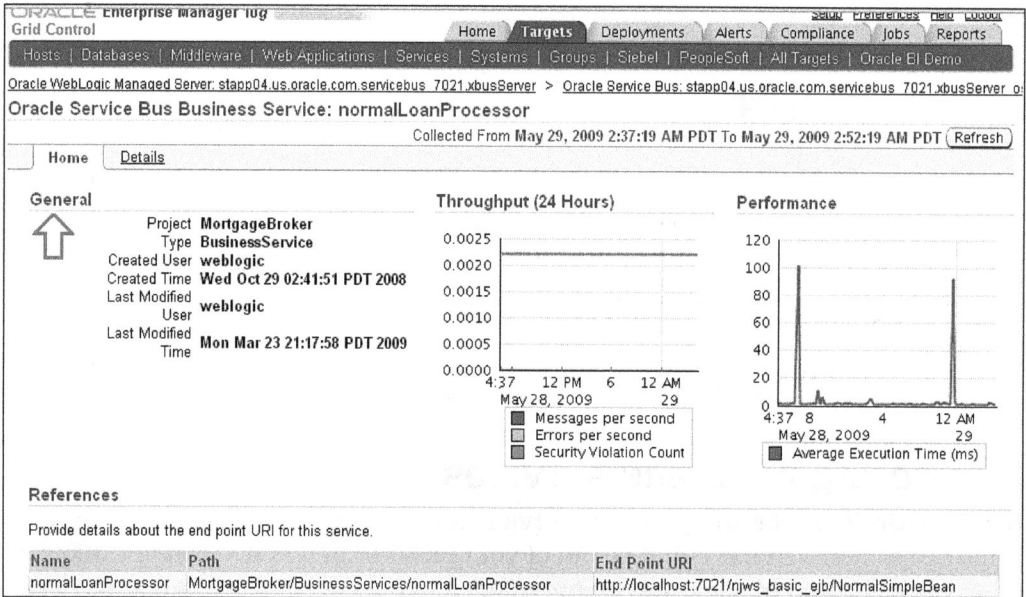

We defined the EM model for monitoring OSB service, where we had one aggregate service that was composed of infrastructure service and availability service. SOAP test for business services are added to same availability service. So, availability service for OSB proxy service includes tests for proxy service and business service endpoint.

Configuration management for Oracle Service Bus

OSB configuration collections from Enterprise Manager include following configuration parameters:

- Configuration for proxy services: It includes a flag for enabling tracing, monitoring, and metric aggregation intervals
- Configuration for business services: It includes a flag for enabling tracing, monitoring, and metric aggregation intervals
- Configuration for business service transport: Load-balancing algorithm, transport type

To see the collected configuration, click on the **View Configuration** link on the OSB homepage. We'll leave it as an exercise for you to complete. You can also compare the configuration of one OSB with another OSB, this is also very similar to the configuration of BPEL PM — we will leave that as an exercise for you to complete too.

Lifecycle management for Oracle Service Bus

In this section, we will cover how to provision the OSB services. In previous chapters, we learned about deployment procedures, software library, and gold images.

In a development environment, developers can build new OSB services through Eclipse IDE or through the OSB administration console. The OSB administration console is a web-based application for OSB configuration and it can also be used to define new OSB services.

To deploy OSB services in a staging or production environment, administrator needs to extract services from the development environment and deploy them to the production environment. Besides deployment in new environment, administrators may need some environment-specific customizations on the services.

Enterprise Manager provides deployment procedures and using which you can:

- Extract OSB services from a reference environment and build gold image
- Provision new OSB service from a reference environment, and apply customizations
- Provision new OSB service from gold image and apply customizations

How to use this feature

1. Go to the **Deployments** tab on the Enterprise Manager homepage. On this page click on the **Deployment Procedures** link.

2. On the next page, you will see a list of all deployment procedures. Search for the deployment procedure by the name **Oracle Service Bus Resource Provisioning**.

3. From the search results, select the radio button next to **Oracle Service Bus Resource Provisioning,** and click on the **Schedule Deployment...** button on top of the table.

4. This will start a wizard to provision OSB services. The first screen of this wizard is shown below, where you will need to provide the source for provisioning, it could be a reference environment or a software library.

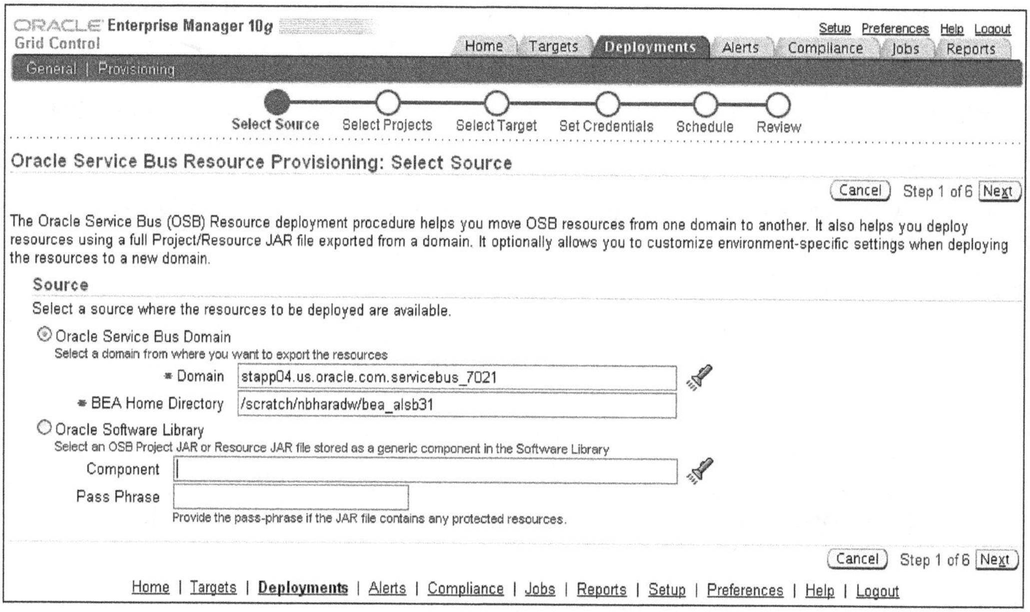

5. In the second step, you will be asked to select the projects that you want to migrate from the source domain. You can select only at **Project** level, all of the services under a project will be selected. The screenshot below shows such a page:

Oracle Service Bus Resource Provisioning: Select Projects

Cancel Back Step 2 of 6 Next

Resource Summary: stapp04.us.oracle.com.servicebus_7021

Select the projects that you want to export and deploy on the target Oracle Service Bus domain. The selected projects are exported to a JAR file and moved to the target host for deployment.

○ Previous 1-7 of 12 ▾ Next 5 ⊘

Select All | Select None

Select	Project Name	Services
☑	HelloWorld	BusinessService/HelloWorld/BusinessServices/HelloWorldBusinessService ProxyService/HelloWorld/ProxyServices/HelloWorldProxy ProxyService/HelloWorld/testproxy/testproxy
☐	MesagingServiceType_Binary	BusinessService/MesagingServiceType_Binary/MyBusinessServices/BinaryBusinessService ProxyService/MesagingServiceType_Binary/MyProxySvs/BinaryProxyService
☐	MortgageBroker	BusinessService/MortgageBroker/BusinessServices/CreditRatingService ProxyService/MortgageBroker/ProxyServices/loanGateway2 ProxyService/MortgageBroker/ProxyServices/loanGateway3 ProxyService/MortgageBroker/ProxyServices/loanGateway1 BusinessService/MortgageBroker/BusinessServices/loanSaleProcessor BusinessService/MortgageBroker/BusinessServices/managerLoanReviewService BusinessService/MortgageBroker/BusinessServices/normalLoanProcessor
☐	Project1	BusinessService/Project1/MyGoogleSearchBusinessSvs ProxyService/Project1/GoogleProxy1
☐	TelecomProviderProcessing	BusinessService/TelecomProviderProcessing/sample/TelecomProvider ProxyService/TelecomProviderProcessing/services/TVTestService ProxyService/TelecomProviderProcessing/services/PhoneTestService

6. In the third step you will be asked to provide the destination domain where you want to deploy the project and services selected in the previous screen. You can also select the customization file that you want to apply after migrating the services.

7. There are other options for advanced cases, but for this exercise you can ignore them. The following screenshot shows such a page.

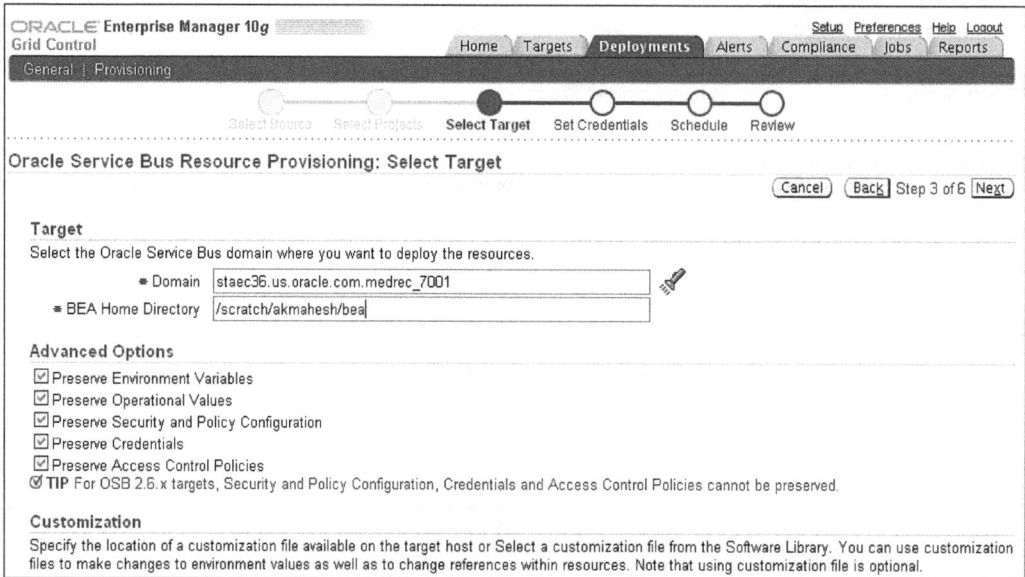

8. On the next two screens you will be asked to provide host and domain credentials for the source and destination domain, and a schedule for deployment.

9. On the final screen you can review all the selections made so far and submit the deployment procedure. Once the deployment procedure is completed, the selected projects will be deployed in the destination domain at scheduled time.

OSB best practices

- Monitor the whole OSB eco system not just the OSB
- Monitor the availability and performance of proxy service endpoints and business service endpoints
- Define the threshold for metrics at endpoints and flow components
- Keep the gold image of configuration — it will help in troubleshooting
- Keep OSB projects and customization files in the software library and use deployment procedures to deploy the OSB projects

Summary

In this chapter we learnt about complexity in managing Oracle Service Bus. Through some exercises we saw how EM can simplify these complexities. The key takeaways before you move to the next chapter is:

- OSB is used to integrate disparate services.
- We need to manage the whole OSB eco system, as the availability and performance of OSB is dependent on the availability and performance of any related component.
- You can do basic monitoring of OSB services using metrics. For OSB we have metrics at proxy service, business service, and message flow level.
- For advanced monitoring you need to monitor performance of proxy, business service endpoints and BPEL eco system. Enterprise Manager provides a model to support that.
- Enterprise Manager provides very fine-grained metrics for message flow, where throughput, and error metrics are available for each step in message flow.
- You can use configuration management to keep track of configuration changes.
- The software library can be used to keep OSB resources and customization files.
- You can use deployment procedures for moving OSB services from one environment to another environment.

In this chapter and the last few chapters we learnt about monitoring of middleware targets like Oracle Application Server, WebLogic Server, BPEL, OSB, and so on. In all these chapters we have also learnt about monitoring of middleware targets that can suggest a problem. But what do we do to fix the problems in applications running on these targets? In our next chapter you will see how to diagnose the issues in application and pinpoint the problem area.

9
Managing Identity Manager Suite

With most applications deployed over the web, identity and access management have become challenging for most IT Administrators. Oracle Identity and Access Management Suite has become a popular choice for organizations needing to manage identities for both custom and packaged applications. Your business may completely depend upon the identity and access management infrastructure and any performance or availability issues may cause severe disruption to your business.

In this chapter, you will learn about:

- Oracle Identity and Access Management Suite and its components
- Discovery and monitoring of different components of Oracle Identity and Access Management Suite

The Oracle Identity and Access Management Suite is a part of the Oracle Fusion Middleware family and includes several products. We can categorize Oracle's Identity and Access Management products into three broad categories:

- Directory services
- Access management
- Identity management

The components such as Directory Integration Platform, Oracle Single Sign-on Server, and so on, come under the Identity Infrastructure components.

The following table shows the products and brief descriptions about them:

Product Name	Purpose
Oracle Internet Directory	LDAP V3-compliant directory service. Serves as the central user repository for identity and access management deployment.
Oracle Virtual Directory	Facilitates the integration of applications into existing identity infrastructures.
Oracle Access Manager	Provides Web-based identity administration, as well as access control to Web applications and resources running in heterogeneous environments. It provides the user and group management, delegated administration, password management and self-service functions.
Oracle Identity Manager	Automates user provisioning, identity administration, and password management.
Oracle Identity Federation	Enables cross-domain single sign-on and allows companies to manage user identities in order to access resources managed by another domain.

It is really beyond the scope of this book to go into the details of each component of the Oracle Identity and Access Management Suite. Refer to the documentation at `http://download.oracle.com/docs/cd/B28196_01/idmanage.htm` for details.

Note that different components of Oracle Identity and Access Management may run on different Java EE application servers, such as Oracle WebLogic Server or a third-party application server, such as IBM Websphere and Jboss Application Server. Refer to the latest certification matrix in **My Oracle Support** time for the latest certification for such combinations.

Oracle Identity Management targets

Oracle Identity and Access Management Suite has several components and hence these components are represented as several targets with in Enterprise Manager. The following table describes the targets that are monitored for the Oracle Identity and Access Management Suite:

Target Type	Description
Access Manager — Access Server	Representation of the Access Server component of Access Manager.
Access Manager — Identity Server	Representation of the Identity Server component of Access Manager.
Access Manager — Access System	Access System is the composite target that includes the Access Server and the underlying host, database and the LDAP Server.
Access Manager — Identity System	Identity System is the composite target that includes the Identity Server and the underlying host, database, and the LDAP Server.
Identity Federation Server	Representation of the Identity Federation Server.
Identity Federation System	Identity Federation System is the composite target that includes the Identity Federation Server and the underlying host, database and the LDAP Server.
Identity Manager Server	Representation of the Identity Manager Server.
Identity Manager Repository	Representation of the Identity Manager Repository.
Identity Manager System	Identity Manager System is the composite target that includes the Identity Manager Server, application server, Identity Manager repository and the underlying hosts, database and the LDAP Server.
Oracle Internet Directory	Representation of Oracle Internet Directory.

Oracle Virtual Directory is not currently supported through Grid Control. However, you can build a JVM target to monitor the Oracle Virtual Directory. We will learn about building a JVM target in the extensibility chapter of this book.

Discovery of Oracle Identity and Access Management Suite

You have to manually discover the components of Identity and Access Management Suite from Grid Control. The different components such as Access Server and Identity Server for Access Manager, Identity Manager Server, and Identity Federation Server are discovered separately.

You have to make sure that the Oracle Management Agent is installed on the hosts to manage those components.

For discovery, first select **Add Identity and Access Management Suite** from the top menu or **All Targets** page. Then select the appropriate target type, for example Oracle **Access Server,** as shown in the following screenshot and enter the **Host Name**, in which the EM agent is running, in order to monitor the target you want to discover.

Note that the Oracle Internet Directory is not discovered as a part of Identity Manager Suite but it is discovered automatically when Oracle Application Server Farm containing Oracle Internet Directory. If you want to monitor Oracle Internet Directory from Grid Control you have to install the plug-in by downloading it from `http://www.oracle.com/technology/software/products/ias/htdocs/101401. html`. We will discuss the discovery of the following components in this chapter:

- Access Manager
- Identity Manager
- Identity Federation

Discovery of Access Manager

The discovery and management of Oracle Access Manager components-both Access Server and Identity Server-requires the SNMP agent. The SNMP agent is an optional component and must be installed on the machine where either the Access Server or Identity Server is running. You can refer to the *Oracle Access Manager Installation Guide* at `http://download-west.oracle.com/docs/cd/B28196_01/ idmanage.1014/b25353/snmp.htm` for details.

Ensure that you have enabled SNMP monitoring for your Access Manager components, and that you have registered your SNMP agent with your component and restarted the component.

Access Server

For discovering the Access Server, you need to enter the connection details for the access server, as shown in the following screenshot:

You have to enter the username and password for the agent host. You have to appropriately select if the management agent is running on a remote machine rather than the SNMP host. You have to enter the home directory for the access server home, for example `/oracle/oam/10.1.4/access,` the version of the access server, for example. **10.1.4**, and the port number and community name for the SNMP host.

The discovery process will find the complete topology of your Identity Server, for example, the associated databases such as Oracle or Microsoft SQL Server and LDAP servers. You have an option to either create a new Access Manager — Access System or add the discovered components to an existing system. We learnt earlier that a system allows Administrators to manage related components/targets as a single entity.

Discovery of Identity Server

The discovery process for the Identity Server component of Access Manager is similar to the process for Access Server. Enterprise Manager discovers the associated databases and LDAP server, and allows you to create a new Identity system or add these to an existing system.

Identity Manager Server

The Identity Manager Server runs on an application server such as Oracle WebLogic Server and requires a database repository. The associated application server and the databases have to be discovered prior to the discovery of Identity Server. Refer to Chapter 4 — *Managing Oracle WebLogic Server*, for the discovery of Oracle WebLogic Server. If your Identity Manager Server runs on a third-party application server such as JBoss then you have to refer to Chapter 11 — *Managing Non-Oracle Middleware*, for the discovery of third-party middleware.

You have to enter the details as shown in the following figure for the discovery of Identity Server Manager.

You have to select the underlying application server target, the database and its credentials, library path, and host credentials. Finally, it allows you to create the Identity Manager System, as shown next:

Add Oracle Identity Manager: Discovery

Select the Application Server where Identity Manager Server is deployed and the database that Application Server targets and Database targets show only previously discovered targets.

* Application Server Target	emgc-amp6.us.oracle.com.oim.mys
* Configured Database Target	idm.us.oracle.com
* Database User Name	XLADMIN
* Database Password	••••••••
* Identity Manager Library Path	\Oracle Identity Manager\xellerate\lib
* Host User Name	Administrator
* Host Password	••••••

☐ Save as preferred credentials

Identity Federation Server

The Identity Federation Server runs on an Oracle Application Server and depends on an LDAP directory such as Oracle Internet Directory and database to store user data. The associated application server discovered prior to the discovery of Identity Federation Server. Refer to Chapter 5, *Managing Oracle Application Server*, for the discovery of Oracle Application Server. The discovery of Identity Federation Server is quite straightforward and it just requires a selection of Application Server Install and credentials for the server host. Enterprise Manager will automatically discover the underlying database and LDAP server and you will be prompted to create Identity Federation System at the end of the discovery.

ORACLE Enterprise Manager 10g
Grid Control

Hosts | Databases | Application Servers | Web Applications | Services | Systems

Add Identity Federation Server: Discovery

In order to add Oracle Identity Federation Target, you need to select the Application server must discover them first.

* Application Server Target	oif_idm.emgc-amp6.us.oracle.com
* Host User Name	Administrator
* Host Password	••••••

Monitoring Identity and Access Management Suite

You can monitor the performance of each component of Identity and Access Management Suite by navigating to the homepage for each target type. For example, if you want to monitor the health of your Identity Manager Server, you can navigate to **All Targets** and then search for **Identity Manager Servers** and navigate to its homepage. For example, the following screenshot shows the homepage for Identity Manager Repository. The homepage provides some important metrics such as SQL Response time and the number of users provisioned, locked, deleted, and so on. Like all targets, the alerts show up in the homepage.

You can similarly navigate to the homepages of other components of Oracle Identity and Access Management Suite to monitor those components. You can view all of the metrics available for a target type by navigating to the **All Metrics** of the Target homepage. For example, the following figure shows the all metrics view of Access Manager — Access Server component.

Access Manager - Access Server: tdsadminoid02.oracleads.com:6035_Access Server >				
All Metrics				
				Collected From Target Jul 2, 2009 1:46:19 AM CDT
Expand All | Collapse All				
Metrics	Thresholds	Collection Schedule	Upload Interval	Last Upload
▼ tdsadminoid02.oracleads.com:6035_Access Server				
▷ Audit log rotation time	Not Applicable	Every 15 Minutes	Every Collection	Jul 2, 2009 1:46:19 AM CDT
▷ Audit request	Not Applicable	Every 15 Minutes	Every Collection	Jul 2, 2009 1:46:19 AM CDT
▷ Directory Server Live connection	None	Every 15 Minutes	Every Collection	Apr 29, 2009 11:06:07 AM CDT
▼ Failed Authentications	Not Applicable	Every 15 Minutes	Every Collection	Jul 2, 2009 1:45:46 AM CDT
Failed Authentications (since last collection)	Not Applicable			
Total Failed Authentications	Not Applicable			
▼ Failed Authentications (%)	None	Every 15 Minutes	Every Collection	Jul 2, 2009 1:45:46 AM CDT
Failed Authentications (%) (since last collection)	Not Set			
Total Failed Authentications (%)	Not Set			
▼ Failed Authorizations	Not Applicable	Every 15 Minutes	Every Collection	Jul 2, 2009 1:45:46 AM CDT
Failed Authorizations (since last collection)	Not Applicable			
Total Failed Authorizations	Not Applicable			
▼ Failed Authorizations (%)	None	Every 15 Minutes	Every Collection	Jul 2, 2009 1:45:46 AM CDT
Failed Authorizations (%) (since last collection)	Not Set			
Total Failed Authorizations (%)	Not Set			
▼ Request Processed by Access Server	Not Applicable	Every 15 Minutes	Every Collection	Jul 2, 2009 1:45:46 AM CDT
Request Processed (since last collection)	Not			

Each target types provide performance pages that help you to monitor key performance metrics for those targets. We will not bore you to death by showing you the homepages and performance pages of all components and instead we will leave that as an exercise for you to explore.

Enterprise Manager allows you to set metric thresholds for several metrics. Like other targets, you can navigate to those by selecting **Metric and Policy Settings** for each target type. For example, you can set critical and metric thresholds for several metrics such as **Active Invocations**, **Active Session Count**, and so on, for Identity Manager Server, as shown in the following screenshot:

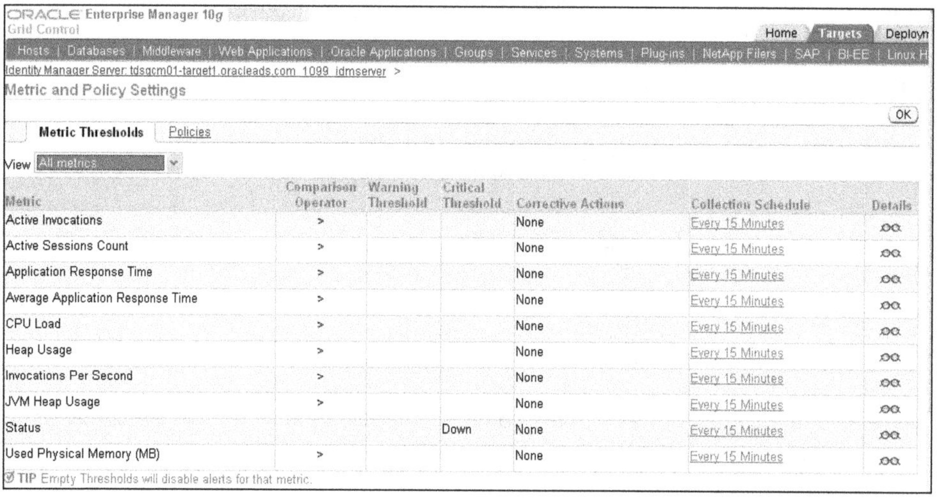

Besides monitoring the Identity Management components, you can also monitor the health of the complete infrastructure. We learnt earlier in this chapter that you build systems for each of these component types during the discovery process. This provides visibility of the health of the dependent components, and helps to diagnose problems quickly. The following figure shows the components of the **Identity Manager System**.

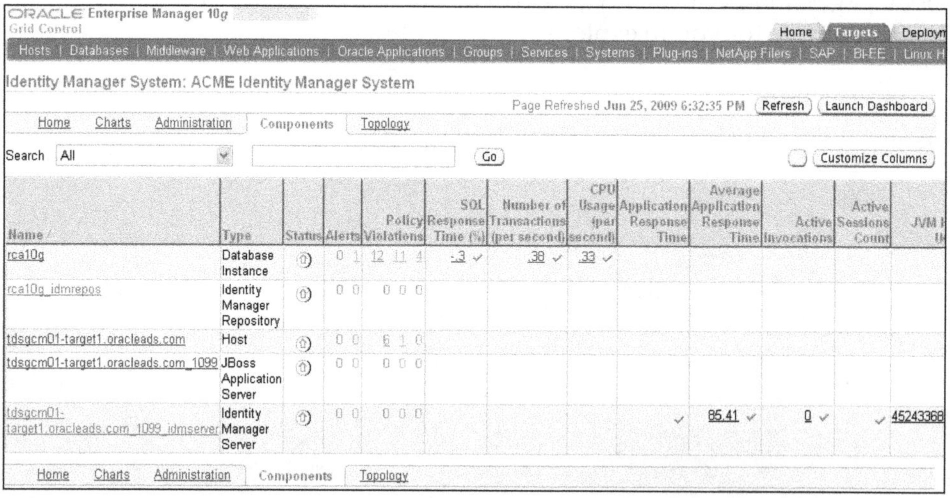

As you can see in this case the Identity Manager Server runs on JBoss application server and depends on the Oracle database. You can view the alerts, policy violations, and some of the key metrics for the components. You can customize these systems to suit your need. For example, you can create a system that contains all identity manager components that you use in your environment.

Service level management

The performance and availability of the Identity and Access Management system is crucial for most organizations. A down or degraded service level for these systems may greatly impact on the performance of several applications that depend on the Identity and Access Management Suite. Enterprise Manager allows you to create service and establish service level and monitor these services for any service level violations. You can create a generic service or web application service for any of the identity management component that you are monitoring.

We learnt how to create a web application service for an application deployed in WebLogic Server in Chapter 4—*Managing Oracle WebLogic Server*. You can use the same approach to build a service for your identity system.

For example, the following figure shows a service that we had built for Oracle Access Manager:

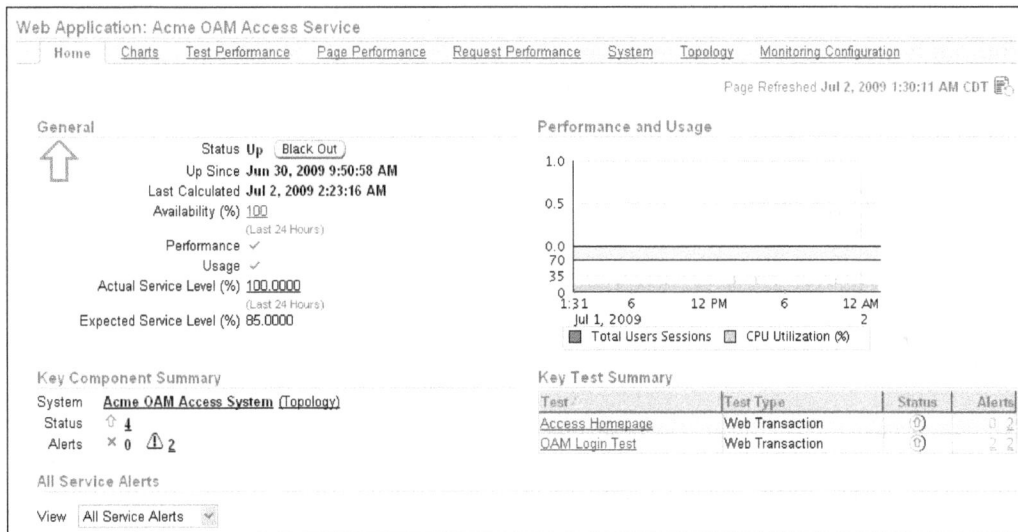

We have two service tests for this service and the OAM Login test verifies the availability and performance of users that are logging into applications using Oracle Access Manager. The following screenshot shows the details of the service test:

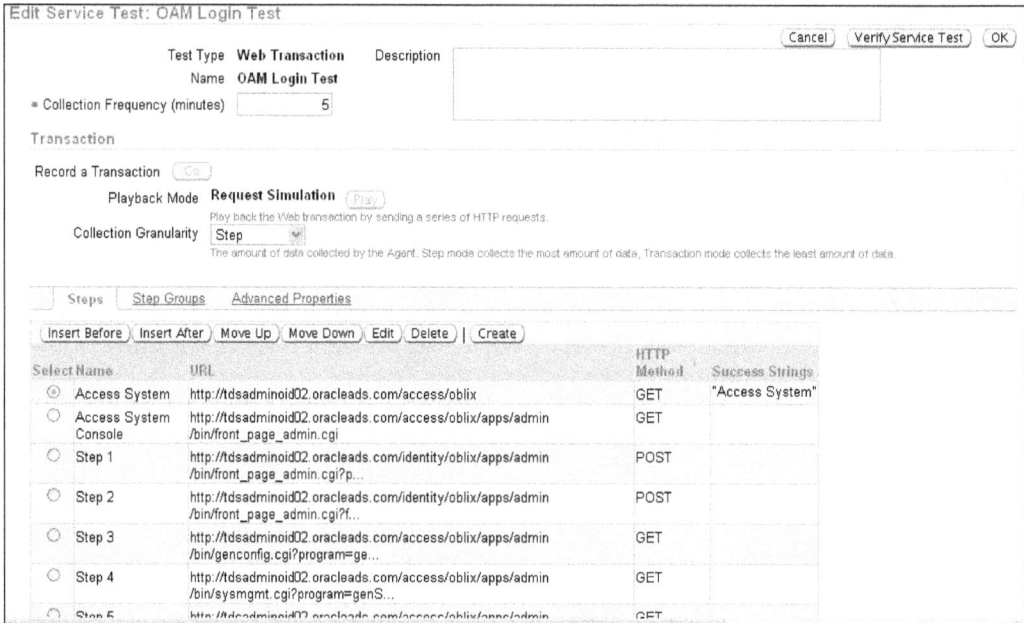

You can build similar service tests for other components of the suite to ensure their availability and performance. This will make sure that your Identity and Access Management System Suite meets the service level that you agreed upon.

Configuration management

Enterprise Manager allows you to track configurations and compare configurations between two different versions of the same target or two entirely different targets of the same type. Enterprise Manager has only configuration management capabilities for Access Manager components.

You can access the configuration management capabilities of Access Server and Identity server by accessing the relevant link from their homepages. The following figure shows the configuration history for Access Server:

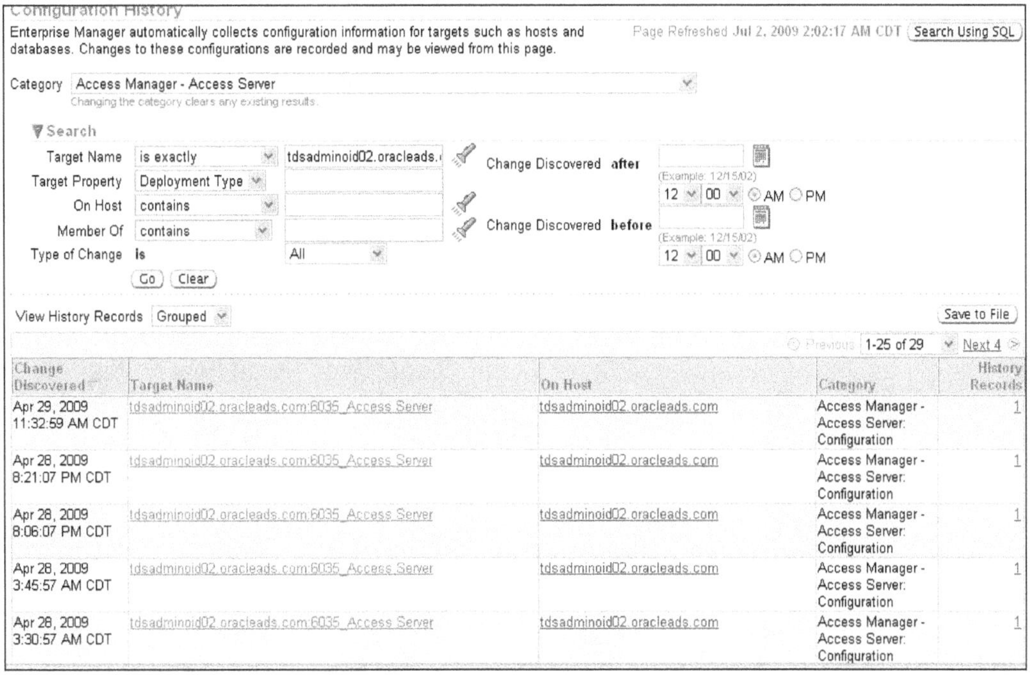

You can see that the configurations have been changed on several dates. You can click on the history records to view the changes as shown in the following figure where the **Number of listener threads** parameter was changed from 27 to **0**.

Similarly, you can compare the configurations between two different versions of the configuration files or between two different servers; for example the test and production servers. The following screenshot shows the comparison between two different versions and the differences:

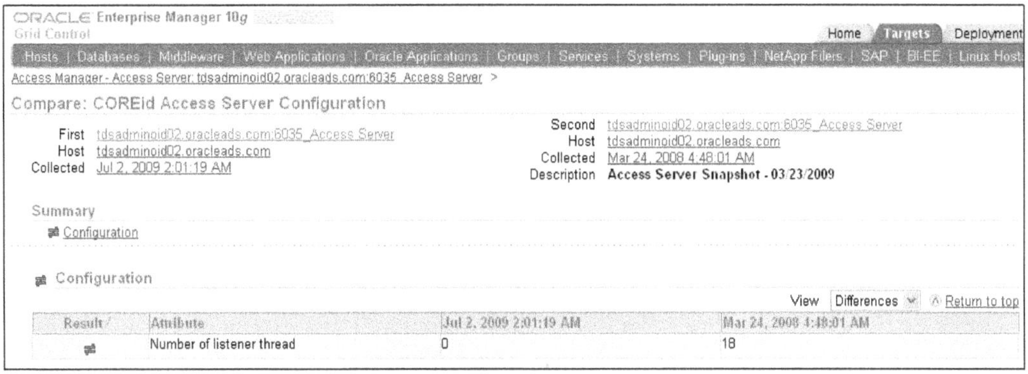

Many of the performance problems are caused by configuration changes and Enterprise Manager helps you to track down the root causes of these by configuration tracking and configuration comparison features.

Summary

Oracle Identity and Access Management Suite provides management of identities and access control for enterprise business applications. Ensuring the performance and availability of these components is critical to your business. The Identity and Access Management Suite comprises of several components and it is a difficult task to ensure the management of these. In this chapter, you learnt how to discover these components and how to monitor the performance and service level of these applications. You also learnt how to manage the configurations of Oracle Access Manager components. We will learn about the management of coherence cluster in the next chapter.

10
Managing Coherence Cluster

Oracle Coherence is an in-memory caching solution that enables organizations to predictably scale mission-critical applications. Oracle Coherence comes with several editions or flavors. You can either use Coherence as a caching solution within your enterprise applications as a shared library, or as an external data grid solution providing distributed data management capabilities. The Coherence product does not come with a management console providing a visibility gap to the Coherence cluster. Effectively, managing your Oracle Coherence environment is critical to maximizing application availability and ensuring a high **Quality of Service** (QoS). In this chapter, we will learn:

- What an Oracle Coherence cluster is
- How to discover a Coherence cluster
- Monitoring and management of a Coherence cluster
- Provisioning of a Coherence cluster and nodes

Coherence overview

A Coherence cluster is a set of Coherence nodes that work together to provide a distributed caching service. A node may be an application server instance or a Java process running Coherence binaries. Coherence functionality is based on the concept of cluster services. Each node can either provide or consume a number of named services. The services may either be caching or data service, connectivity services, management service, and so on. A node providing a caching service is often referred to as a storage node and a node providing management node i.e. hosting the Mbean server is referred to as a management node. For more about Coherence, refer to the *Coherence documentation* in the Oracle Technology Network at: http://download.oracle.com/docs/cd/E14526_01/index.htm

Oracle Coherence comes with several flavors or editions. Take a look at the Oracle Technology Network for the features offered by each edition: `http://www.oracle.com/technology/products/coherence/coherencedatagrid/coherence_editions.html`.

The following figure shows the architecture for each editions of Coherence:

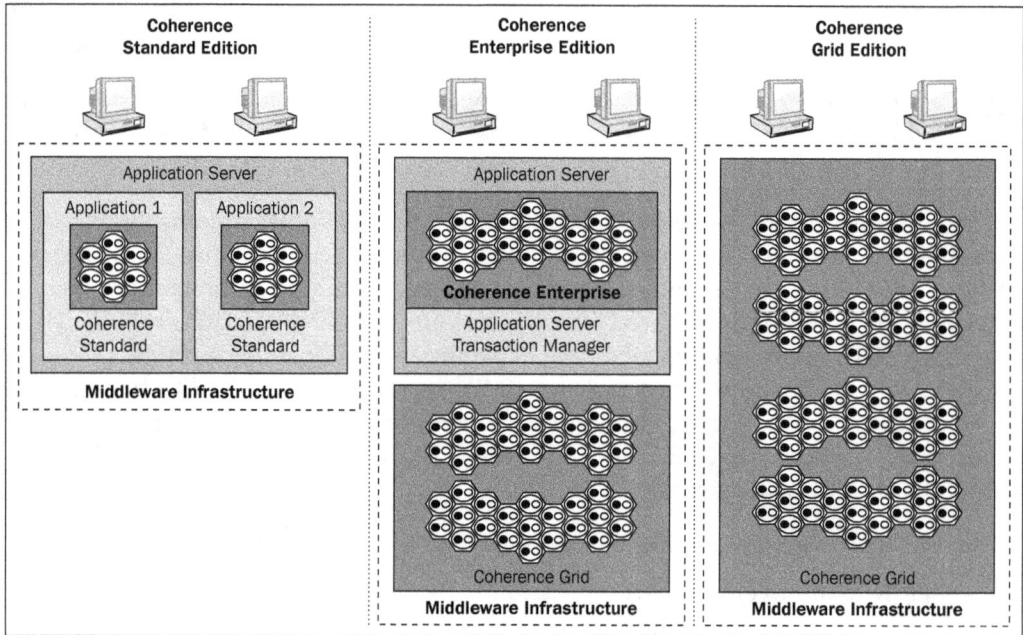

You can use Enterprise Manager to monitor your Coherence cluster.

> Enterprise manager supports only Coherence Enterprise Edition and Grid Edition. You have to enable management service for your Coherence cluster to monitor from Enterprise Manager Grid Control.

Discovery of the Coherence cluster

A Coherence cluster usually has a large number of nodes that may run on multiple hosts. As we discussed earlier, a node could either be a storage, proxy, or management node and each node is nothing but a JVM process. For example, a Coherence node may have 16 nodes, where 14 may be storage nodes and one may be a management node and another a proxy node. The management node hosts a JMX server, and Oracle Enterprise Manager depends on the management node for discovering and monitoring the Coherence cluster. The Oracle Management Agent talks to the management node for collecting metrics, propagating runtime configuration changes, and so on.

Enterprise Manager discovers the entire cluster in a single step and requires a single agent to monitor the entire cluster.

> The agent can either be local or remote where management node is running. The agent box should be able to communicate with the host running the management node.

You have to start management nodes and other Coherence nodes with special start-up parameters. The *Coherence Developer's Guide* documents contain material on how to enable JMX for Coherence cluster (`http://download.oracle.com/docs/cd/E13924_01/coh.340/e13818/managejmx.htm#BABICAAI`).

The management node provides an aggregated view of monitoring metrics by collecting it from other nodes. If you have a large number of nodes in the cluster, the metrics collection may take a long time. Enterprise Manager ships some binaries, called Bulk Mbean, that makes collection and aggregation of metrics much faster and we recommend that you use those binaries to start your management node. These JAR files (`bulkoperationsmbean_11.1.1.jar`, `coherenceEMIntg.jar`) are shipped in the OMS. You have to copy these JAR files to your server where you are starting the management node.

Starting Coherence management node using bulk management Mbeans

You have to start your management node before you can discover the cluster. If you want to use bulk management Mbean, copy those to your server where you have a management node. You have to modify your start script to include the `coherenceEMIntg.jar` and `bulkoperationsmbean_11.1.1.jar` files.

For example, the following is an example of a script to start Coherence 3.4
management node using the bulk management Mbean:

```
CLASSPATH=$COHERENCE_HOME/coherence/lib/coherence.jar
CLASSPATH=$CLASSPATH:/em/lib/coherenceEMIntg.jar:/em/lib/
bulkoperationsmbean_11.1.1.jar
$JAVA_HOME/bin/java -cp $CLASSPATH $JVM_OPT $SYS_OPT oracle.sysman.
integration.coherence.EMIntegrationServer > $COHERENCE_HOME/mgmtnode.
log >> $COHERENCE_HOME/mgmtnode.err &
```

You have to make sure that you specified the following option in your start script
when you start the management node:

```
com.sun.management.jmxremote.port=portNum
```

You will need this port number while discovering the Coherence cluster. The agent
talks to the management node using this port.

See the *Coherence Developer's Guide* for additional options that you can use to start the
management node, for example, security credentials.

Now that we have learned how to use the set-up required for starting up the
management node, we will move ahead and discover the Coherence cluster.

The Coherence Target Model

Before we discover Coherence Cluster, let us understand the target model for
Coherence. In Coherence cluster, nodes, caches, connection managers, and so on,
seem to be the perfect fit to be considered as a target. However, from Enterprise
Manager's perspective, only the Coherence cluster is a managed target. Coherence
nodes, caches, and so on are not real targets from an EM perspective. However, each
of these entities' nodes, caches, and so on have homepages and you can have alerts
appear on these pages whenever an alert is generated.

Discovering Oracle Coherence

Before you discover the Coherence cluster, you have to make sure that the
Management Agent is running and discovered. You have to also ensure that the
Coherence management node is up and running. If you have multiple management
nodes in the cluster, ensure that your primary management node is up and running.
Check the certification matrix at My Oracle Support to verify if the Coherence
version you are using is certified with Grid Control.

To discover the Coherence cluster, log on to the Enterprise Manager Grid Control as an administrator that has **Add target** privilege. Then select the middleware targets and select **Add Oracle Coherence** page.

Then select the host name where Oracle Management Agent is running, which you will use to discover/monitor the Coherence cluster.

On the next page, you have to enter the details for connecting to the management node for Oracle Coherence as in the following screenshot:

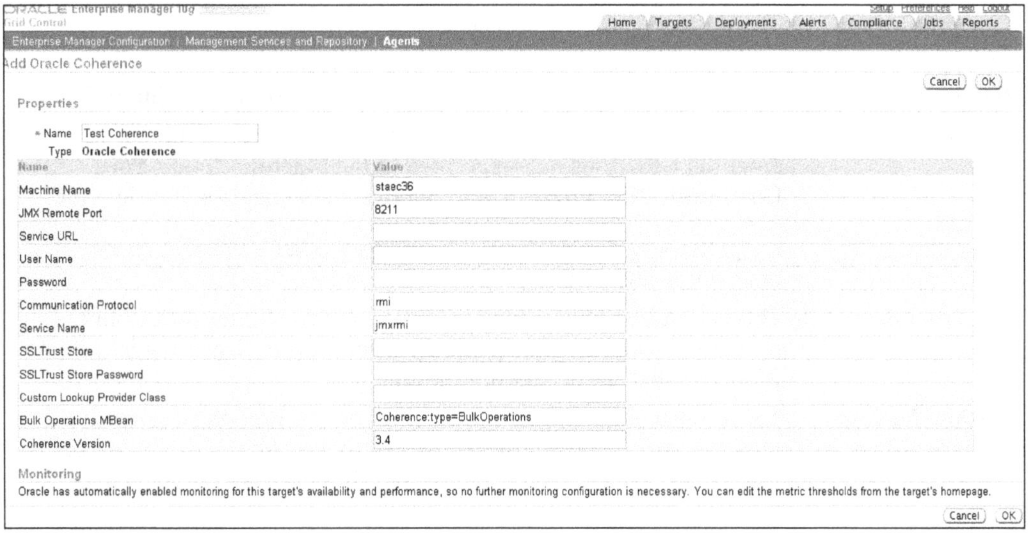

The important parameters are the **Machine Name** and **JMX Remote Port** for the Coherence management node. You have to ensure that these parameters are supplied correctly for monitoring to work. Select the default value **Bulk Operation Mbean** if you have started the managed node with bulk management Mbean. You have to select the appropriate version for the Coherence cluster.

The other parameters are optional and only required if you have enabled these when starting your management node. The following table provides the description for other optional parameters for discovery:

Parameter	Description
User Name and **Password**	The credentials required for connecting to the Coherence JMX Server. The User Name and password specified `$JDK_HOME/jre/lib/management/jmxremote.password file.`
Communication Protocol	The protocol used for JMX connection. The default is **rmi**.
Service Name	The service name used for the connection. The default is **jmxrmi**.
Service URL	The JMX Service URL that will be used for JMX connection. If you enter the URL, the values specified in the **Machine Name**, **Port**, **Communication Protocol**, and **Service Name** fields will be ignored. Example: service:jmx:rmi://hostname:3001/jndi/rmi://hostname:9001/server
SSLTrustStore	This is required only when you have enabled SSL for JMX Connection for your Coherence Management Server. This indicates the SSL store where trusted certificates are stored.
Custom Lockup Provider Class	This is used only when the above JMX connection details are dynamic and must programatically be looked up, for example from some LDAP server. You have to enter the class that implements JMXLookUp.
Bulk Operations MBeans	Oracle has supplied the Bulk MBean to improve the performance of the MBean server and the default value (**Coherence: type=BulkOperations**) should be used if you use those JARS to start your Mbean server.

You can select **OK** to add the Coherence cluster and it will be added as a target. If the monitoring properties are not correct, then you will get errors when trying to monitor from Enterprise Manager. You can select monitoring configuration and enter the correct configuration for monitoring. If you have multiple management nodes in your cluster and your management node goes down, you can switch to another management node by changing the monitoring configuration to point to another management node.

Monitoring of Coherence cluster

You can monitor the entire Coherence cluster as a single target. The Coherence cluster homepage provides important aspects of the Coherence cluster. You can monitor availability and performance of the cluster from this page, as shown in the following screenshot:

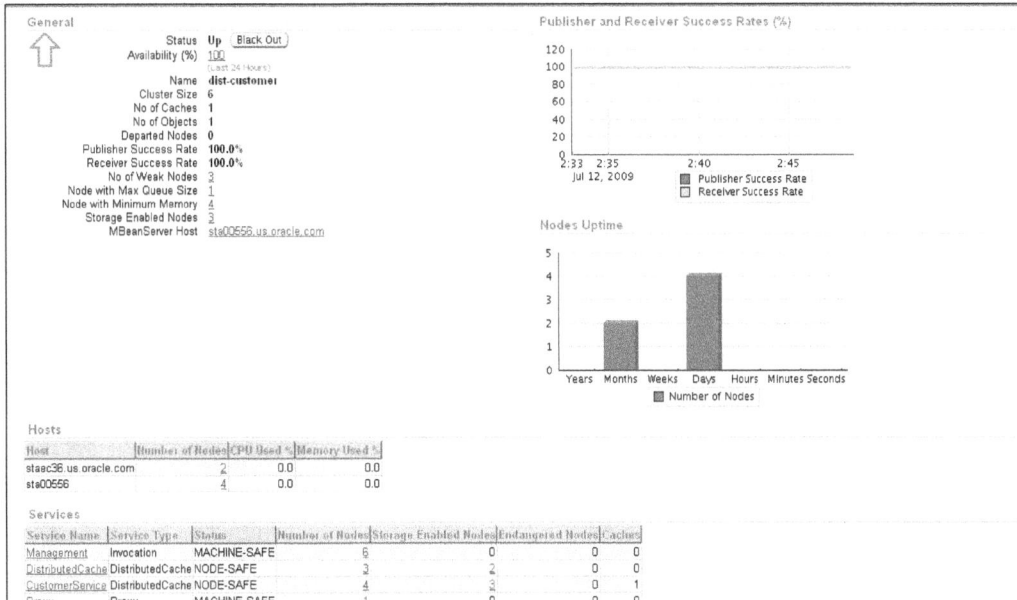

The publisher and receiver success rate provides the health of the network and looks at how the nodes are communicating with each other. If the **Publisher and Receiver Success Rates** are significantly down, you have to worry about the health of the cluster because the nodes are not effectively communicating with each other.

It provides the number of nodes, objects, hosts, the CPU and memory usage and status of the services. For a caching service such as Distributed Cache, you should not see the status as **ENDANGERED**. Also, you will get an alert if any of the service status is **ENDANGERED**. It will appear in the Cluster homepage along with other metric alerts. You can use a notification mechanism such as email, if you want to get an email. We talked about setting up email as a notification method in Chapter 4, *Managing Oracle WebLogic Server*.

Setting up the metric threshold

You can implement proactive monitoring for Coherence by setting the metric threshold. You can set up both warning and critical threshold for the Coherence cluster. Enterprise Manager allows you to select several Coherence metrics, such as node or cache specific metrics. You can select this by clicking on the **Metric and Policy Settings** link from the Coherence cluster page. The following screenshot shows how you can set the warning and critical threshold. You can set the value for warning and critical thresholds. EM uses the comparison operator to compare with the warning or critical threshold and if the comparison evaluates to true then an alert is raised.

Metric	Comparison Operator	Warning Threshold	Critical Threshold	Corrective Actions	Collection Schedule	Edit
Cache Hits Delta	>			None	Every 300 Seconds	
Cache Hits Delta Sum	>			None	Every 300 Seconds	
Cache Misses Delta	>			None	Every 300 Seconds	
Cache Misses Delta Sum	>			None	Every 300 Seconds	
Cache Size Delta	!=	0	0	None	Every 300 Seconds	
Cluster Size Delta	!=	0	0	None	Every 300 Seconds	
Memory Available (MB)	<			None	Every 300 Seconds	
Publisher Success Rate	<			None	Every 300 Seconds	
Publisher Success Rate (Delta Time)	<			None	Every 300 Seconds	
Receiver Success Rate (Delta Time)	<			None	Every 300 Seconds	
Receiver Success Rate (Delta Time)	<			None	Every 300 Seconds	
Request Timeout Count	>			None	Every 300 Seconds	
Request Timeout Count Delta	>			None	Every 300 Seconds	
Request Total Count	>			None	Every 300 Seconds	
Request Total Count Delta	>			None	Every 300 Seconds	
Send Queue Size	>			None	Every 300 Seconds	
Status			Down	None	Every 1 Minute	
Status HA	Matches		ENDAN(	None	Every 300 Seconds	
Store Reads Delta						
dist-customer;8;CustomerService	>	1000	2000	None	Every 300 Seconds	
All others	>			None	Every 300 Seconds	
Store Reads Delta Sum	>			None	Every 300 Seconds	
Store Writes Delta	>			None	Every 300 Seconds	

Even then you can customize the metric rule to run against a specific monitored target. For example, you can set a metric threshold for **Store Reads Delta** only for a specific cache service, as shown in the previous screenshot. How do you do that? We leave that as an exercise for you. (A hint: Select **Edit** and then add **Monitored Objects**.)

Monitoring Coherence node

A Coherence node is a JVM process that is a member of Coherence cluster and it provides a clustered/distributed caching service. Therefore, it is important to monitor the health of the Coherence nodes. From the Coherence Cluster homepage, you can navigate to the **Nodes Performance** page, and see the performance of the top nodes as in the following screenshot:

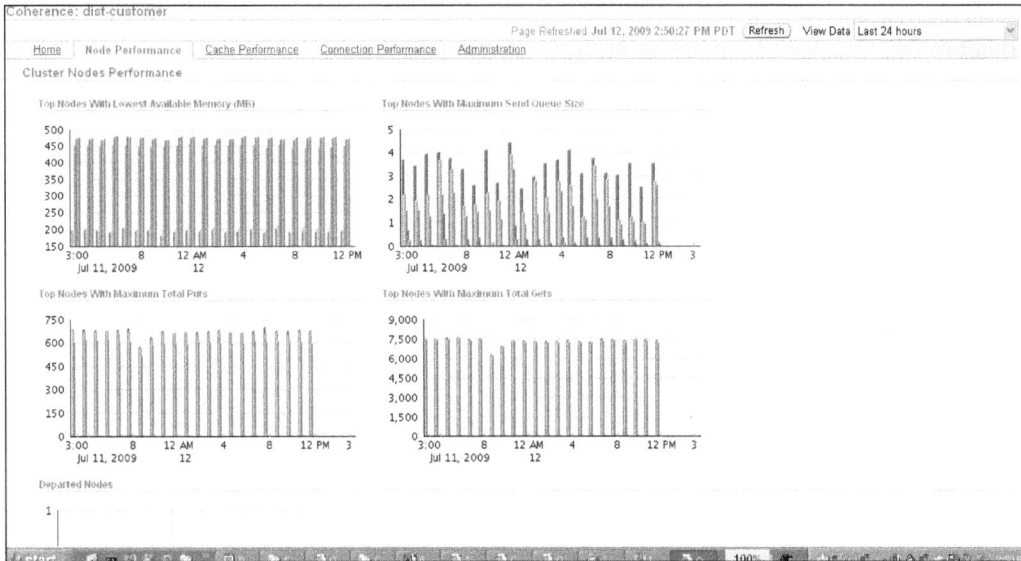

Coherence: dist-customer

The top nodes are the nodes that may have potential issues, for example, nodes with less memory or a large queue size. On this page, only the top nodes are shown. You can see both the real time and historical metrics. The historical metrics are useful to perform a trend analysis. You can navigate to the bottom of the page to see all nodes in a tabular view, as in the following screenshot:

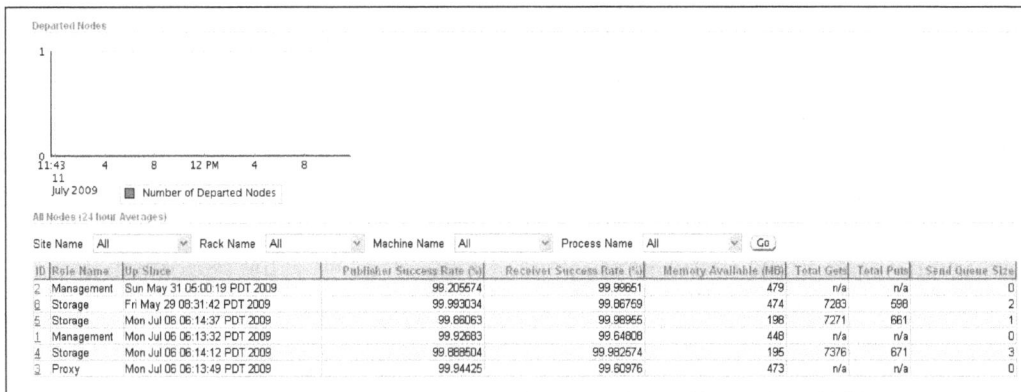

ID	Role Name	Up Since	Publisher Success Rate (%)	Receiver Success Rate (%)	Memory Available (MB)	Total Gets	Total Puts	Send Queue Size
2	Management	Sun May 31 05:00:19 PDT 2009	99.205574	99.99651	479	n/a	n/a	0
6	Storage	Fri May 29 08:31:42 PDT 2009	99.993034	99.86759	474	7283	598	2
5	Storage	Mon Jul 06 06:14:37 PDT 2009	99.86063	99.98955	198	7271	661	1
1	Management	Mon Jul 06 06:13:32 PDT 2009	99.92683	99.64808	448	n/a	n/a	0
4	Storage	Mon Jul 06 06:14:12 PDT 2009	99.888504	99.982574	195	7376	671	3
3	Proxy	Mon Jul 06 06:13:49 PDT 2009	99.94425	99.60976	473	n/a	n/a	0

The tabular view provides you with a way to compare how the nodes are performing compared to each other. However if you have a large number of nodes, it will be difficult to compare them to each other. We will discuss later in the chapter about how you can use Enterprise Manager to compare performance and configuration of two nodes.

You can drill down to a specific node by clicking a node in the graph or in the table to get to the node's homepage as in the following screenshot:

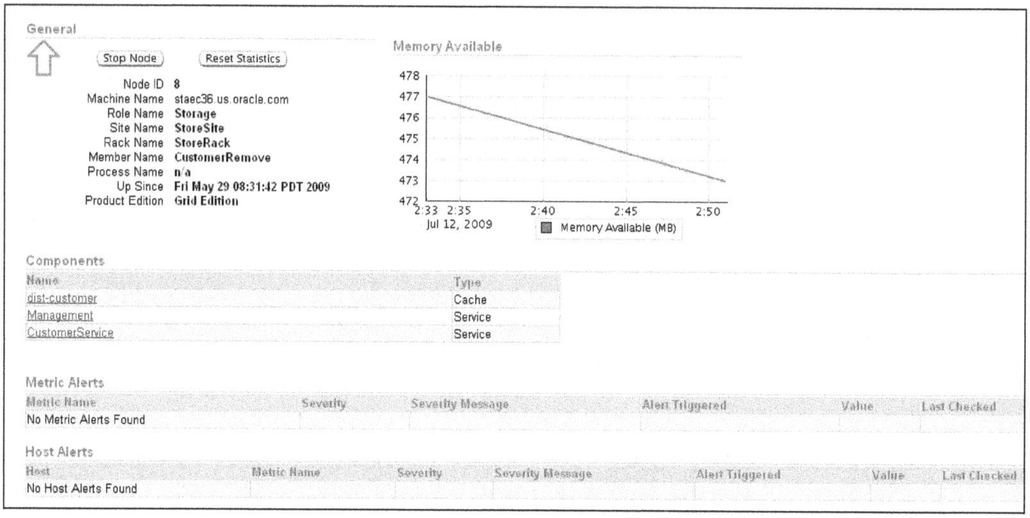

The node homepage provides the health of a node and the cache or service it offers. You can see the host and metric alert and take the appropriate action. It provides operations such as stop and reset statistics.

> Note that the stop operation does not actually stop the JVM process running the node but it evicts the node from the cluster. For example, you may decide to stop/evict the node if you find out that the node is not performing to expectations. When you evict the node, it will depart the node and it may join back later. When a node departs or joins a cluster, the cached data automatically gets repartitioned and the data gets redistributed.

You can navigate to the **Performance** page of a cluster to view the performance details for the cluster. The **Performance** page for the cluster provides several crucial metrics that indicate the health of the node such as gets, puts, memory available, stored reads, and so on, for the last 24 hours or the selected period.

You can also view the health of the underlying JVM process, such as heap memory and garbage collection data and network connections, as shown in the following screenshot:

This data provides you with an insight into the node's JVM process, and helps you diagnose issues that may be due to a JVM problem, for example garbage collection data.

Monitoring Coherence cache

Coherence cache is the most important aspect of the cluster. Coherence provides a distributed caching service, and applications read and store objects from these caches, without having to know about the actual location of this data. A cache may be distributed across multiple storage nodes or JVMs and each of these are called cache partitions. Enterprise Manager provides excellent capabilities to monitor caches. You can navigate to the cache performance page.

By default, you will see the top five caches compared to each other and you can change the view by all caches or view by nodes.

You can drill down to a specific cache and view its performance. The **Performance** page shows the performance of each cache's partitions compared to the other, as shown in the following figure:

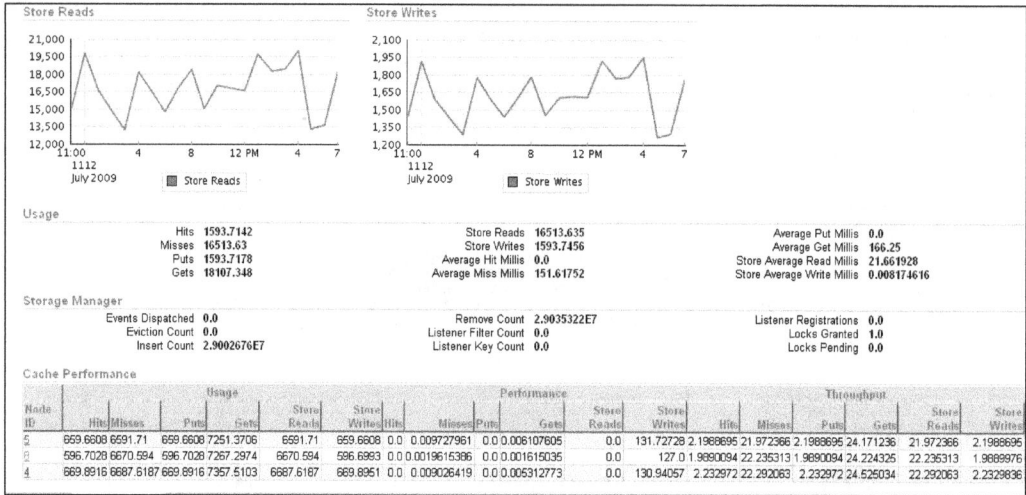

You can compare usage, performance, and throughputs for each cache partition. This helps you to quickly gauge how nodes are performing and take remedial steps.

Monitoring connections and connections managers

You can monitor the health of connections and connection managers using Enterprise Manager. This provides you with an insight into the health of proxy connections. You can monitor each connection and how these are using the cluster. For example, one particular connection may be overloading the cluster with too much data and this may be it slowing down. You can find out who the client is, as Enterprise Manager can help you to find the IP address and you can even choose to close the connection.

We leave navigating and monitoring of connections and connection managers as an exercise for you to complete in your own time.

Comparing and propagating changes

Most of the performance degradation in a running system is due to configuration changes and Enterprise Manager can help you to track down the configuration and performance differences between two different nodes, two caches, connection managers, or connections. Think about the case where, for example, you rolled out some changes to the cache configurations of your storage nodes and, by mistake, you did not propagate that change to one node and that node is not performing as expected. You can then use the compare configuration feature. You can access this either using the **Administration** link from the Coherence cluster page or each component page, for example node or cache. You can select the two nodes or caches to compare and you will see the comparison as in the following page:

You can compare both configuration and performance between two nodes and track down the difference between them.

You can then use the real-time configuration change propagation feature of Enterprise Manager. You can navigate to the real-time configuration change page, either by navigating to **Administration** link from your component homepage, or the cluster homepage. For example, the following figure shows the configuration change for a node.

You can change a configuration for example, log level for a node. You can even propagate this change to the entire cluster. You have to be careful as some changes may slow down the performance of the cluster.

> Note that these changes are for real-time only and do not get persisted. The changes are only temporary and are lost when a node is restarted.

Provisioning the Coherence cluster

Your cluster may have a large number of nodes and you may be adding new nodes to the cluster depending on the increasing load on your cluster. Enterprise Manager can help you automate the provisioning of Coherence cluster. You can either provision a completely new cluster or add new nodes to the cluster by using the Coherence provisioning deployment procedure. You can schedule the coherence node provisioning by selecting it from the homepage.

> Ensure that you have installed management agent in the hosts/machines where you want to provision new Coherence nodes and these hosts are discovered from Enterprise Manager.

The Coherence provisioning deployment procedure can install Coherence, copy your application binaries, cache configuration files and startup scripts and start a new coherence node.

You have to upload your coherence binaries, startup script, application jars, and so on to the software library.

You can schedule a Coherence node provisioning deployment procedure by selecting the appropriate deployment procedure. You have to first select the appropriate source in the first step, as shown in the following screenshot:

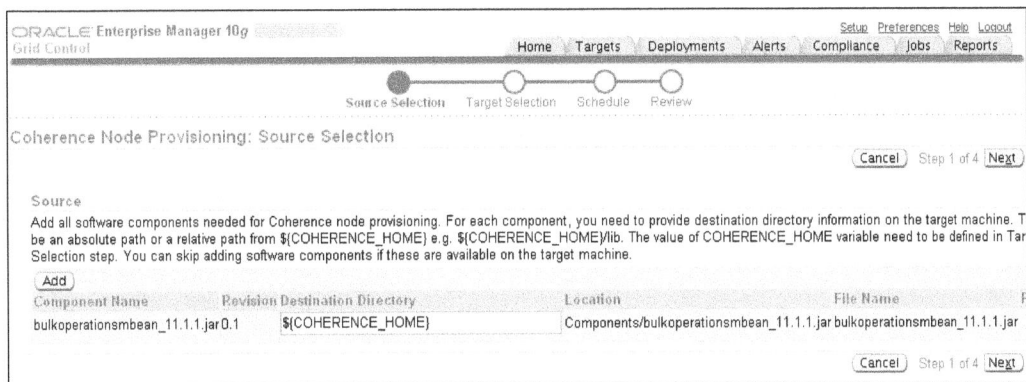

In this step, you can select the appropriate software components such as the application components that you need as a part of your Coherence node.

Then you can choose whether you want to add a new node to the cluster or add a completely new cluster. For example, if you have a test cluster and you want to move that to UAT or the production environment you can chose this option. When you add a new Coherence cluster, it is automatically discovered by Enterprise Manager.

In the next step, you can select the node details. In this step, you have to select the hosts where you want to provision new nodes, number of nodes, and node types, as shown in the following screenshot:

You have to enter the home directory and the path of the startup script that will be used to start the node. If you have selected more than one node, then Enterprise Manager will automatically derive the names and the home directory.

> We recommend that you enter the node details such as **Site Name**, **Role Name**, and **Rack Name** even if these are optional parameters. These parameters are used to uniquely identify a node, as the node number is dynamic in nature and gets changed whenever it gets started or rejoins the cluster.

After entering these details you can schedule the deployment. The deployment procedure will run and then provision the node or cluster. The deployment procedure framework is extensible in nature, for example you can build a new procedure to roll out application patches to all the nodes in your cluster.

Summary

Coherence cluster is a very popular technology that provides distributed caching services. In this chapter, we learnt how to discover a Coherence cluster from Enterprise Manager. You can now monitor a Coherence cluster either by using a local or remote management agent. Bulk Operation Mbean is recommended for better performance in metrics collection and aggregation when you have a large number of Coherence nodes. Enterprise Manager monitors Coherence cluster by talking to a single management node. We can use Enterprise Manager to monitor the health and performance of Coherence cluster and learned how to monitor and diagnose issues in different entities such as nodes, caches, services, and so on. We also learned configuration comparison and rolling out real-time configuration changes. We can use Coherence node provisioning feature to create a new Coherence cluster or add new nodes to an existing Coherence cluster.

Today heterogeneous systems are very common and you would expect that there will be some non-Oracle middleware in your IT shop. In the next chapter, we will learn how you can monitor a third-party middleware such as IBM, Websphere, Jboss, or Microsoft Middleware. So, see you there!

11
Managing Non-Oracle Middleware

You cannot expect your IT organizations to have only Oracle middleware and databases. The Service Oriented Architecture has become popular because it simplifies the integration of several heterogeneous platforms and systems. Even if you primarily run on Oracle software you may get some non-Oracle middleware platforms along with a packaged application or due to a merger/acquisition with another company. You would expect that the management solution that you implement will help you to monitor your non-Oracle middleware and databases. You may remember from our discussion that Oracle Enterprise Manager provides an extensible mechanism known as plug-in architecture to build additional monitoring capabilities.

In this chapter, we will learn how Oracle Enterprise Manager provides you with the ability to manage non-Oracle middleware.

You will learn about the following:

- Monitoring of open source middleware Apache HTTP Server, Tomcat, and JBoss Application Server
- Monitoring of IBM WebSphere Application Server and IBM WebSphere MQ
- Monitoring of Microsoft middleware such as Microsoft IIS, .NET, and so on

Non-Oracle middleware support

We can broadly categorize non-Oracle middleware into two categories. The middleware platform that is primarily popular with Java applications and also with software that has been built using the Microsoft platform.

Oracle provides two types of plug-ins to monitor non-Oracle software:

- The first type of plug-ins are integrated with Oracle Enterprise Manager Grid Control and do not require a separate installation.

- Some of the plug-ins are released separately in Oracle Technology Network, and require installation. Let's refer to these types of plug-ins as standard plug-ins.

The following screenshot shows an instance of Oracle Enterprise Manager Grid Control managing non-Oracle middleware, which is being being monitored along with Oracle middleware installations:

All Middleware							
dev.oracleads.com	Oracle Application Server Farm	n/a	16 (↑16)				
farm	Oracle Application Server Farm	n/a	3 (↑3)				
VIS12Cluster	Oracle Application Server Cluster	n/a					
cdb_app.tdscontentdb.oracleads.com	Oracle Application Server		4 (↑4)	1521.58	10.1.2.0.2	8.03
EnterpriseManager0.tdsgcm01.oracleads.com	Oracle Application Server		5 (↑5)	2021.73	10.1.2.3.0	31.72
IDM_INFRA.tdsadminoid02.oracleads.com	Oracle Application Server		7 (↓2 ☼1 ↑4)		10.1.2.0.2	
PSFT_IAS.tdspsft01.oracleads.com	Oracle Application Server		3 (↑3)	626.36	10.1.2.0.2	3.71
soademo.tdscamm01-soa.oracleads.com	Oracle Application Server		2 (↑2)	769.21	10.1.3.1.0	26.58
soademo.tdssoaob2.oracleads.com	Oracle Application Server		2 (↑2)	937.2	10.1.3.1.0	4.49
soademo.tdssoaob3.oracleads.com	Oracle Application Server		2 (↑2)	1024.37	10.1.3.1.0	3.96
tds_federation.tdsadminoid02.oracleads.com	Oracle Application Server		3 (↑3)	335.71	10.1.2.0.2	7.92
VIS12_tdsebizxii01.tdsebizxii01.oracleads.com	Oracle Application Server		4 (↑4)	547.97	10.1.3.0.0	11.09
tdsats00-weblogic1.oracleads.com.medrec_7011	Oracle WebLogic Server Domain	n/a	1 (↑1)			
tdscamm01-soa.oracleads.com.camm_domain_80	Oracle WebLogic Server Domain	n/a	1 (↑1)			
tdsgcbea01.oracleads.com.MedRecClusterDomain	Oracle WebLogic Server Domain	n/a	3 (↑3)			
tdsgcweb01.oracleads.com.tdsgcweb01Network	IBM WebSphere Application Server Cell	n/a	3 (↑3)			
CLUSTER1	IBM WebSphere MQ Cluster		2 (↑2)			
IIS6_tdsintsieb1	Microsoft IIS 6.0		↑			
JBoss402Partition	JBoss Partition	n/a	2 (↑2)			
ms_activedir_tdsgcwin02	Microsoft Active Directory		↑			
ms_biztalk_tdsgcwin01	Microsoft BizTalk Server 2004		↑			
ms_dotnet_tdsgcwin01	Microsoft .NET Framework		↑			
ms_iis6_tdsgcwin01	Microsoft IIS 6.0		↑			
TDS_COHERENCE	Oracle Coherence		↑	716.0	3.4	
tdsgcm01-target1.oracleads.com_1099	JBoss Application Server		↑		4.0.3SP1(build: CVSTag=JBoss_4_0_3_SP1 date=200510231054)	

It is evident from the previous screenshot that Oracle Enterprise Manager supports a large amount of middleware such as JBoss Application Server, Microsoft IIS, .Net, Active Directory, IBM WebSphere, and JBoss Application Server. The following table shows the names of the plug-ins and their types. For the actual version of these supported products, check the certification matrix in My Oracle Support.

Middleware	Plug-in Type
Apache HTTP Server	Integrated
Apache Tomcat	Standard
IBM WebSphere Application Server	Integrated
IBM WebSphere MQ	Integrated
JBoss Application Server	Integrated
Microsoft Active Directory	Standard
Microsoft BizTalk Server	Standard
Microsoft Commerce Server	Standard
Microsoft IIS	Standard
Microsoft Internet Security and Acceleration Server	Standard
Microsoft .NET Framework	Standard

Looking at the previous table, we can divide this middleware support in to three categories:

- Open source middleware
- IBM middleware
- Microsoft middleware

Managing open source middleware

Oracle supports the management of most popular open source middleware, such as Apache HTTP Server, Apache Tomcat, and JBoss Application Server. We will discuss the management of each of these functionalities.

Managing Apache HTTP Server

Apache HTTP Server is the most popular version of the web server. Your organizations may be using Apache HTTP Server as the web server for your applications. For example, many customers use Apache HTTP Server as the load balancer for WebLogic Server. Even Oracle HTTP Server is based on the Apache HTTP Server. However, Oracle HTTP Server is significantly pre-instrumented for performance monitoring and is automatically discovered when an Oracle Application Server instance is discovered.

Let us discuss how you can discover Apache HTTP Server from Enterprise Manager. In order to discover Apache HTTP Server, you have to navigate to the **Agent** page for the host where Apache HTTP Server is running and then, from the **Add** drop-down list select **Apache HTTP Server,** as shown in the following figure:

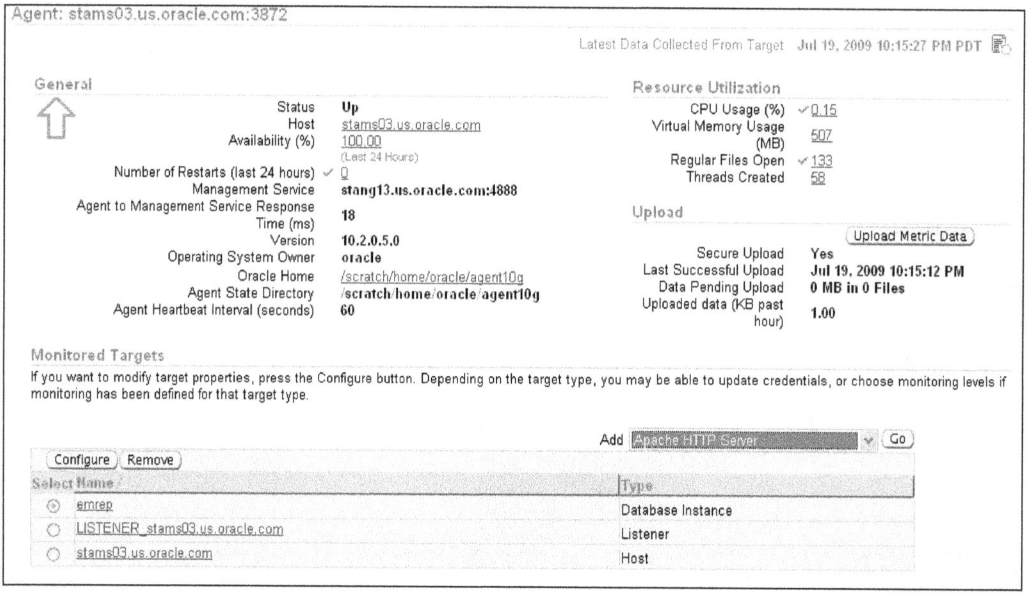

After you click on **Go**, you will be prompted by the discovery page, as shown in the following screenshot. You have to enter the details for the HTTP server. Only the paths to the `config` file directory and `bin` directory are required. The other parameters are optional, and required only when you want to use the End-User Monitoring feature. Oracle recommends using another product named Oracle Real User Experience Insight to monitor the end-user experience.

After you complete these details, the Apache HTTP Server will be discovered.

> You should avoid this approach to discover Oracle HTTP Server because although Oracle HTTP Server is a variant of Apache HTTP Server it has been pre-instrumented by Oracle and is automatically discovered with Oracle Application Server.

You can monitor the health of Apache HTTP Server and get notified when the server goes down. Note the generic Apache HTTP Server is not pre-instrumented and hence Grid Control cannot provide a lot of performance metrics similar to Oracle HTTP Server.

> For that reason, we recommend that you use Oracle HTTP Server instead of Apache HTTP Server.

The following page shows the homepage for Apache HTTP Server.

Besides the status monitoring, Enterprise Manager provides configuration management capabilities. You can view the configuration details for an Apache HTTP Server or compare it with a previous version or another server. You can access these details from the homepage.

Managing Apache Tomcat

Apache Tomcat is a very popular open source web container to deploy Java EE based web applications. Enterprise Manager Grid Control provides a plug-in to monitor Apache Tomcat Server. Unlike plug-ins for other non-Oracle application servers such as JBoss or IBM Websphere, the plug-in for Apache is not integrated and you have to install the plug-in on your Grid Control and deploy it to the agents that monitor the Tomcat servers.

Oracle provides several plug-ins in the Oracle Technology Network. You can download the plug-in to monitor Tomcat Server from the following location: `http//www.oracle.com/technology/software/products/oem/htdocs/plugin-apache_tomcat.html`. In this chapter, we will learn how to install the Tomcat plug-in and then monitor the Tomcat server.

Installing the Tomcat plug-in

First you have to download the plug-in JAR file to your local work station. Then you have to install the plug-in on your Oracle Management Server. To install a plug-in you have to perform the following steps:

- Login to Grid Control as a **Super Administrator**
- Navigate to **Setup | Management Plug-ins | Connectors** and then select **Add/Import Management Plug-ins**
- In the **Import Management Plug-ins** page, click on **Browse...** to select the `tomcat_plugin.jar` file that you downloaded earlier, and then click on **List Archive** and you will see the Tomcat plug-in details, as shown in the following screenshot:

- Click **OK** to install the Tomcat plug-in and you will get a confirmation message that the plug-in was installed
- You have to deploy the plug-in to the management agents that you want to use to monitor Tomcat

> Note that each plug-in adds one or more target type and the management agent has no knowledge of the target type. Therefore, the metadata files for the target types need to be pushed to each agent that will monitor the new target-types, for example in our case it is Tomcat.

- You can easily do that by selecting the target agents for the plug-in, as shown in the following figure:

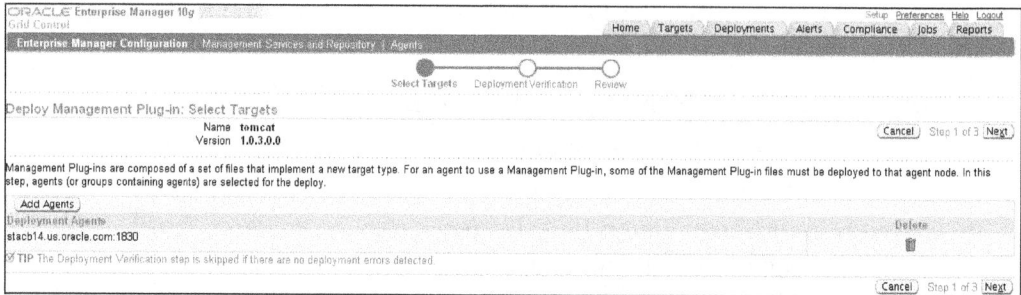

- After you select an agent and click on **Finish**, OMS will push the new metadata files for Tomcat to the agent that you selected and this agent will be able to monitor that Tomcat server.

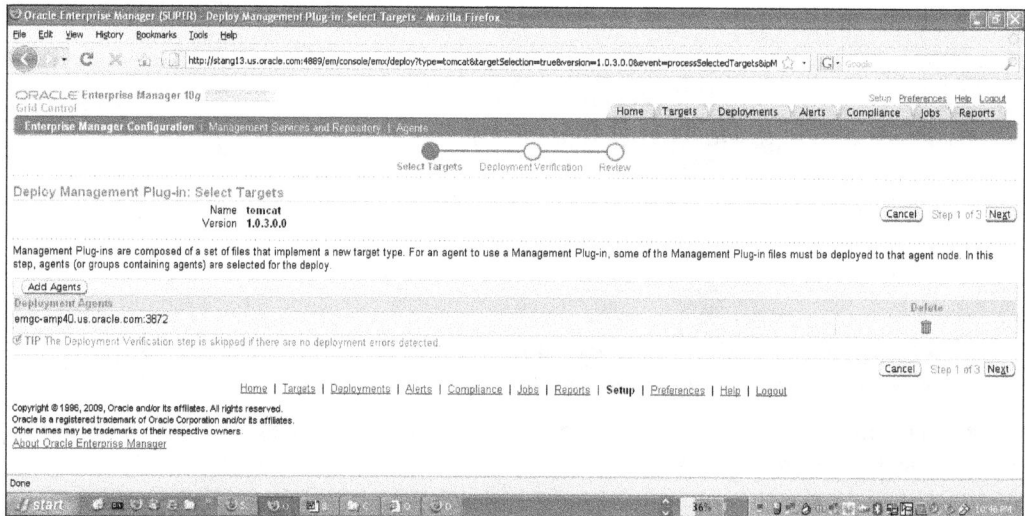

Discovering Tomcat Server

You have to enable JMX in your Tomcat server to discover and monitor from Oracle Enterprise Manager. You have to modify the start script for your Tomcat server to enable JMX Mbean server. To enable JMX, you have to add the following parameters to your startup script:

```
-Dcom.sun.management.jmxremote=true \
    -Dcom.sun.management.jmxremote.port=%my.jmx.port% \
    -Dcom.sun.management.jmxremote.ssl=false \
    -Dcom.sun.management.jmxremote.authenticate=false
```

Look at the Tomcat documentation at `http://tomcat.apache.org/tomcat-5.5-doc/monitoring.html` for details about enabling JMX and options that make sense with respect to your environment.

To discover a Tomcat server from Grid Control, you have to navigate to the **All Targets** page, and then click on **Add Apache Tomcat Server**, and you will get the discovery screen, as shown in the following screenshot:

You have to enter the name of the **Host** where Tomcat server is running, and the JMX **Port Number** that you specified when you enabled JMX for your Tomcat server. If you used any advanced JMX configurations for your server, you have to enter those while discovering your Tomcat server.

After you confirm, the Tomcat Server will be discovered. If you enter any incorrect configuration, you will get errors while navigating to the Tomcat homepage. You have to use the **Monitoring Configuration** link to modify the configuration details before you can monitor the Tomcat servers.

The monitoring of Apache Tomcat is similar to any other targets and we leave that for you as an exercise to complete in your own time.

Managing JBoss Application Server

JBoss Application Server is a popular Java EE application server for deploying enterprise Java applications. You may remember from our discussion in Chapter 9, *Managing Identity Manager Suite*, that some Fusion Middleware components such as Oracle Identity Manager Server runs on JBoss Application Server and you may be running OIM on JBoss AS. In this section, we will learn about the discovery and monitoring of JBoss Application Server.

> Ensure that you have enabled JMX for your JBoss Application Server for monitoring with Enterprise Manager Grid Control. You have to also ensure that Jboss application server is enabled with JSR 77 management. This requires the MEJB application to be deployed.

The Java options to enable JMX are similar to those for Tomcat that we learnt about in the previous section. Please refer to JBoss server documentation for complete start-up options.

You can either have a local or remote agent to monitor JBoss Application Server. You have to copy the relevant JBoss client JAR files to the agent location if the agent is running in a remote location.

Launch the JBoss discovery page either from the **All Targets** page or **Middleware Targets** page by selecting **JBoss Application Server** on the **Add Target** drop-down menu, and clicking on **Go** and you will get the discovery page, as in the following screenshot:

If the agent is on the same machine then you have to enter the install home for JBoss. Ensure that the operating system user that owns the management agent has read and executed privileges on the JBoss binaries. If the agent is running on a remote box then copy the required JAR files to the agent box. You need the following JAR files to be copied to the library path: `jboss-management.jar`, `jnp-client.jar`, `jbossall-client.jar`, and `dom4j.jar`.

You have to enter the port number for the **JNDI Port** that the agent will communicate with to monitor the server. The **Username** and **Password** fields are optional and are required only if you have enabled security credentials for JBoss server.

On the next page, you have to enter the credentials for the agent host and then confirm selection and this should discover the JBoss Servers running on the host and then on confirmation it will add the JBoss Server to Enterprise Manager.

You can see the JBoss Application Server by navigating to **All targets** | **Middleware**. You can monitor the JBoss Application Server by navigating to its homepage, as shown in the following screenshot:

If you see the status of the JBoss Application Server immediately after the discovery, then it may be shown as down. If you see the status to be down, then recycle the Management Agent.

You can monitor the health and performance of JBoss Application Server from Enterprise Manager. Enterprise Manager provides several performance metrics for applications, services, and resource usage. We leave the monitoring tasks, such as setting thresholds or generating reports, as an exercise for you.

Managing IBM middleware

Oracle Enterprise Manager supports monitoring of two middleware offerings from IBM. Those are IBM WebSphere Application Server and IBM WebSphere MQ. IBM WebSphere Application Server is one of the leading Java EE application servers in the market, whereas IBM WebSphere MQ is a very popular messaging provider. Your organization may be using either of these software along with other Oracle middleware. For example, Oracle SOA Suite may be deployed on IBM WebSphere.

We will first learn about the discovery, monitoring, and configuration management aspects of IBM WebSphere Application Server and then IBM WebSphere MQ.

Managing IBM WebSphere Application Server

Oracle Enterprise Manager uses JMX to monitor IBM WebSphere Application Server, which is similar to other Java EE servers. When you discover a WebSphere Cell, it automatically discovers servers and clusters in the cell. An IBM WebSphere Cell is analogous to a WebLogic Server Domain. Note that Enterprise Manager monitors only servers and clusters and does not monitor agents required by WebSphere such as a node agent.

You can monitor an IBM WebSphere Application Server Cell either using a local or remote management agent. The agent can be running on the same or different host where WebSphere deployment manager is running. The agent host should be able to communicate with the deployment manager host. Check the certification matrix at **My Oracle Support** (https://metalink.oracle.com) for the versions of WebSphere supported from Enterprise Manager.

If your agent is local to the deployment manager host then you have to make sure that the agent user has read and executed privileges on the WebSphere binaries. If the agent is remote, then you have to copy the client JAR files i.e. com.ibm. ws.admin.client_6.1.0.jar and com.ibm.ws.runtime_6.1.0.jar.

The discovery mechanism for WebSphere is similar to other middleware and you can invoke the discovery screen from middleware target page by selecting **Add IBM WebSphere Cell**. You will get the the discovery screen, as shown in the following page:

Add IBM WebSphere Application Server Cell: Host

In order to add an IBM WebSphere Application Server Cell to Enterprise Manager, you must first specify details of the host on which the
IBM WebSphere Deployment Manager is running. If only one cell is found on the host, the Select Cell step will be skipped.
| Cancel | Step 1 of 5 | Next |

* Deployment Manager Host `tdsdil01-d1.oracleads.com`

* Version `5.x`

Port `7008`
SOAP Connector Port

Trusted Keystore Filename
Specify the absolute path of the Trusted Keystore file name. This is required if the port is
SSL enabled.

* Deployment Manager Username `admin`

* Password

☑ Agent is running on a host other than the Deployment Manager.

Agent Host `tdsebizxii01.oracleads.com`

Deployment Manager Home Directory `/mylibrary/ibmwas/lib`
Specify the absolute path of the directory where Deployment Manager is installed.

☑ TIP The Deployment Manager credentials are used to collect metric data for this target, and will be stored as Monitoring Properties
for the target. If you want to change the password, click the Monitoring Configuration link on the respective server home page.

| Cancel | Step 1 of 5 | Next |

In this environment, our agent is remotely located and we have copied all client JAR files to `/mylibrary/ibmwas/lib directory`.

After you enter the appropriate value during the interview phase and then credentials for the agent host, Enterprise Manager will retrieve all servers and clusters. You can choose those servers or clusters that you want to manage from Grid Control.

> Note that the servers that you want to monitor from Enterprise Manager should be Up during the discovery process. If you add a new server or cluster to a previously discovered cell, make sure that you refresh the cell by clicking on **Refresh IBM WebSphere Cell** from its homepage.

Enterprise Manager provides capabilities to monitor the performance of WebSphere Application Servers, resources, and applications. It also provides configuration management capabilities, such as configuration tracking and comparison. Enterprise Manager allows you to configure threshold settings for several metrics and you can use alert notification for any other middleware targets such as WebLogic Server.

We leave exploring these functionalities for WebSphere as an exercise for you to complete.

Managing IBM WebSphere MQ

IBM WebSphere MQ is widely used in many organizations either as a messaging server or to integrate applications. It is highly likely that you may be using WebSphere MQ with WebLogic Server or Oracle Fusion Middleware SOA Suite. Enterprise Manager allows you to discover and monitor WebSphere MQ.

In this section, we will the learn about the discovery mechanism for WebSphere MQ. You can either use an agent running on the same host where IBM WebSphere MQ is installed, or on a remote host.

You can navigate to the the Websphere MQ discovery screen by clicking on **Add IBM WebSphere MQ** from the **All Targets** page.

The following screenshot shows the discovery screen for WebSphere MQ:

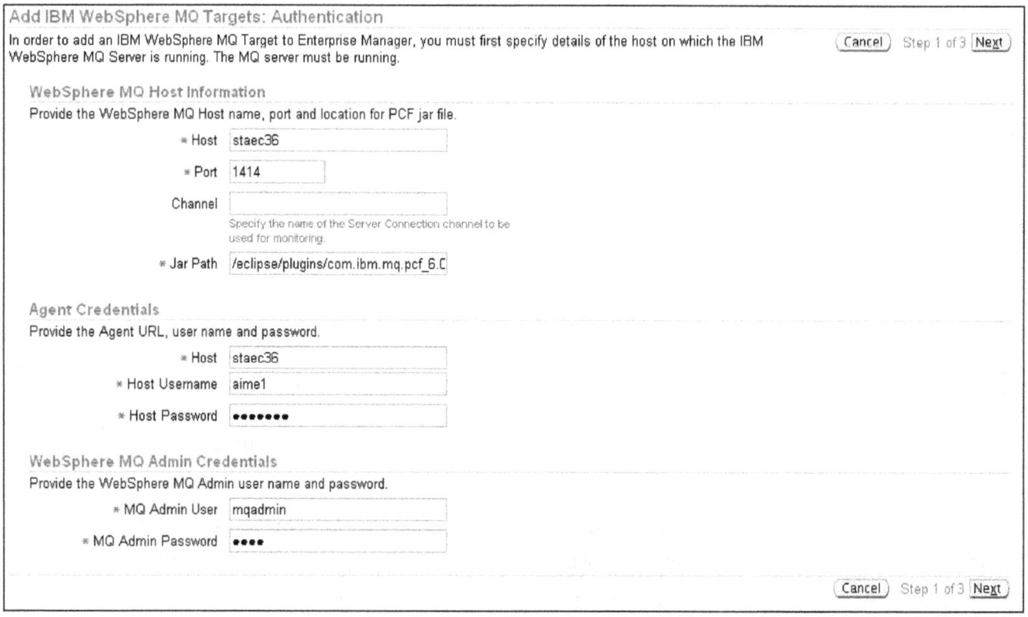

Most of the fields in the discovery screen are self-explanatory, except the **Jar Path**. Unlike other middleware where we provided the directory that contained all of the JAR files, this WebSphere MQ discovery requires the complete classpath as shown next as an example:

```
%MQ_HOME%/eclipse/plugins/com.ibm.mq.pcf_6.0.0/pcf.jar:%MQ_HOME%/
Java/lib/com.ibm.mq.jar
```

It will discover the Queue Manager Clusters, Queue Managers, Queues, and Channels for the WebSphere MQ install. You can monitor performance of these components and make the most of the benefits of most of the Grid Control features such as historical performance metrics, alert notification, and so on. We leave you to do these as an exercise.

Best practices for managing non-Oracle Java middleware

Now that we have concluded the management of non-Oracle Java middleware, here are some best practices that we recommend to get the best out of Enterprise Manager.

- You can monitor multiple installs of non-Oracle middleware targets running on multiple hosts from a single agent. If you are monitoring a large number of application server targets, do not use the agent to monitor more than 25-30 application server instances.

- Do not use an agent to monitor different types of Java targets, for example do not use an agent to monitor both JBoss Application Server and IBM WebSphere. The agent communicates with the application servers using JMX and requires client-side JAR files provided by application servers and there could be conflicting classes that could cause classloading errors at the agent side. This will result in metric collection error.

- Avoid monitoring different versions of the same application server from the same agent, unless your application server supports connecting to different versions using the same client JAR files.

Managing Microsoft Middleware

Many organizations use heterogeneous software platforms. The Service Oriented Architecture allows integration between heterogeneous platforms. For example, if you have built a service using a Microsoft platform, you will be able to consume that service in Oracle Fusion Middleware. Also, you may be using Microsoft Active Directory as the LDAP provider for your Identity Management Suite. So, there is a likelihood that your organization may be using Microsoft's Middleware platform. As we discussed earlier, Oracle provides several plug-ins to monitor Microsoft middleware such as Microsoft .NET, IIS, Active Directory, and so on.

> You have to download the appropriate plug-in from Oracle Technology Network at http://www.oracle.com/technology/software/products/oem/htdocs/system-monitoring-connectors.html. Oracle recommends that you use the latest plug-in available.

Installing Plug-ins

Each plug-in is available separately and needs to be installed separately. For example, if you want to monitor Active Directory and IIS, then you have to download the plug-ins for both Active Directory and IIS separately and install those on Grid Control.

We learnt about installing the Tomcat plug-in earlier in this chapter. Just to recap, following are the steps to install a plug-in that you can use for Microsoft middleware:

1. Download the plug-in JAR file from OTN to your local desktop
2. Login to Grid Control as a **Super Administrator**
3. Navigate to **Setup | Management Plug-in** and **Connectors,** and then select **Add/Import Management Plug-in**
4. In the **Import Management Plug-in** page, click on **Browse** to select the respective plug-in JAR file, for example `microsoft_active_directory_plugin.jar` that you downloaded earlier, and then click on **Archive** and you will see the plug-in details
5. Click **OK** to install the plug-in, and you will get a confirmation message saying that the plug-in was installed
6. You have to deploy the plug-in to those management agents that you want to use to monitor the respective target

Discovery of Microsoft middleware

- You can add new instances of Microsoft middleware, for example Active Directory or IIS or .NET Server from Grid Control. Discovery of each of these servers requires installation of the appropriate plug-in. The discussion of discovery of each of these targets is beyond the scope of the book and the steps can be generalized as follows:

- Deploy the plug-in to the agent that you want to use to monitor your target. Most of these targets can be monitored either with a local or remote agent.

- To discover a target instance, navigate to the Agent page and then select Add for the appropriate target type, for example Microsoft Active Directory.

- This will take you to the **Target Discovery** page. You have to enter the agent credentials and target specific information to complete the discovery of the target.

Monitoring Microsoft middleware

Each Microsoft middleware target has its homepage and performance page that you can use to monitor the health and performance. For example, the following figure shows the homepage for Microsoft Active Directory.

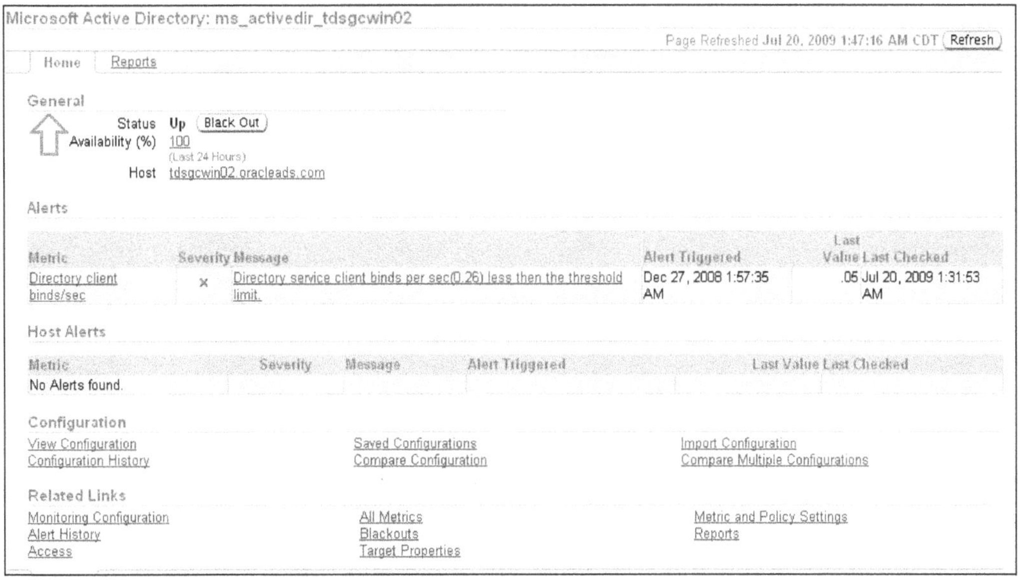

Enterprise Manager provides performance monitoring and configuration management capabilities for Microsoft middleware targets. Similarly, you can use Enterprise Manager to set metric thresholds for alert notifications. The following screenshot shows the metrics available for setting thresholds for Active Directory.

Metric	Comparison Operator	Warning Threshold	Critical Threshold	Corrective Actions	Collection Schedule	Details
Active threads	>			None	Every 15 Minutes	
Client sessions	<			None	Every 15 Minutes	
CPU Load Percentage	>			None	Every 10 Minutes	
Database file size (GB)	>			None	Every 2 Hours	
Database Log File Size (GB)	>	15	20	None	Every 2 Hours	
Directory client binds/sec	<	5	10	None	Every 15 Minutes	
Directory searches/sec	<			None	Every 15 Minutes	
Directory server binds/sec	<			None	Every 15 Minutes	
Global Catalog evaluations/sec	<			None	Every 15 Minutes	
Inbound bytes total/sec	<			None	Every 15 Minutes	
Inbound Objects/sec	<			None	Every 15 Minutes	
Input/Output data bytes per second	>			None	Every 15 Minutes	
KDCA requests/sec	<			None	Every 15 Minutes	
Kerberos Authentications/sec	<			None	Every 15 Minutes	
LDAP directory searches/sec	>			None	Every 15 Minutes	
LDAP new connections/sec	<			None	Every 15 Minutes	
LDAP server binds/sec	<			None	Every 15 Minutes	
Lost and Found objects count	>			None	Every 2 Hours	

We have discussed these topics numerous times, such as for Oracle WebLogic Server and this same steps apply here. We leave these for you to explore on your own.

Service Level Monitoring for third-party targets

We discussed Service Level Management earlier in this book. Also, we learnt about creating service level and service tests in Chapter 4, *Managing Oracle WebLogic Server*.You can use Service Level Management features with third-party targets. For example, you can use the Service Level management feature to monitor service level of a web application running in JBoss Application Server or service level for an LDAP search in Microsoft Active Directory.

We will summarize the steps for Service Level Management in order to recap, using an example of Active Directory:

1. Create a system for the underlying infrastructure components/targets that provide the service. For example, the Active Directory System includes the Active Directory Server and the host.

2. Create a service, either a generic service or a web application service based on the service. For example, we have the Active Directory Service which is a generic service, as shown in the following screenshot:

3. Then you have to define how you measure the availability and performance of the service. This may depend upon the system availability or on a service test. For example, we have a service test for LDAP Search that determines the availability and performance and usage metrics for the service.

4. You can define the beacons for the service test to measure the availability from different geographical locations.

5. You can leverage all reporting capabilities such as system and services dashboards for services that depend upon non-Oracle middleware.

Summary

You can manage broadly three types of middleware with Oracle Enterprise Manager. These can be classified as open source middleware, IBM, and Microsoft middleware. Enterprise Manager supports the management of non-Oracle middleware by providing various plug-ins. Plug-ins for all open source middleware, except Tomcat, are integrated with Enterprise Manager. You can manage IBM WebSphere Application Server Cell and Websphere MQ with Enterprise Manager. Enterprise Manager also provides several plug-ins for managing Microsoft Middleware. You have to install these plug-ins as a super administrator and deploy them to an agent before you can monitor a plug-in target. You get all the benefits of alert notification, historical performance metrics, configuration, and configuration management with plug-ins. You can also use Service Level Management with third-party targets. In the next chapter, we will learn how you can diagnose problems in the JVM or Java EE applications.

12
Java and Composite Applications Monitoring and Diagnostics

Application hangs and performance issues appear in many applications in the production environment. These problems in production applications cause availability and service level issues. Diagnosing these application performance issues is very challenging for application administrators and support personnel. Often these issues are hard to reproduce in a test and development environment, and most diagnostic tools are too inadequate to be used in the production environment. Oracle Enterprise Manager has two products: **Composite Application Monitor and Modeler (CAMM)** and **Application Diagnostics for Java (AD4J)** that are used to diagnose application issues.

CAMM allows you to diagnose performance issues in composite applications, whereas AD4J allows you to diagnose issues such as memory leak and application in Java applications and the underlying JVM.

In this chapter, you will learn how you can effectively use these two tools to diagnose application issues.

We will discuss the following:

- Architecture and components of CAMM
- Monitoring and diagnosing Java EE and Composite Applications with CAMM
- Architecture and components of AD4J
- Diagnosing Java resource problems with AD4J

Composite Application Monitor and Modeler

The modern SOA applications are very complex in nature. They depend on services either within the application and/or external services. These could be either a remote EJB running on another application server or on a BPEL process or ESB service. Due to the dynamic nature of today's applications some of the application dependencies are not defined in deployment descriptors and may be defined using Java annotations that are buried inside the application code. Therefore, it is difficult to get a complete understanding of a composite application for administrators and support personnel. CAMM provides a model-driven diagnostics approach and provides a topological view of the composite applications by showing the application dependencies. In this section, we will learn about CAMM, supported products and its architecture, and how you can use this to diagnose application issues.

> The CAMM product was a part of the ClearApp acquisition and is not yet integrated with Enterprise Manager Grid Control. CAMM has its own management server, agent, and requires its own repository database and applet-based management console.

Supported products

At the time of writing, CAMM supports several Oracle and non-Oracle middleware products. Besides the traditional application servers some notable products supported by CAMM are:

- Oracle BPEL Process Manager
- Oracle Electronic Service Bus
- Oracle Service Bus aka BEA AquaLogic Service Bus
- Oracle WebLogic Integration
- Oracle WebLogic Portal
- IBM WebSphere Portal

Refer to the certification matrix available on My Oracle Support (http://metalink.oracle.com) for the latest versions supported products.

CAMM architecture

The deployment architecture of CAMM is similar to Oracle Enterprise Manager. If you look at the deployment architecture for CAMM, it has two primary components: CAMM **server** and **agent**.

The CAMM server constitutes three main components: CAMM **manager**, **database**, and **user interface**.

- The CAMM manager is the core analytical engine, which performs heavy-duty processing of collected data and enables the user interface for administration.

- The CAMM database is the repository used by CAMM manager to store analyzed data and the application model. The CAMM repository database can either be an Oracle or MySQL database.

- The CAMM user interface is the primary administration console used for monitoring. This is currently a Java applet-based console.

- The CAMM agent is an application that gets deployed to each managed application server target such as WebLogic Managed Server or WebSphere server. The CAMM agent collects data from the managed server and tracks the contextual relationship and summarizes data in real time.

The following figure shows the typical deployment architecture for CAMM.

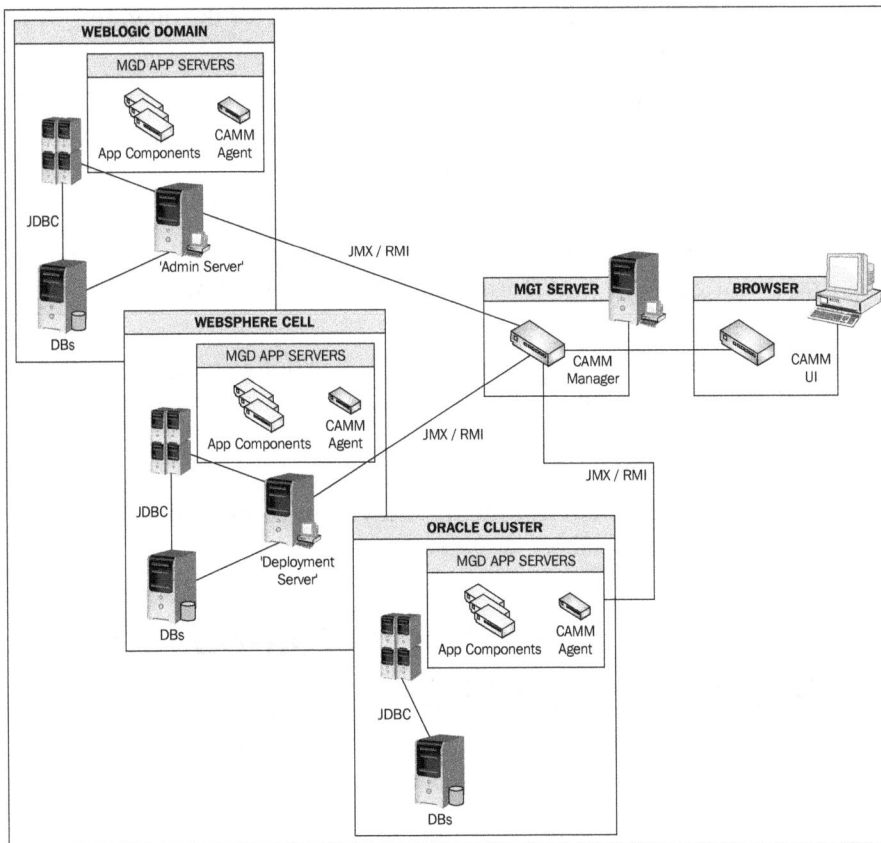

Installation and configuration

The installation and configuration of CAMM is similar to that of Enterprise Manager. You have to configure the repository database, install CAMM manager and the agents. We will provide you with some quick tips about the installation process but, the detailed coverage of CAMM is beyond the scope of this book.

You can install and configure CAMM in two operation modes: **service mode** and **application mode**. The actual CAMM manager runs as an UNIX daemon or Windows service in this mode. This is the default mode and recommended for a production deployment. The UI runs in a web container in this mode.

When you run CAMM in a standalone application mode, the CAMM process is started and the user interface is rendered automatically. You can use this mode to quickly debug the problems in a server. The CAMM process is stopped when you exit the user interface.

The actual installation is documented in the *CAMM Installation Guide* (`http://download.oracle.com/docs/cd/E14670_01/doc.10205/e14147/toc.htm`) and we recommend that you review the certification guide for the operating system requirements and certified targets.

You can download CAMM from Oracle Technology Network at `http://www.oracle.com/technology/software/products/camm/index.html`.

Here are the few quick tips that you want to follow for the installation:

- Install CAMM manager on a dedicated server. It requires a good processing power to perform mathematical modeling and analyze application relationship.

- The CAMM repository database has to be configured prior to the installation. You can use a separate schema in the EM repository database as the CAMM repository.

- The agent installation requires a special setup and privileges in different application server environments and you have to ensure that you have those privileges on those targets.

Monitoring and diagnosing Composite Applications with CAMM

You can use CAMM to monitor application performance, service level objects, and to help you to detect application bottlenecks.

The primary benefit is that it automatically determines the contextual relationship between components and services, and provides a graphical model for application.

- You have to start CAMM manager before you can start the console. In Windows, you can start the console by accessing the **Start CAMM manager** option.

- In UNIX, you have to start CAMM manager as follows:

  ```
  nohup ./$CAMM_INSTALL_DIR/bin/acsera.sh &
  ```

- You can access the CAMM console in a browser by accessing `https://hostname:port/qvadmin`

Note that the default port for CAMM console is 5560, so if you are in the same box where CAMM manager is running and CAMM is running on the default port, then you can access the console using `https://localhost:5560/qvadmin`

You will get the CAMM console rendered as an applet as follows:

If the agents are deployed on the servers that you want to monitor, then it will automatically discover the components and create the nodes as shown in the previous screenshot. For example, this instance of CAMM has discovered BPEL processes, ESB, OSB, and so on.

The initial top-level view illustrates all of the active entities being monitored by CAMM. You can open a specific node e.g. OSB to monitor business services and proxy services and some important metrics such as arrivals, completions, response time, and so on, as shown next:

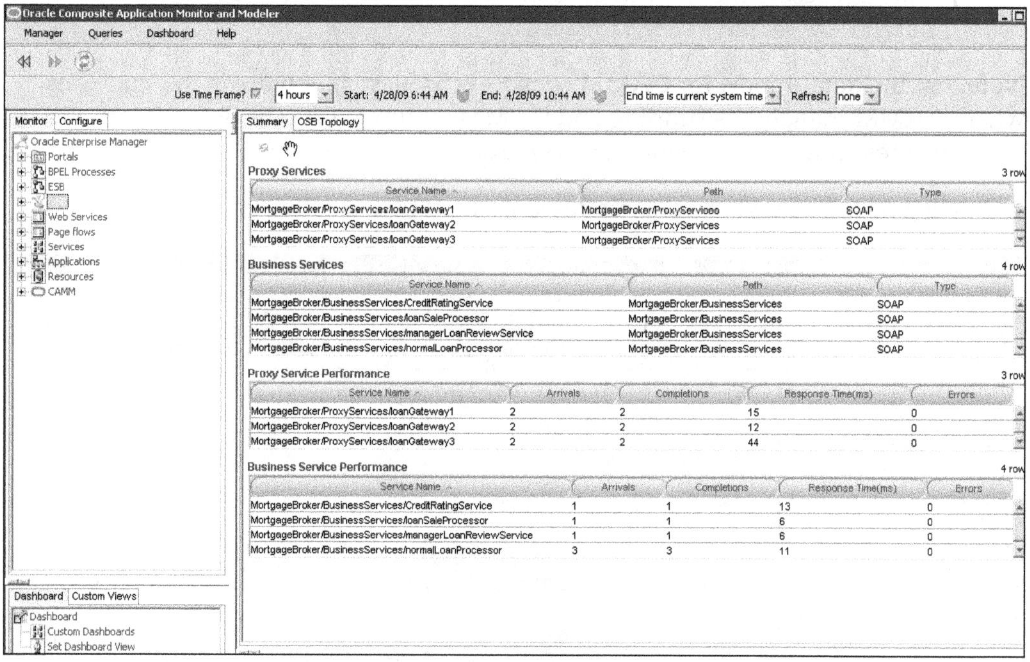

The most important aspect of monitoring by CAMM is the topological view that shows the high-level topology, showing the call interactions, both defined and current, between different services and components they may be invoking. You can view the topological view of a component by clicking on the topology for that specific component e.g. **OSB Topology** will provide a topological view, as shown in the following screenshot:

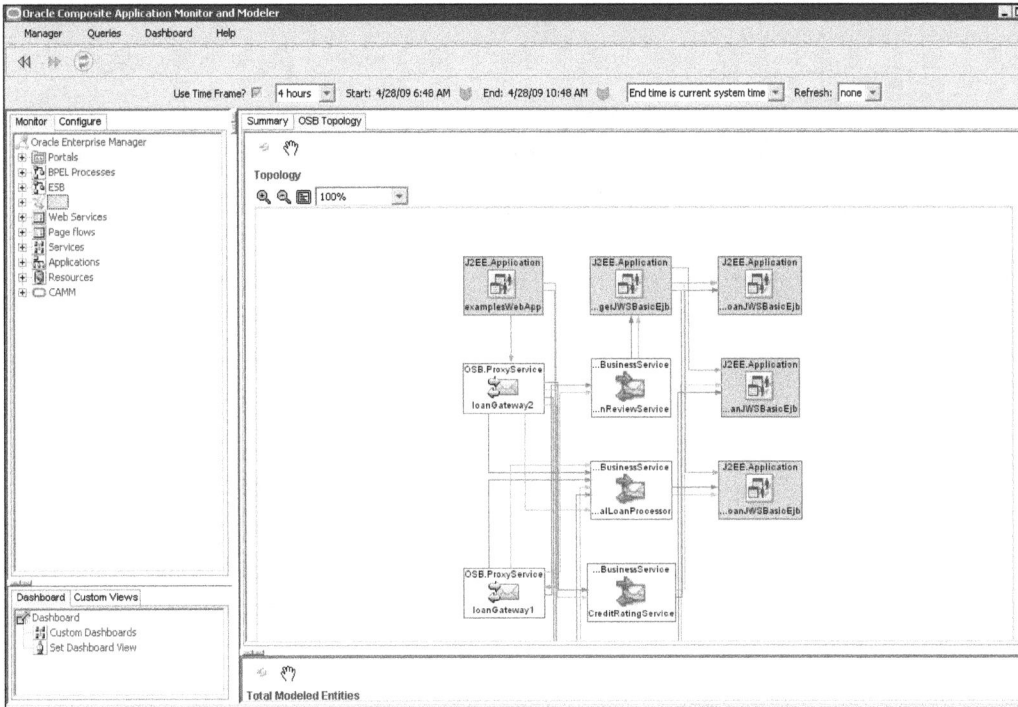

The topology view is great for administrators to understand the actual application topology. You can further drill down to a specific service by clicking on a business or proxy service and view the call interactions and diagnose problems in composite applications.

For example, you can view what service is taking the longest time to respond, as shown in the following screenshot:

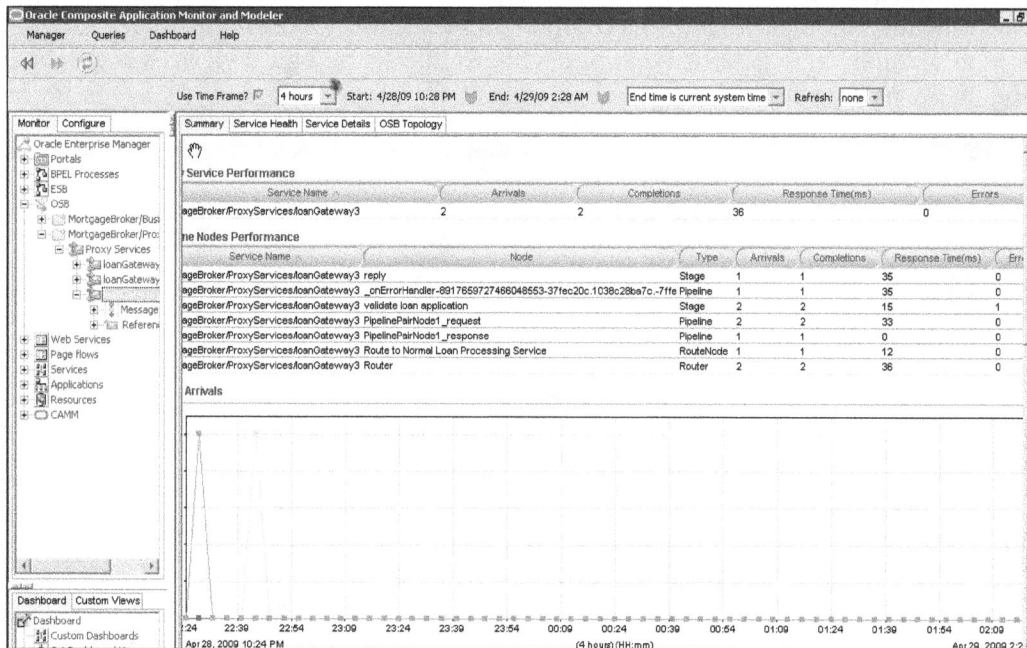

CAMM allows drilling down to a specific method and allows you to view a method-level performance and track down the SQL/JDBC being generated by a specific method.

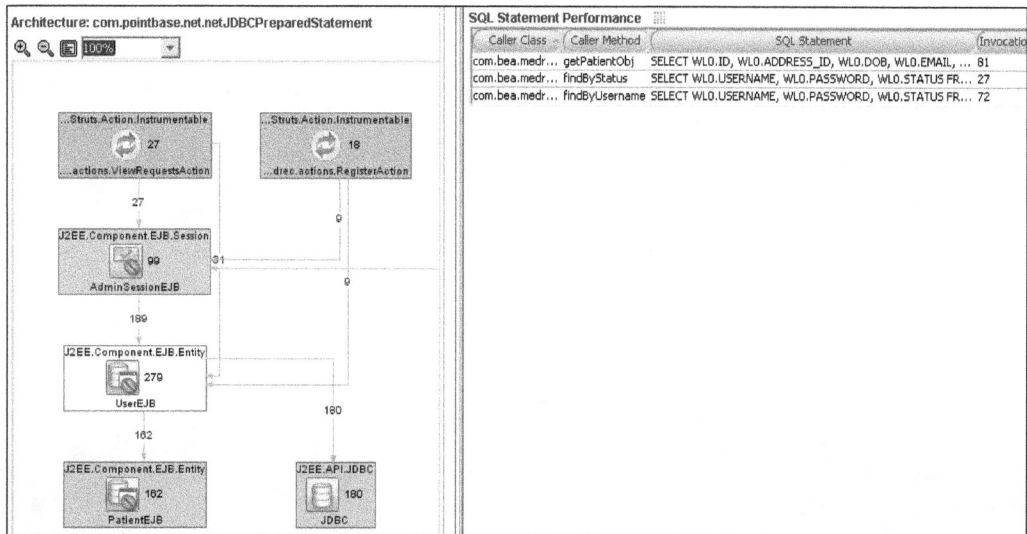

We leave other aspects of CAMM as an exercise for you to do, as it can help you to find out memory leaks and trace specific transactions.

Application Diagnostics for Java (AD4J)

The Application Diagnostics for Java product allows users to diagnose production issues in Java applications. It helps you to diagnose JVM issues such as thread deadlock/contention and memory leak. The AD4J product was acquired from a small privately held company named Auptyma, and this is still a standalone product with its own installer.

AD4J Architecture

The architecture of AD4J product is similar to EM Grid control. The management console runs on Apache JServ and it requires a database repository. You can either use an Oracle database and PostgresSQL as the repository. You have to install an agent in the JVM or application server to monitor the JVM process. The agent is a WAR file that you can deploy to the server. If you want the correlation between the application server JVM and the database tier, you have to install the database agent in the database host.

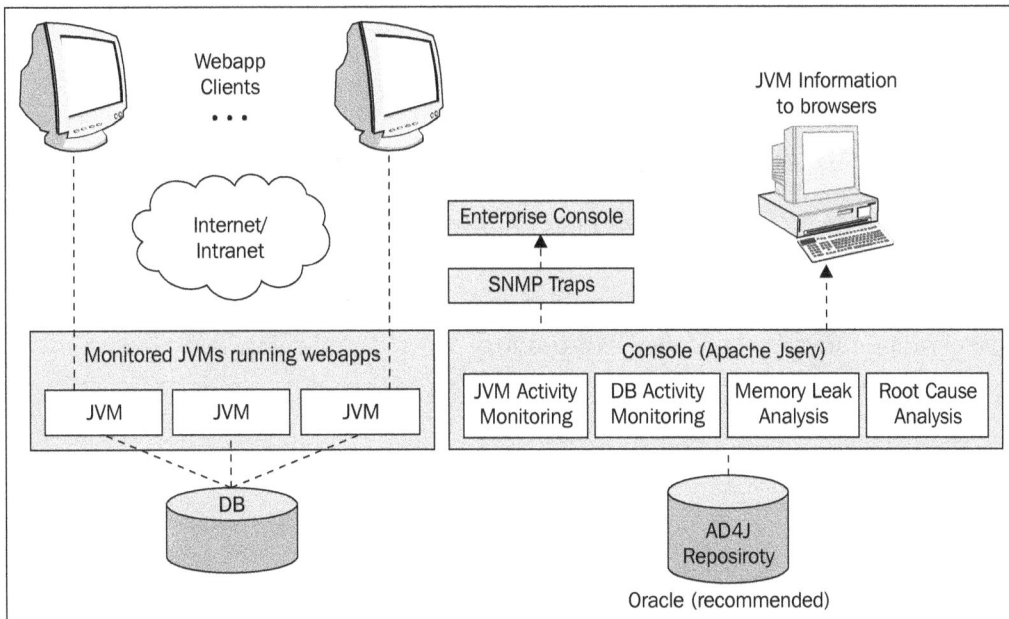

> Note that the AD4J database agent is different from the actual EM Management agent. The database agent is supported only on UNIX platforms.

Installation and configuration

AD4J Console is supported only on Windows 32-bit, Linux, and Solaris platforms. The agents are supported on numerous JVMs. The AD4J agents are for a very specific version of JVM and you have to check the certification matrix to verify whether your JVM is certified. You can download AD4J from OTN from the following location:

`http://www.oracle.com/technology/software/products/oem/htdocs/jade.html`

The installation of AD4J Console is straightforward and is documented in the AD4J Install Guide at `http://download.oracle.com/docs/cd/B16240_01/doc/install.102/e11085/toc.htm`. The installation steps require you to create the database schema and tables.

Starting up AD4J Console

As we discussed earlier, AD4J Console runs on Apache JServ, and hence, you need to start the Apache HTTP Server to access the AD4J Console.

In UNIX/Linux, you can start AD4J Console as follows:

`$AD4J_HOME/jamserv/bin/apachectl start`

The console runs on the default port of 3500, and you can access the AD4J Console at `http://hostname:3500`

If the AD4J repository is not created/configured, AD4J Console will prompt you for the connection details about the DB repository and create the database objects.

When you access AD4J Console, you have to logon as the administrator, and then you will get the homepage as follows:

You will see the JVMs monitored by the AD4J. You can download the agent from AD4J Console by clicking on the download AD4J agent menu. You can select the appropriate agent, and then deploy the agent into your application server using the appropriate deployment tool for your server. For example, if you are using Oracle WebLogic Server, you can deploy `jamagent.war` using WebLogic Server Console.

If you are running multiple managed servers in a WebLogic Server Domain, you have to activate the application in all managed servers that you want to monitor from AD4J. The JVM process for the application server is automatically discovered in the AD4J Console as soon as the agent is deployed.

> If your application accesses an Oracle database, the AD4J agent allows you to perform cross-tier tracing to the Oracle database. The DB agent is only supported in UNIX platforms.

Diagnosing Java applications

In this section, we will learn how to diagnose problems in your Java applications and JVM using AD4J.

You can see several important metrics such as CPU usage, locks, database,and network waits, top requests, and methods. The cost indicates the number of method invocations and requests. You will see various metrics for each of JVM being monitored. The following table shows the description for each of these metrics:

Metric Name	Description
CPU	CPU utilization on the JVM.
OSR	OS indicator of how quickly you can get the CPU when you need it.
Mem	The percentage of the JVM Heap used.
Run	Threads using the CPU.
DB	Threads waiting for DB activity to complete.
Lock	Thread waiting for the JVM synchronization lock.
Net	Threads waiting for Network Activity.
Obj wait	Idle Threads, which have called Network Wait.
Sleep	Idle Threads, which are sleeping.

There is much compelling JVM data provided by AD4J that may feel unimportant to you as an administrator, but they may be very useful for developers. You can look at the detailed usage scenarios of AD4J at `http://www.oracle.com/technology/products/oem/pdf/oraclead4j_usagescenarios.pdf`.

Diagnosing application hangs

You can use AD4J to diagnose problems such as application hangs or lack of speed. If your application appears hanging or running slow, you can view the active threads or the threads waiting for **Lock** or **DB Wait** for the JVM. You can view all active threads and see their status, as shown next:

You can then click on the thread name to view the call stack for a thread and find the methods being invoked. This will be useful for developers in order to find the line of code being executed.

Call Stack		
Class Method	**File**	**Line**
java.net.SocketInputStream->socketRead0	Native Method	
java.net.SocketInputStream->read	SocketInputStream.java	129
oracle.net.ns.Packet->receive		
oracle.net.ns.DataPacket->receive		
oracle.net.ns.NetInputStream->getNextPacket		
oracle.net.ns.NetInputStream->read		
oracle.net.ns.NetInputStream->read		
oracle.net.ns.NetInputStream->read		
oracle.jdbc.driver.T4CMAREngine->unmarshalUB1	T4CMAREngine.java	978
oracle.jdbc.driver.T4CMAREngine->unmarshalSB1	T4CMAREngine.java	950
oracle.jdbc.driver.T4C8Oall->receive	T4C8Oall.java	434
oracle.jdbc.driver.T4CPreparedStatement->doOall8	T4CPreparedStatement.java	181
oracle.jdbc.driver.T4CPreparedStatement->execute_for_rows	T4CPreparedStatement.java	629
oracle.jdbc.driver.OracleStatement->doExecuteWithTimeout	OracleStatement.java	1153
oracle.jdbc.driver.OraclePreparedStatement->executeInternal	OraclePreparedStatement.java	2932
oracle.jdbc.driver.OraclePreparedStatement->executeUpdate	OraclePreparedStatement.java	3004
jadetest.Inventory->updateAvailQty	Inventory.java	74
jadetest.Cart->confirmqty	Cart.java	52
checkout->_jspService	_checkout.java	82
com.orionserver.http.OrionHttpJspPage->service	OrionHttpJspPage.java	56
oracle.jsp.runtimev2.JspPageTable->service	JspPageTable.java	350
oracle.jsp.runtimev2.JspServlet->internalService	JspServlet.java	509
oracle.jsp.runtimev2.JspServlet->service	JspServlet.java	413
javax.servlet.http.HttpServlet->service	HttpServlet.java	853
com.evermind.server.http.ResourceFilterChain->doFilter	ResourceFilterChain.java	65
jadetest.filter4->doFilter	filter4.java	16
com.evermind.server.http.EvermindFilterChain->doFilter	EvermindFilterChain.java	16
jadetest.filter3->doFilter	filter3.java	16
com.evermind.server.http.EvermindFilterChain->doFilter	EvermindFilterChain.java	20
jadetest.filter2->doFilter	filter2.java	16
com.evermind.server.http.EvermindFilterChain->doFilter	EvermindFilterChain.java	20
jadetest.filter1->doFilter	filter1.java	16
com.evermind.server.http.ServletRequestDispatcher->invoke	ServletRequestDispatcher.java	659

You can drill down to the method and see its details. You can view and diagnose if a method is executing any JDBC SQL statement. In the next section, we will discuss, how you can use AD4J.

However, the most interesting task for you is to perform an elapsed time analysis. You can view the call stack trace by lock or by percent and AD4J will display the percentage elapsed for each method. You can quickly find out the culprit method that is taking an unusually long time.

Tracing a thread

You can trace an active thread and diagnose problems in the thread. You can click on the trace link on an active thread and specify the poll interval. AD4J will trace the thread and then view the result for the trace. You can find CPU utilization, heap usage, and garbage collection time; thread state and request state, as shown in the following figure:

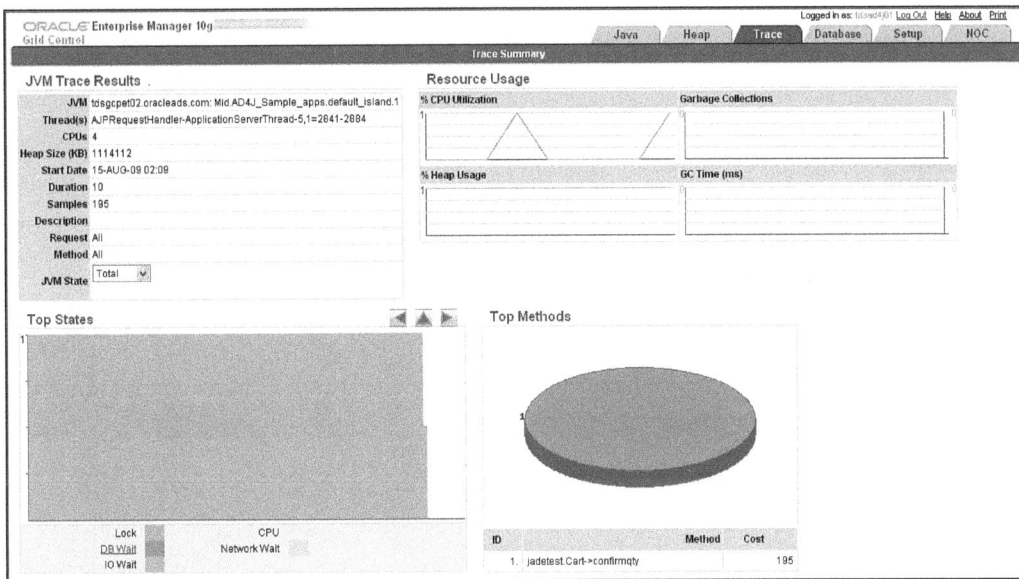

Cross-tier diagnostics

You can diagnose the application problem that is due to a problem in the database tier. For example, your Enterprise Java applications may be running slowly either because the SQL is taking an unusually long time to execute, because of a full table scan or there is a network issue. If a thread is waiting for a JDBC call to return, you will see the state as **DB Wait**.

You can drill down and view the SQL statement that is being executed. It further allows you to run the explain plan to see if the SQL statement is causing any full table scan.

Detecting and analyzing memory leaks

You can use AD4J to analyze memory leaks and also to take heap dumps without impacting the performance of your applications. You can take heap dumps at two different times and compare those and detect memory leak. The following shows a comparison between two different heaps:

AD4J provides several interesting features such as tracing active thread capabilities and we leave that as an exercise for you to explore.

Summary

In this chapter you learned about the monitoring and diagnostics for composite applications and Java resource problems. The Composite Application Monitor and Modeler (CAMM) provides a model-driven diagnostics approach to diagnose Composite Applications whereas AD4J allows you to diagnose JVM resource problems by providing a deep diagnostics approach. Besides monitoring production applications, these products can be handy for you during the development and testing phase. In the next chapter, you will learn how to use extensibility features of Enterprise Manager. We will demonstrate by creating a monitoring plug-in for Sun Java Web Server.

13
Building Your Monitoring Plug-in

In the initial chapters, we learned about the Enterprise Manager Grid Control architecture, features, sub-systems, and so on. We learned that Enterprise Manager provides a centralized console for the monitoring and managing of the whole data center. We saw that Enterprise Manager provides a monitoring and management support for many commonly used middleware platforms and applications. There are a lot of middleware products and platforms on the market and there can be products where Enterprise Manager doesn't provide monitoring and management support out-of-the-box. To support centralized management for such products, Enterprise Manager provides an extensibility framework. Using this framework, vendors of other products and end-users can add management support where not available.

Management support built using an extensibility framework is packaged as a monitoring plug-in. These plug-ins can be deployed an existing Enterprise Manager installation. There are many plug-ins available from the Oracle website—some built by Oracle; others built by third party vendors. These plug-ins provide monitoring support for Microsoft SQL server, Checkpoint Firewall, NetApp Filer, and many other products. For a complete list of plug-ins, please refer to the Oracle website.(`http://www.oracle.com/technology/products/oem/extensions/ index.html`)

To build such a monitoring support, you will need to learn how to build a management plug-in. In this chapter, we'll see the steps and artefacts required to build a monitoring plug-in. We will be building this monitoring plug-in for Sun Java Web Server.

But the overall objective of this chapter is to learn about the extensibility framework of Enterprise Manager. It'll help if you know about the basic usage and architecture of SUN Java Web Server or any other Web Server, but no need to worry if you don't—we'll start with an overview of Sun Java Web Server.

In this chapter, we'll cover:

- A brief introduction of Sun Java Web Server. We'll introduce you to SUN Java WebServer, typical usage, and deployment
- The working of plug-ins—plug-in artefacts, deployment, and lifecycle
- An exercise—monitor Sun Java Web Server by deploying some sample files from the code bundle
- Overview of the artefacts used for monitoring in the exercise
- Packaging and deploying the plug-in
- Advance features of plug-in

Introducing Sun Java Web Server

A web server serves content using the HTTP protocol. The web server receives client requests over HTTP protocol and responds back in HTTP protocol. The web server can serve static or dynamic content based on configuration and software associated with the web server deployment.

In a typical production environment, the web server acts as a gateway for all of the incoming traffic. Usually, all static content including HTML and images are stored on the same host where the web server is running. Any request for this static content is served by the web server over HTTP. For dynamic content, the web server passes a request to some application server; the application server generates and returns dynamic content to the web server, and the web server delivers it back to the client over HTTP protocol.

The web server also provides support for secure transmission by providing encryption over HTTP protocol. The web server supports SSL over HTTP for communication between the client and the web server, and if the web server is a separate host to the application server then it may also use SSL for communication between the web server and the application server or servers.

Besides serving the purpose of HTTP gateway, Sun Java Web Server provides some more services such as support for executing servlets based applications, and so on. It also provides high availability support through clustering.

For this exercise, we'll focus on a very simple deployment of Sun Java Web Server, we'll be using Sun Java Web server version 7.0. In this deployment, we'll have one instance of admin server and one instance of web server. Admin server is used to manage the configuration of one or more web servers.

How plug-ins work

We learnt in Chapter 1, *Enterprise Manager Grid Control*, about targets, target metadata, and target collection file. Target is an entity managed by the Enterprise Manager Grid Control. For each target type there is a target metadata file that defines the properties for the target, the metrics that need to be collected for a target and the mechanism to collect those metrics. For each target type there is a collection file that defines at what frequency metrics should be collected and at what frequency metrics should be persisted. You may want to revisit Chapter 3, *Enterprise Manager Key Concepts and Subsystems*, before we continue with this chapter. Once you have familiarized yourself about the purpose of these entities, let's use them to see how plug-ins work.

Plug-in artefacts

There are two types of artefacts for a plug-in:

1. Mandatory artefacts: Target metadata and Target collection are the mandatory artefacts; with these artefacts all of the monitoring metrics can be collected, but very limited monitoring interface will be available.

2. Optional artefacts: Optional artefacts are used to provide enhanced monitoring interfaces like extra charts on the homepage, or a report linked from the homepage. The following type of optional artefacts can be defined:

   - Charts Definition file: Using this file you can define what metrics you want to show on time series charts, you can define the types of charts, height, width of charts and so on

   - Reports Definition file(s): You can define some SQL, using that, reports on historical metric data can be made available from the target homepage

   - Jobs Definition file(s): You can define jobs that can be scheduled from the Enterprise Manager Grid Control

   - Scripts/Binary executable: You can package some scripts, executable — these scripts/executable can be used to fetch monitoring metrics or perform some operation through the job system

Management Plug-in Archive (MPA)

All the artefacts for a plug-in can be packaged in an archive; this archive forms the basic deployment unit of management plug-in functionality. This archive is referred to as **Management Plug-in Archive** or **MPA**. Enterprise Manager provides a utility to build MPA from all the artefacts. Management server recognizes the format of this JAR file. This JAR file can be shared between developers. All the plug-ins available from Oracle website are available only in this format.

Plug-ins can be versioned—this helps to keep track of various versions of plug-ins, just like any other software module and is highly recommended.

Plug-in deployment

You can import a plug-in on the Management server using the import interface provided by the Enterprise Manager Console. Once this plug-in is imported onto the Management Server you can further deploy it onto one or more agents.

Monitoring targets using a plug-in

Once the plug-in is deployed on a management server and agents—you can add a target by using the **Add Target** feature provided on the agent homepage. To use this generic UI you need to select the type of target that you want to add and provide the required properties. For example, if you want to monitor a web server you will need to provide the URL, using Agent can monitor the availability of the web server.

Exercise—monitor Sun Java Web Server

In this exercise, we will monitor Sun Java Web Server using some sample code available with the book. After the exercise in the next section, we'll describe the code used for this exercise.

Pre-requisites

You will need a setup of Enterprise Manager Grid Control. Besides the Enterprise Manager setup, you will need one more host where you can install Sun Java Web Server. On the additional host you will need to install an additional agent. You may want to refer to Chapter 2 for this installation.

Once you have this setup ready, install Sun Java Web Server on the host where you installed the additional agent. Note down the following details about this installation of the web server:

- Installation directory
- Admin server host and port
- User-ID and password to authenticate with Admin Server
- Configuration and node name of the setup
- URL for the web server

Exercise steps

This exercise involves some setup on the agent side followed by some configuration through Enterprise Manager Console.

Setup on agent side

By following instructions, please replace `${AGENT_ORACLE_HOME}` with the actual path of Oracle Home where the Enterprise Manager Agent is installed.

- Copy `metadata\sun_javawebserver.xml` to `${AGENT_ORACLE_HOME}\sysman\admin\metadata` directory.
- Copy `default_collection\sun_javawebserver.xml` to `${AGENT_ORACLE_HOME}\sysman\admin\default_collection` directory.
- Create directory `emx\sun_javawebserver` under `${AGENT_ORACLE_HOME}\sysman\admin\scripts` folder.
- Copy `scripts\emx\sun_javawebserver\sunws.pl` to `${AGENT_ORACLE_HOME}\sysman\admin\scripts\emx\sun_javawebserver` directory.
- Execute `${AGENT_ORACLE_HOME}\bin\emctl stop agent`.
- Execute `${AGENT_ORACLE_HOME}\bin\emctl start agent`.
- Copy `admin\admin.pwd` to any directory and remember that directory. Open admin.pwd file and replace welcome1 with the password that you use to authenticate with Admin Server of SUN Java WebServer. This file will be used for executing the `wadm` utility provided by Sun Java Web Server.

Configuration from Enterprise Manager Console

Login to Enterprise Manager console; navigate to the homepage of the agent where we did the setup steps as defined earlier. From this page you can select **SUN Java Webserver** from the drop-down menu and click on **Go**. The following image shows the agent page where you can select the option to add **SUN Java Webserver**.

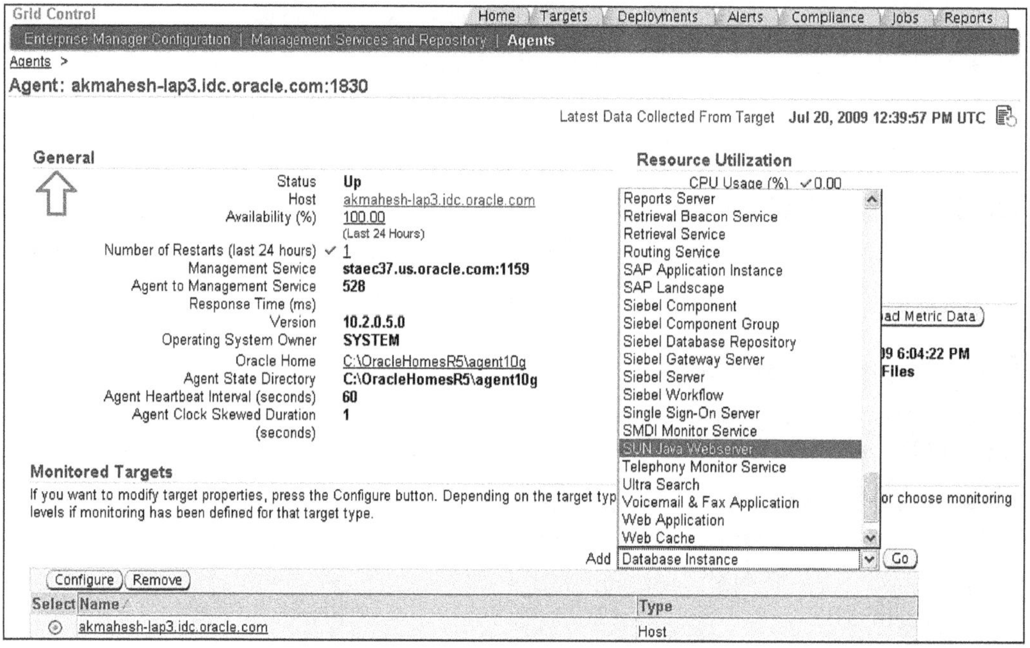

Once you select **SUN Java Webserver** from the drop-down menu, as shown in the previous image and click on the **Go** button, you will see the following page:

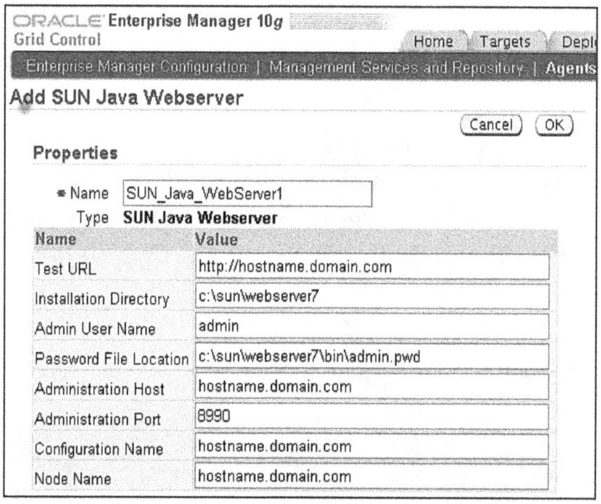

On this page, you will need to provide the following details:

- **Name**: The name that you want to give for the Sun Java Web Server target
- **Installation Directory:** The directory where the web server is installed
- **Administration Host**: The hostname/ip-address where Admin Server is running
- **Administration Port**: The communication port for Admin Server
- **Admin Server User**: The user-ID to authenticate with Admin Server
- **Password file Location**: The file that contains password to authenticate with Admin Server
- **Configuration Name**: The name of the configuration used by the web server
- **Node Name**: Name of node where the web server is running
- **Test URL**: The URL to check if the web server is up

After providing all of the details click on **OK**, after a few seconds you will be redirected to the agent homepage with a confirmation message displayed on the page, which is shown in the following screenshot:

On the same page, you will see that the new target is listed under the **Monitored Targets** section, as shown in the following screenshot:

Number of Restarts (last 24 hours)	1		Threads Created	18
Management Service	staec37.us.oracle.com:1159		**Upload**	
Agent to Management Service Response Time (ms)	571			(Upload Metric Data)
Version	10.2.0.5.0		Secure Upload	**Yes**
Operating System Owner	**SYSTEM**		Last Successful Upload	**Jul 20, 2009 6:04:22 PM**
Oracle Home	C:\OracleHomesR5\agent10g		Data Pending Upload	**0.23 MB in 5 Files**
Agent State Directory	**C:\OracleHomesR5\agent10g**		Uploaded data (KB past hour)	**0.00**
Agent Heartbeat Interval (seconds)	60			
Agent Clock Skewed Duration (seconds)	1			

Monitored Targets

If you want to modify target properties, press the Configure button. Depending on the target type, you may be able to update credentials, or choose monitoring levels if monitoring has been defined for that target type.

Add | Database Instance | ▼ | (Go)

(Configure) (Remove)

Select	Name /	Type
⦿	akmahesh-lap3.idc.oracle.com	Host
○	LISTENER_akmahesh-lap3.idc.oracle.com	Listener
○	SUN_Java_WebServer1	SUN Java Webserver

Under **Monitored Targets,** you will see the target listed with its name and target type. Click on the target name link, and you will be redirected to the homepage for a newly discovered target, as shown next:

Status	**Up** (Black Out)	
Availability (%)	Not Applicable (Last 24 Hours)	
Host	akmahesh-lap3.idc.oracle.com	

Alerts

Metric	Severity	Message	Alert Triggered		Last Value	Last Checked
No Alerts found.						

Host Alerts

Metric	Severity	Message	Alert Triggered	Last Value	Last Checked
Filesystem Space Available (%) for C:\	⚠	Filesystem C:\ has 8.52% available space, fallen below warning (20) or critical (5) thresh...	Jul 8, 2009 12:14:51 PM	8.21	Jul 20, 2009 6:16:45 PM

Related Links

All Metrics	Metric and Policy Settings	Alert History
Blackouts	Monitoring Configuration	Reports
Access	Target Properties	

Home

On this page, you will see the status and availability of the new web server target. In the beginning, availability for the last 24 hours will be listed as **Not Applicable**. But after some time, you can see the availability details for this target.

On the same page, you can see the alerts related to this target and the host on which this target is running.

There are some useful links under **Related Links** section:

- **Monitoring Configuration**: You can use this link to see or update any of the target properties.

- **Metric Policy Settings**: You can set the thresholds for the metrics by using this link.

- **All Metrics:** You can also see all collected metrics for this target by clicking this link under **Related Links**. The following screenshot shows the page listing all the **Metrics**:

Metrics	Thresholds	Collection Schedule	Upload Interval	Last Upload
▼ SUN_Java_WebServer1				
▼ Response	All	Every 1 Minute	Every 60 Collections	Jul 20, 2009 6:16:49 PM IST
UpDown Status	Set			
▼ VirtualServerStats	None	Every 1 Minute	Every Collection	-
New 404 Errors since last collection	Not Set			
New Requests since last collection	Not Set			
bytesReceived	Not Applicable			
bytesTransmitted	Not Applicable			
count200	Not Applicable			
count2xx	Not Applicable			
count3xx	Not Applicable			
count404	Not Applicable			
count4xx	Not Applicable			
count5xx	Not Applicable			
countErrors	Not Applicable			
countRequests	Not Applicable			

From this page, you can click on the various links to see current or historical metrics. We'll leave that as an exercise for you.

Exercise summary

In this exercise, we built the monitoring support for Sun Java Web Server. The steps to build that monitoring support were:

- Copy required artefacts on agent side. These artefacts included a metadata file, collection file, and the script to get the monitoring data.
- Discover the web server target by providing required details. These details included the web server install directory, admin server host and port.

Let's spend some time understanding the artefacts that we used for this exercise. In the next section, we'll learn about those artefacts.

Overview of artefacts used for monitoring of Sun Java Web Server

Now, we have seen how to monitor the Sun Java Web Server with the code sample provided with the book. Let's spend some time to understand the code sample that we used in the exercise.

Target definition

First, we need to find out what is the runtime entity or process that we want to monitor. A very basic set up of Sun Java Web Server has an Admin Server process and a Web Server process. The Admin Server process can be used only for administration and it doesn't serve any content or application service. The web server process is used for serving content to the real end-user. So, the web server process is the entity that we want to monitor, as this impacts content delivery for the end-user.

You will remember from the earlier chapters that all managed entities should be modeled as a target, so we will model the web server process as a target.

The first step of target modeling is naming the target type; we need an internal name and an external name. The internal name is a unique string that will represent the unique target type, and the external name is an end-user friendly name that explains about the target type. For this exercise, we will use `sun_javawebserver` as an internal name and `SUN Java Webserver` as the external name.

After the name, we need to define the attributes for the target type, these attributes serve two purposes — (a) identify a target (b) provide connection details to a target. For this exercise, we'll define following attributes for Sun Java Web Server:

- Target Name: The name of the target
- Installation Directory: The directory where the web server is installed
- Admin Server Host: The hostname/ip-address where Admin Server is running
- Admin Server Port: communication port of Admin Server
- Admin Server User: User-ID to authenticate with Admin Server
- Password file: File that contains the password to authenticate with Admin Server. Please refer to the web server documentation for more details on this
- Configuration Name: Name of configuration used by the web server
- Node Name: Name of node where the web server is running
- Test URL: The URL to check if the web server is up

In subsequent sections, well see how these properties can be defined in the required XML format.

Target metrics

Then next step is to define the metrics and mechanism to get those metrics. The most import metric for a managed entity/target is the Status metric. Status metric indicates whether the target is up or not.

Some targets expose the status metric; for some targets we need to derive the status metric by performing some operation on the target. For the web server, we'll calculate the Status metric by accessing a URL on the web server, if URL access is successful we can say that the web server is up and serving content.

We also learnt in Chapter 3, *Enterprise Manager Key Concepts and Subsystems*, about fetchlets — fetchlets provide the mechanism for gathering metrics. There are different fetchlets out-of-the-box for gathering metrics using different protocol. For gathering the status metric of the web server we'll use URLTiming fetchlet. This fetchlet takes web server URL as input and returns the status of URL by accessing it over HTTP protocol.

Besides status metrics, we want to get some more metrics for the web server. For this exercise, we will capture various metrics for each virtual server that include:

- Total Number of requests served by the virtual server
- Total Number of bytes served by the virtual server
- Total Number of Errors
- Total Number of 4XX errors — i.e. error codes between 500 and 599
- Total Number of 404 errors — since 404 indicate all the unknown URLs
- Total Number of 5XX errors — i.e. error codes between 500 and 599
- Total Number of 200 requests – requests served with 200 code – 200 code represents success in HTTP protocol.

These metrics are exposed through the `wadm` utility of the web server. We'll use `OSLineToken` Fetchlet to capture these metrics. For more details on `wadm` utility, please refer to the web server documentation on the Sunwebsite.

Target artefacts

So far, we have defined the target model, metrics, and the mechanism to gather those metrics. The next step is to put that definition and metrics in artefacts that can be deployed through Enterprise Manager.

Usually, all of these artefacts are packaged and uploaded to the management server and the management server deploys artefacts to different directories on the agent.

During the development time we need to put these artefacts manually into a different location. We saw this in the previous section where we copied the metadata file and other files into various locations. Once we have tested these artefacts we can package them using the command line utility provided by Enterprise Manager.

Target metadata

The metadata file name should be the same as the internal name for the target so, in our case the metadata file name is `sun_javawebserver.xml`. This metadata file needs to be copied in the `sysman\admin\metadata` folder in the EM agent, Oracle Home. If you want to write this metadata file from scratch we suggest that you copy one of the existing metadata files in `sysman\admin\metadata` folder and make the changes to that file to suit your needs.

Let's look at sections of metadata file—you can write your own metadata file or use sample metadata file available as part of a code bundle. At a broad level, metadata file can be defined in three sections the top section that has some details about the target type and version, the metric section that defines the metrics to be collected and mechanism to collect those metrics, and the properties section that defines the attributes required by a target.

Top section

This section declares what `dtd` is used for validating the structure of the metadata file. It also defines the internal name, external name and version of metadata file. Internal names are defined by `TYPE` attribute, the external name is defined by `DISPLAY` element, and the metadata version is defined by `META_VER` attribute. The following code snippet shows the top section of the sample file from the code bundle:

```
<?xml version='1.0'?>
<!DOCTYPE TargetMetadata SYSTEM "../dtds/TargetMetadata.dtd">
<TargetMetadata META_VER='1.0' TYPE='sun_javawebserver' >
<Display>
  <Label NLSID='sun_java_webserver'>SUN Java Webserver</Label>
</Display>
```

> Please note `META_VER` indicates the version of target metadata – whenever you make changes to the metadata file please increase this number. For example you can start with number 1.0 and continue with 1.1 or 1.2 and so forth.

Metric section

Each metric defines a group of performance indicators for a given target. These indicators are represented as columns under metrics. For each metric we need to define all of the columns for the metric and mechanism to gather the metrics. The mechanism to collect metrics is defined in `QueryDescriptor` tag through `FETCHLET_ID` attribute.

The most important performance indicator for any target is the status of that target; we'll first model this indicator. We'll define a metric called Response which will have the status of performance indicator. A web server status is up when you can access the web server URL using HTTP protocol. To find the status of the web server we'll use URLTiming fetchlet, this fetchlet will access web server URL periodically to check the web server status. In the following code snippet that is taken from a sample metadata file, you will see the metric definition that includes all of the columns and the fetchlet to be used.

```
<Metric NAME="Response" TYPE="TABLE">
  <Display>
    <Label NLSID="SUNWS_response">Response</Label>
  </Display>
  <TableDescriptor>
    <ColumnDescriptor NAME="Timing" TYPE="NUMBER" IS_KEY="FALSE"
                      TRANSIENT="TRUE">
      <Display>
        <Label NLSID="test_url_time">Test URL response time </Label>
      </Display>
    </ColumnDescriptor>
    <ColumnDescriptor NAME="Status" TYPE="NUMBER" IS_KEY="FALSE">
      <Display>
        <Label NLSID="apache_resp_stat">UpDown Status</Label>
      </Display>
    </ColumnDescriptor>
  </TableDescriptor>
  <QueryDescriptor FETCHLET_ID="URLTiming">
    <Property NAME="url0" SCOPE="INSTANCE">TestURL</Property>
    <Property NAME="verbose" SCOPE="GLOBAL">0</Property>
    <Property NAME="singlerow" SCOPE="GLOBAL">y</Property>
  </QueryDescriptor>
</Metric>
```

Besides Response metric we have another metric VirtualServerStats that is a group of virtual host performance indicators. For this metric we are using OSLineToken fetchlet. Through this fetchlet a perl script is invoked, this perl script gets metrics for all virtual servers, and prints into a format that can be parsed by OSLineToken fetchlet. This script is also part of a plug-in and needs to be deployed in the sysman\admin\scripts\emx\ sun_javawebserver folder under EM Agent Oracle Home. You can get that script from the sample code bundle.

Properties section

After metrics you can see the properties section that starts with
`InstanceProperties`—these are the properties required by the target for metric
collection. The following listing shows two such properties; the first property is the
URL for the web server that can be accessed to find the status of the web server. The
next property is the install directory for the web server.

```
<InstanceProperties>
  <InstanceProperty NAME='TestURL'>
    <Display>
      <Label NLSID='testurl'>Test URL</Label>
    </Display>
  </InstanceProperty>
  <InstanceProperty NAME='InstallDirectory'>
    <Display>
      <Label NLSID='instDir'>Installation Directory</Label>
    </Display>
  </InstanceProperty>
```

Target collection

The collection file name should be the same as the internal name for the target so
the metadata file name is `sun_javawebserver.xml`. The collection file needs to be
copied in the `sysman\admin\default_collection` folder in EM agent Oracle Home.

Now we will visit each section of the collection file—you can write your own
collection file or use a sample collection file available as part of the code bundle. On
a broad level, the collection of each metric can be defined in two sections—the first
section defines the collection frequency and upload frequency. The second section
defines the mathematical operators to be used for Metric threshold evaluation.

Collection schedule

This section defines what metric needs to be collected, how frequently it should
be collected, and how frequently it should be persisted. The `IntervalSchedule`
element defines the collection frequency. The `UPLOAD` attribute defines the sample
ratio of the collection that should be persisted, `1` indicates that each sample should
be persisted, `2` indicates that every second collection should be persisted with and so
forth. In the following example, we are collecting `VirtualServerStats` metric every
1-minute and we persist with every collection of metrics.

```
<CollectionItem NAME = "VirtualServerStats"  UPLOAD="1">
  <Schedule>
    <IntervalSchedule INTERVAL = "1" TIME_UNIT = "Min"/>
  </Schedule>
```

Metric thresholds & operators

This section defines the mathematical operator to be used for metric thresholds evaluation. For example, the following code snippet shows that for metric column `NewRequests`, we should use "Greater than"—`GT`—the mathematical operator for evaluating the metric threshold.

This section can also be used to define some out-of-the-box metric thresholds; it also contains the alert message that is sent out as a notification whenever a metric threshold is violated.

```
<Condition COLUMN_NAME="NewRequests" CRITICAL="NotDefined"
WARNING="NotDefined" OPERATOR="GT" MESSAGE_NLSID="New_Reqs"
MESSAGE="New Requests are %value%"/>
```

Packaging and deploying a plug-in

So far we have seen how to monitor a target using various definition files. In this section, we'll see how we can package those files into an archive. This archive can be used to deploy the monitoring support on multiple hosts through Enterprise Manager Console.

Packaging

We'll use `emcli` command utility to package all the files required for the management plug-in. One sample command is listed next—for more details on `emcli` command and all other options, you can refer to the Enterprise Manager documentation.

```
emcli add_mp_to_mpa -mpa="/tmp/sun_javawebserver.jar"
-mp_version="1.0"
-ttd="/tmp/metadata/sun_javawebserver.xml"
-dc="/tmp/default_collection/sun_javawebserver.xml"
-file="MONITORING_SCRIPT:/tmp/sunws.pl"
-func_desc="Management Plug-in version 1.0 for SUN Java Webserver"
```

Please note that `/tmp` is a temporary location where we can copy the files (downloaded from the Packt website).

Deploying

In the next few pages, we'll see how we can upload a plug-in archive to Management Server and deploy it to different agents.

To deploy a plugin—go to the **Set Up** section from the EM console homepage. In the **Setup** section, you will see the **Management Plug-in** option on the left-hand side, once you click on that you will see the page as shown in the following screenshot:

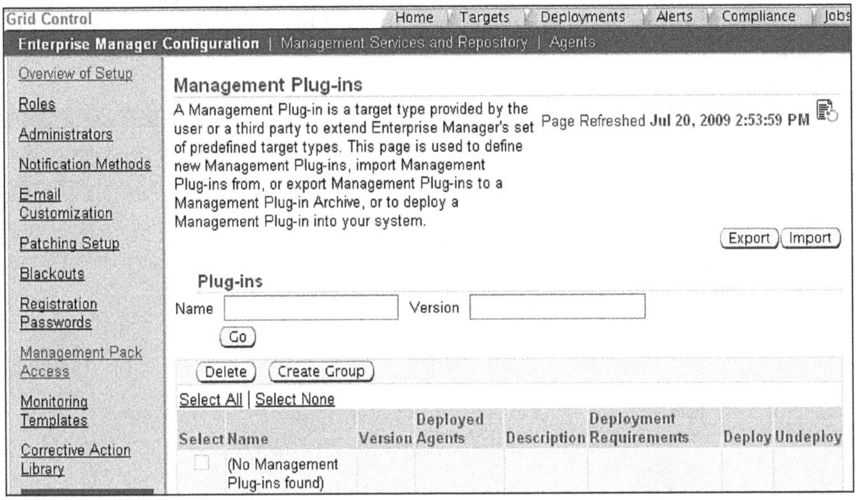

On this page, click on the **Import** button and on the next page you can import a plug-in archive.

On this page, you can upload a plug-in archive from a local machine to the management server. Once you have selected the plug-in archive, click on the **List Archive** button and you will see the details about the plug-in.

The following screenshot shows one such page:

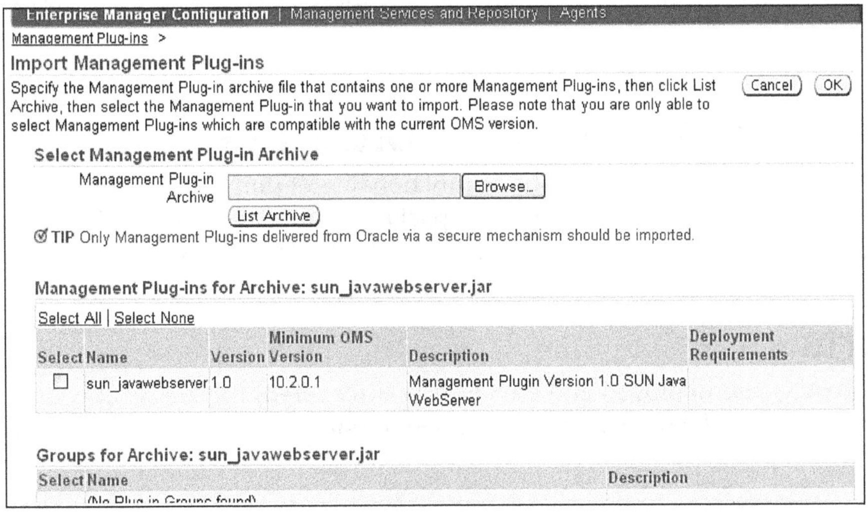

From this page, you can select the plug-ins that you want to import by selecting the check-box next to it. After selecting the checkbox next to **sun_javawebserver** plug-in, click on **OK**. On the next page you will see the confirmation message and all of the plug-ins available for deployment. From that page, you can start deployment by clicking on the **Deploy** button next to a plugin. The following screenshot shows one such page:

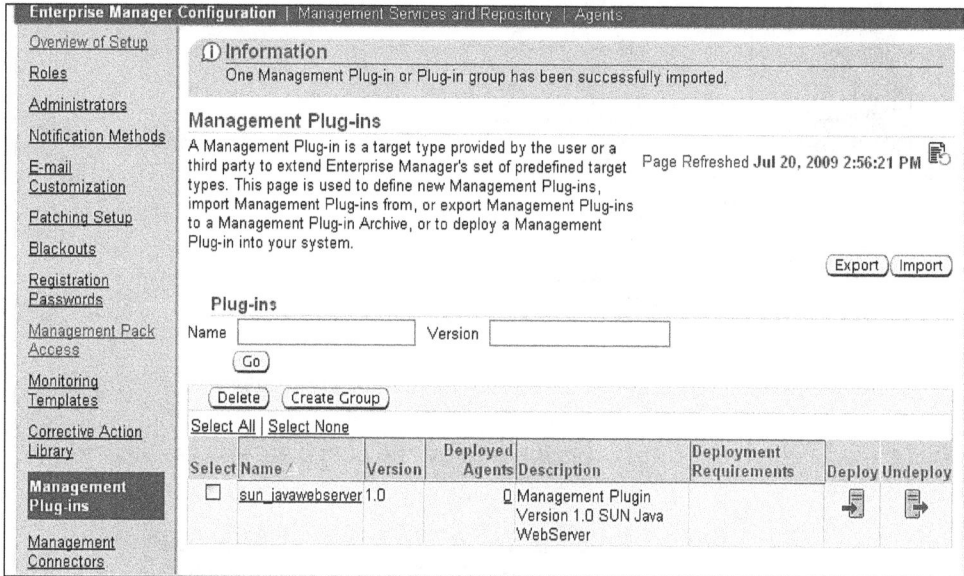

Once you click on **Deploy**, you will see a few screens that show where you can select the agents and where you want to deploy the plug-in. Once the deployment is completed for the selected agents—you can use those agents to monitor the Sun Java Web Server.

Advance features for plug-ins

So far, we have learned about the basic functionality of plug-ins, we saw the various artefacts needed and we also saw how to package and deploy those artefacts. In this section, we'll cover some of the advanced features of plug-ins.

Charts

Once the plug-in is deployed and the target is discovered, we can see the target homepage, and on the homepage, we can see the status and availability metrics.

Wouldn't it be nice if we could add some charts that can show historical data on the target homepage? Plug-ins provide support for adding such charts on the target homepage. All that we need to do is that we define the location of the chart, the data that should go in the chart and the type of the chart. We can define all of this in an XML format and include that file as part of the plug-in archive.

One sample chart file is listed below:

```
<HomepageCharts TARGET_TYPE="sun_javawebserver">
  <ChartSet>
    <TopPane>
      <Chart TYPE="timeSeriesChart">
        <ChartProperty NAME="metric">
                                VirtualServerStats</ChartProperty>
        <ChartProperty NAME="column">NewRequests </ChartProperty>
        <ChartProperty NAME="width">300</ChartProperty>
        <ChartProperty NAME="height">150</ChartProperty>
        <ChartProperty NAME="legendPosition">south</ChartProperty>
        <ChartProperty NAME="titleVisible">true</ChartProperty>
        <ChartProperty NAME="title">Virtual Server
                                        Traffic</ChartProperty>
        <ChartProperty NAME="subtitle"> </ChartProperty>
        <ChartProperty
                    NAME="destination">metricDetail</ChartProperty>
        <ChartProperty NAME="yAxisLabel">Number of
                                        Requets</ChartProperty>
      </Chart>
    </TopPane>
  </ChartSet>
</HomepageCharts>
```

This chart definition can also be included in the Management Plug-in Archive. The following listing shows a command to include the chart definition as a part of the plug-in archive.

```
emcli add_mp_to_mpa -mpa="/tmp/sun_javawebserver.jar"
-mp_version="2.0"
-ttd="/tmp/metadata/sun_javawebserver.xml"
-dc="/tmp/default_collection/sun_javawebserver.xml"
-file="MONITORING_SCRIPT:/tmp/sunws.pl"
-file="HOMEPAGE_DEFINITION:/tmp/charts/charts.xml"
-func_desc="Management Plug-in version 2.0 for SUN Java Webserver"
```

Once you deploy the new plug-in—you will see a chart on the web server homepage, as shown in the following screenshot:

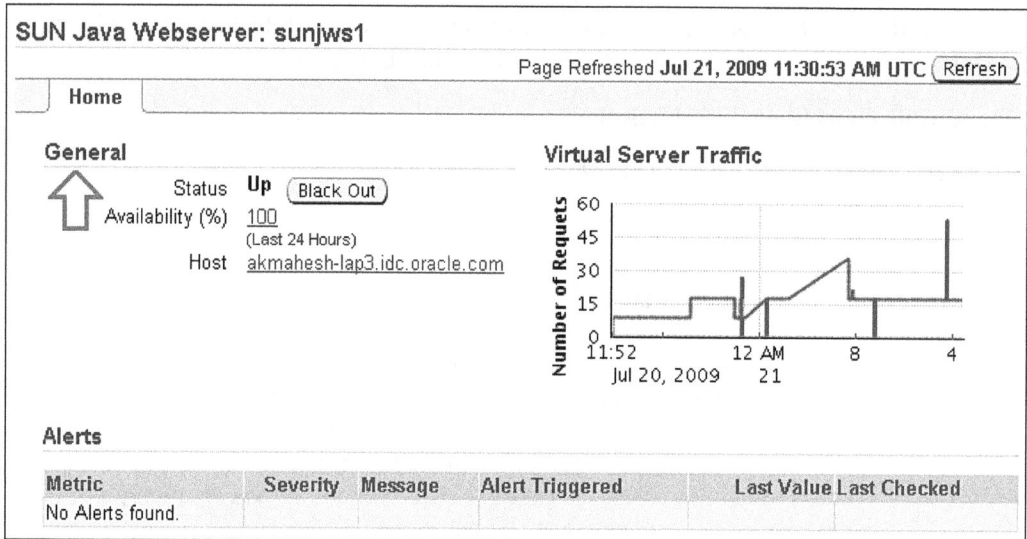

Other advanced features

Along with the chart, there are some more advanced features that can be included in the Management Plug-in Archive.

You can add some reports for a target. These reports are displayed on another tab next to the **Home** tab for the target. These reports are also available from the **Reports** tab of Enterprise Manager Console. You can also package a job definition in the plug-in archive.

The description of those features is beyond the scope of this book. You can get more details about the advanced features from the product documentation.

Summary

In this chapter, we learnt about extending the Enterprise Manager Grid Control monitoring support. Extensibility support is crucial for any system's management product, as there can always be some products that do not have out-of-the-box support.

The key takeaways before you move to the next chapter are:

- Management Plug-ins can be built and deployed on top of Enterprise Management Server
- Management Plug-ins are packaged as Management Plug-in Archive (MPA)
- There are many MPAs available from the Oracle website, some developed by Oracle, others developed by third party vendors
- To create an MPA, we need metadata and collection files
- There are some advanced features like Charts, Reports, and so on that can also be packaged with MPA

In the next chapter, we'll provide the best practices for various aspects of systems' management, such as best practices for monitoring, configuration management and so on.

14
Best Practices for Managing Middleware Components Using Enterprise Manager

As middleware administrators, you have various responsibilities that include provisioning, monitoring, lifecycle management, and so on. We will be providing the best practices categorized by such responsibilities. These best practices cover all aspects of systems monitoring and management, and will help you in building comprehensive approach for systems monitoring and management.

Enterprise Manager provides special support to implement these guidelines for most of the middleware targets, such as one click system creation, out-of-the-box configuration policies and so on. In case some customization is needed, or specialized support is not there, Enterprise Manager provides UI flows to customize or implement a best practice.

In this chapter, we'll provide some best practices for monitoring and managing middleware targets using the Enterprise Manager Grid Control. Some of the best practices were covered in the previous chapters—those practices were more specific to a particular middleware target, for example using deployment procedure to deploy a BPEL suitcase. We will bring together all such best practices for specific targets and generalize those best practices to cover all middleware targets. It will help you in putting together a plan for the management and monitoring of middleware targets.

We will be covering best practices for various responsibilities for a middleware administrator in the following order of management tasks:

- Provisioning
- Routine monitoring
- Configuration management
- Compliance
- Lifecycle management
- Information publishing
- Summary

Provisioning

Provisioning is usually the first step in the lifecycle of an IT resource. Provisioning of an application comprises multiple provisioning operations. These operations include:

- Provisioning of core stack i.e. J2EE server, HTTP server, Identity servers, and so on
- Provisioning of application artefacts i.e. J2EE applications, BPEL processes, OSB services, and so on

Some of the best practices for provisioning are discussed in the sections ahead.

Creating gold images

After the first installation is completed, various required patches are applied, configuration is done, and the system is stabilized; you should create a gold image of the setup and use it for subsequent setups. This image will also help to rebuild a system from scratch just in case the server crashes.

Enterprise Manager provides support for the gold image creation for Oracle products like Oracle Application Server. For other products you can write your own scripts and use them for the gold image creation.

Use software library as central repository

Besides the gold image of core stack, keep all your application artefacts in the software library. The software library is a central repository where you can keep all of the gold images and artefacts; it is very well integrated with the deployment framework.

The software library also provides support for assigning maturity levels to each component. For example, you can put a new J2EE application in the software library and mark it as untested, after testing the QA Manager can mark it beta, after the end-user acceptance, it can be marked as production. The page shown in the following screenshot shows a view of the software library—where you can see **Sample BPEL Suitcase** is production ready, where as **SOA Order Booking** is untested.

Define deployment procedures for all provisioning activities

Implement the deployment policies as deployment procedures. For example, if you want HTTP traffic to be stopped before deploying a new application and want to send an email after deployment, you should put these steps in a deployment procedure and deploy applications using this deployment procedure. This will help you in standardizing the deployment practices and for every deployment you can check logs from the central console.

For some artefacts like BPEL processes and OSB services, deployment procedure is available out-of-the-box. For the other artefacts, you can either customize the existing deployments procedure, or build a new one.

Routine monitoring

Most of the applications today are built with multi-tier architecture, where multiple middleware components are deployed in different tiers. Within each tier, there can be software components distributed on multiple servers. To monitor such applications, you need to monitor all of the components in the different tiers. For example, a typical web-based application serves content through HTTP server, has presentation tier deployed in J2EE container, has business tier deployed in the J2EE container, has authentication data stored in LDAP server, and has persistence in the relational database.

In such a distributed environment, often one or more components can become bottlenecks and can affect the performance of complete application. As a middleware administrator, you need to identify components that are bottlenecks, or can become potential bottlenecks, so that you can take some actions, such as adding more capacity for that component. For example, in a web-based application the HTTP server can be a bottleneck, and you can improve performance of the application by adding more capacity for the HTTP server.

Some of the best practices for monitoring middleware components and applications are listed in the following sections.

Select monitoring indicators and define acceptable limits

Each software component provides lots of performance metrics, but not all of the metrics are useful for each deployment of the component. Vendors provide such metric support so that any possible deployment can be monitored, but you need to monitor metrics that are useful for you. For example, there are two applications deployed, application A provides implementation for many web services and application B provides implementation for Enterprise Java Beans (EJBs). In this case, you should focus on web service metrics for application A and EJB metrics for application B.

Usually, the application developers know about the content of application, but it's very important that administrators also have some details so that they can focus on appropriate metrics.

Define thresholds for all the metrics that you have identified as useful. For many metrics, thresholds are available out-of-the-box, but for some metrics you need to define the thresholds. For example, the acceptable response time for air traffic control application could be in milliseconds whilst the acceptable response time for shopping catalog can be a few seconds.

So, based on the nature of your application, you define the thresholds that indicate acceptable limits for your component. Any such violation of the thresholds is recorded and can be later used for further analysis like capacity planning, and so on. You can also use violation history to tweak your thresholds.

From the Enterprise Manager Console, you can use **Metric and Policy Setting** from any target homepage to view or update the thresholds for the metrics. The following screenshot shows one such page for HTTP server. You can set the warning and critical thresholds for each metric. The following screenshot depicts that the warning threshold for error rate is set at 1% and critical threshold is set at 1.5%:

Hosts | Databases | Middleware | Web Applications | Services | Systems | Groups | All Targets

Oracle HTTP Server: EnterpriseManager0.staec37.us.oracle.com HTTP Server >

Metric and Policy Settings

Cancel OK

Metric Thresholds   Policies

View Metrics with thresholds

Metric	Comparison Operator	Warning Threshold	Critical Threshold	Corrective Actions	Collection Schedule	Edit
Active HTTP Connections	>	135	140	None	Every 5 Minutes	✎
Active HTTP Requests	>	135	140	None	Every 5 Minutes	✎
Active Requests for a Virtual Host	>	135	140	None	Every 5 Minutes	✎
Error Rate (%)	>	1	1.5	None	Every 5 Minutes	✎
Memory Usage (%)	>	80	90	None	Every 5 Minutes	✎
Percentage of Busy Processes	>	85	90	None	Every 5 Minutes	✎
Percentage of Requests Resulted in Internal Errors	>	1	1.5	None	Every 5 Minutes	✎
Percentage of Requests that Were Failures	>	1	1.5	None	Every 30 Minutes	✎
Percentage of Requests that Were Failures	>	1	1.5	None	Every 30 Minutes	✎
Percentage of Requests that Were Failures	>	1	1.5	None	Every 5 Minutes	✎
UpDown Status		Down	None		Every 1 Minute	✎

☑ TIP Empty Thresholds will disable alerts for that metric.

Use monitoring templates

Setting thresholds for multiple targets can be a time-consuming activity. Monitoring templates can be used to define a threshold definition. The monitoring template can be applied to multiple targets of the same type. You can also set a default-monitoring template for a target type. The default template for a target type gets applied to any new target of matching target type. The following screenshot shows a page where you can create, modify, or apply a template to one or more targets:

Setup notification rules

Some events are critical and for such events you need notifications to be sent out to an administrator or system, the rest of the events are still recorded in the repository. You should identify the events that are critical for you and set up appropriate notification rules. Criticality of such events can depend on nature or use of application. For example, if the public website is down, you may want notifications to be sent out, but if the intranet site is down you don't need notifications to be sent out, to achieve this you need to setup notification rules accordingly.

Besides paging or informing the system administrator, these notification rules can be used to communicate the availability of one system to another system. For example, if some application is down you can send out an SNMP trap to another application informing about the non-availability of the former application.

Enterprise Manager provides support for defining notification rules, where you can define rules for all targets of the same type or some individual targets. You can also select the events for which you want notifications.

The following screenshot displays a page where you can create, edit, or delete notification rules:

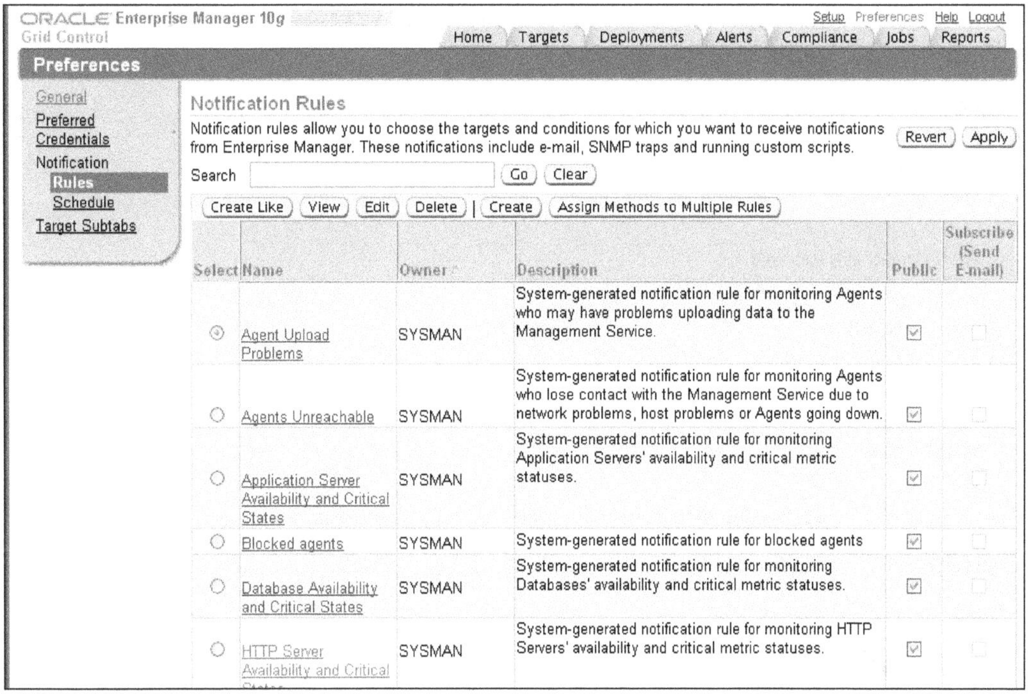

Select one of the notification rules and click on the Edit option, and you will see a page as shown next. From this page, you can select the metrics for which you want to receive notifications. You can also select the policies and jobs for which you want to receive the notifications.

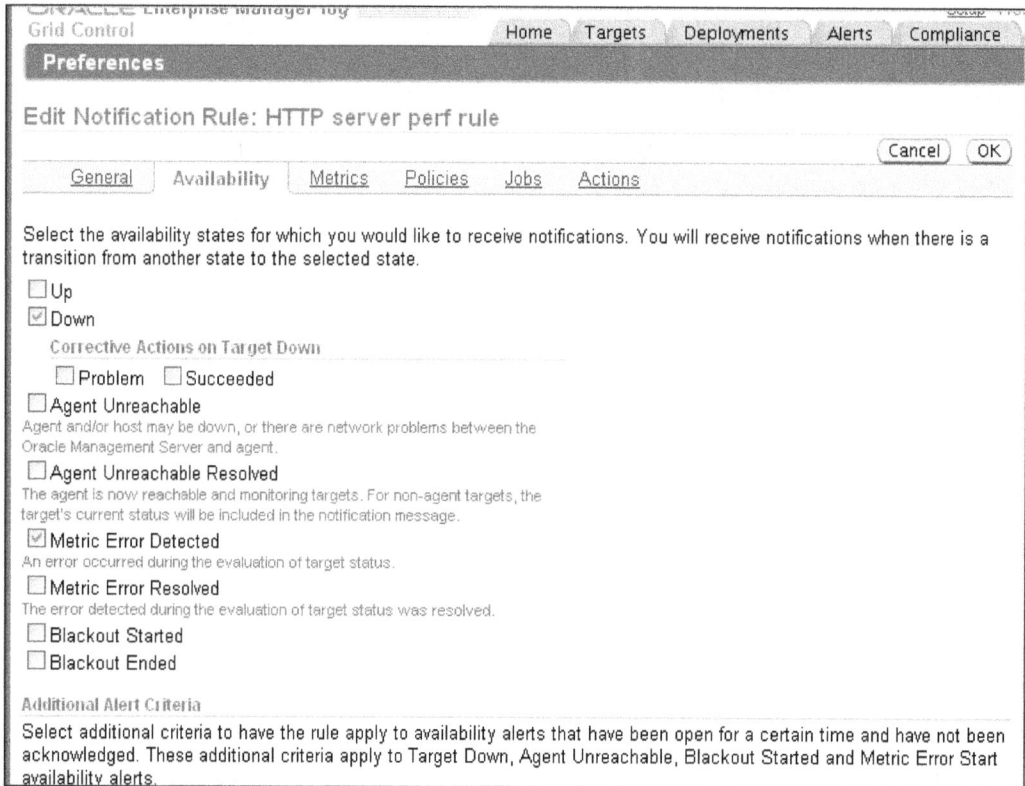

Manage many-as-one

To monitor an application you need to monitor all the related components. You need to have a view where you can see performance of all related components together and should be able to drill down to the performance of individual components. This view also helps in identifying the bottlenecks of a system.

Use the system construct provided by Enterprise Manager for grouping such related components. For many applications like BPEL Process Manager, Enterprise Manager provides a short cut to create a system where the Enterprise Manager identifies all the related components and groups them. For any other application, you can create such a system manually, by identifying and adding all components.

Defining Service Level Agreements (SLA)

Model the services provided by an application using the service construct of EM. You can define the service level agreements for availability and performance of this service. You can use the system metrics and the test metrics for defining these agreements.

Enterprise Manager provides a shortcut to create a service for many applications, for example, the BPEL process manager. However, for the rest you can create services by using the generic services framework.

Define service tests

To monitor actual user behavior, define service tests that repeat the recorded transaction at fixed intervals. For example, in a shopping cart application you can record a web transaction that goes through each step of shopping cart, and you can repeat all the steps of transaction from different geographical locations. Enterprise Manager provides various test types: some can simulate user behavior like the web transaction test, others can be used to monitor a component like the Host ping test.

Have a beacon in each geographical region where your user community resides. By executing recorded transactions from beacons in different regions, you can identify the issues local to a given community; for example, if network traffic is slower in Europe and fine in North America, then the beacon test from Europe will show you significant delays compared to North America. Just looking at the beacon results you can find that network latency issues in Europe are causing a slowdown for users in Europe.

Configuration management

We learned in previous chapters that Enterprise Manager collects configuration data for monitored targets. Enterprise Manager also keeps a history of configuration changes for the monitored targets. Collected configuration data can also be used to ensure configuration compliance across multiple targets.

Some best practices for configuration management are discussed in the next sections.

Save configuration snapshots

Whenever you make configuration changes to a component, save a snapshot of the collected configuration. Such snapshots will be very useful in keeping track of all the configuration operations performed by you. Ideally, save a snapshot after initial installation and one snapshot after every configuration, patching, or upgrade operation.

For some applications you may need to make configuration changes on multiple components—in such cases, save a configuration snapshot for all of the components and use the description field to relate all such snapshots. These snapshots can be very useful in case you want to view and restore configuration changes across components.

You can also use these snapshots to search for a particular configuration item, for example, you can search for all Web Logic Servers that are running on port 7001. The following screenshot explains one such search page:

Enterprise Manager provides support for exporting/importing snapshots to/from the file system. You can use this for saving configuration screenshots outside Enterprise Manager.

Use configuration comparison

Use configuration comparison feature to find configuration differences between two components of the same type. This feature is very handy when an application works in an environment but doesn't work in another environment.

You can also use configuration comparison to compare the configuration of the same component at two points in time.

Configuration compliance

Use configuration policies to enforce configuration compliance in your data center. Enterprise Manager provides many useful out-of-the-box policies. You can use those policies or define new policies for configuration compliance. For example, in Chapter 4, we saw how to define a configuration policy that checks for any Web Logic Server running on a default port (7001).

You can use the compliance score generated by Enterprise Manager to quantitatively define configuration compliance for a target. The following screenshot shows a configuration compliance score for a host target:

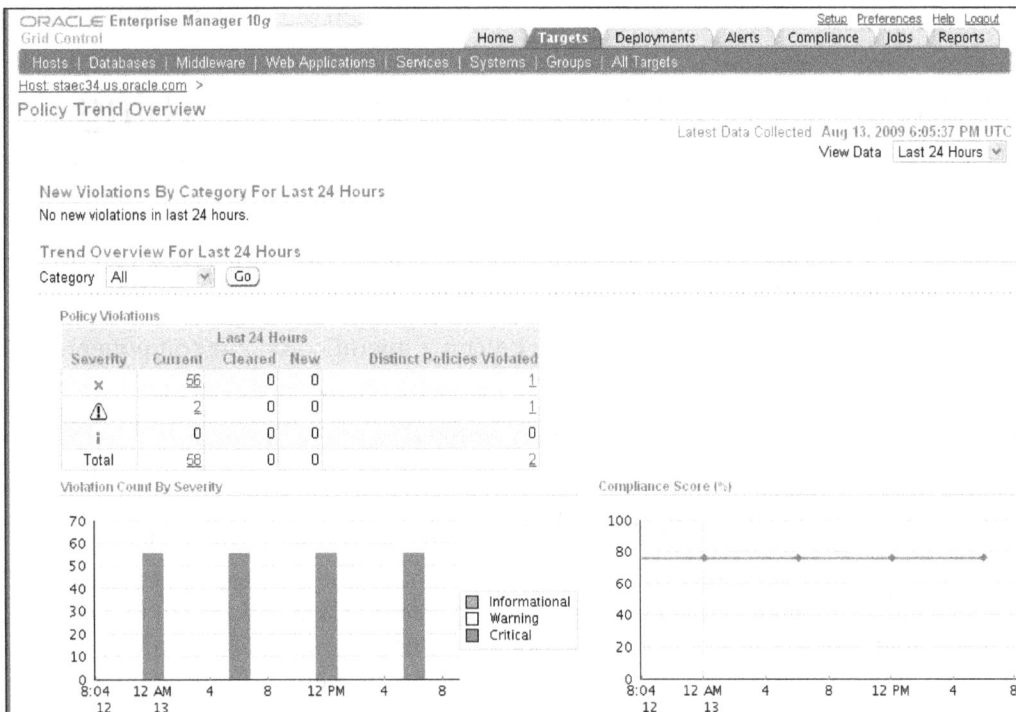

Lifecycle management

There are many routine operations that a middleware administrator needs to take care of. Most of these operations are repetitive in nature (for example, weekly backup of a system). Besides such operations, administrator needs to keep track of any critical patch advisories and needs to apply critical patches.

Some best practices for routine operations are discussed in the next sections.

Using the Critical Patch advisory

Typically, there are patching advisories published every month, these advisories contain all of the recommended patches for all of the products. Manually finding out which patch recommendations are appropriate can be a tedious task and can be prone to error. Also periodically, you will need to check for any new patch advisory.

Configure Grid Control for automatic download of patch advisories. Once these advisories are downloaded, Grid Control will evaluate and suggest only the patches applicable for your environment.

You may want to revisit Chapter 8, *SOA Management – OSB (aka ALSB) Management*, on how to configure Grid Control for automatic download of the patch advisory.

Using deployment procedures for patching

In big data centers, patching multiple servers can be a very time consuming job. Besides the effort in patching, you need to keep track of the servers patched and the servers to be patched.

You can manage such a scenario very easily by using deployment procedures for patching. By using deployment procedures, you can deploy patches on one or more components with the effort required for a patching operation on one component.

You may want to revisit Chapter 8, *SOA Management – OSB (aka ALSB) Management*, on how to use deployment procedures for patching

Use the job system library

Most of the Administrators have some scripts for the routine operation, which they execute manually or schedule through some other mechanisms like crontab. Such a methodology has been in practice for a long time but has some disadvantages, for example, there is no central repository of such scripts or there is no central place where you can see the output of all scheduled operations.

You can use the job system library where you can put the details of an operation to be executed and save that definition as a job. Later, you can pick out a job from the job system library scheduled execution of job definition.

Also this could be very useful where an administrator can define and save a few jobs in the job library, and based on the system requirement, the operator can execute one or more jobs. With this approach, the operator doesn't need to know all the complexity and parameters of jobs.

The following screenshot shows such a page where you can create or submit jobs from the job library:

Using the multi-tasking jobs

Multi-task jobs are used to define complex jobs by combining existing job types. For example, consider a scenario where you need to do a cold backup every day and along with the backup you need to rotate the log files. For this scenario, you can define a multi-task job that consists of shutdown job, backup job, and rotatelogs job. You can schedule this multi-task job to achieve all required operations.

With this approach, you can define modular jobs for simple operations and can combine some or all of them to achieve complex tasks.

Information publishing

Administrators need to publish data about data centers, like usage reports, compliance report, availability reports, and so on. You can leverage information-publishing support from Enterprise Manager to make this task easier.

Some best practices for information publishing are discussed in the next sections.

Using reports for information publishing

There are many out-of-the-box reports that you can use. You can customize or build new reports using wizards provided by the Enterprise Manager Framework. You can use various report content elements and formatting elements to build or customize reports.

Once you have the reports definition that you want, you can define the frequency of report generation. Enterprise Manager schedules the report generation and saves the generated report in the repository. Enterprise Manager can also email those reports as and when generated.

Use database views for publishing information

There are various public database views available in the Enterprise Manager Repository. You can use these views for publishing information from a repository. For example you can use some business intelligence tools to generate reports from public views in a repository.

The benefit of using public views is that across the different releases, view definitions are maintained.

Summary

In the last few chapters, we learned about the Enterprise Manager Architecture and features. We saw how to use those features to manage specific middleware entities. In this chapter, we bring together our learning from different chapters and put across the best practices for middleware monitoring and management.

The key takeaways in terms of best practices from this chapter are:

- Create a gold image of your setup—you can use the gold image for cloning or building a new setup
- Use the software library to store all gold images and application artefacts
- Implement your deployment processes through deployment procedures
- For monitoring, select the metrics you want to monitor and define acceptable limits for those metrics
- Define the notification rules for critical metrics
- To monitor an application, monitor all of the entities that contribute in making the application operational
- Define service to represent services provided by an application
- Save configuration snapshots after all configuration/patching/ upgrade operations.
- Enforce configuration compliance through configuration policies
- Use the jobs library and multi-tasking jobs for routine operations
- Use reports and public view to publish operational/compliance information about data centers

Index

Service Level Agreements. *See* **SLA**
service level management
  about 54, 203, 204
  configuration management 204
service level management, WebLogic Server
  about 82
  availability 83
  Beacon 83
  service, creating 85- 89
  service level 83
  service test 83
  system 83
  system, creating 83, 84
  terminologies 83
service level monitoring
  for, third-party targets 242-244
Service Oriented Architecture. *See* **SOA**
SLA 54
SOA 145
software library 286
software library, provisioning subsystem 54
SQL Server 20
states, Oracle WebLogic Server
  admin 64
  down 64
  running 64
  shutdown 64
  starting 64
subsystems, Enterprise Manager Grid
    Control
  configuration management 49
  information-publishing 56
  job 51
  monitoring 46
  Notification system 52
  provisioning 53
  service level management 54
  target 42
Sun Java Web Server
  about 264
  introducing 264
  monitoring 266
supported products, CAMM
  BEA AquaLogic Service Bus 246
  IBM WebSphere Portal 246
  Oracle BPEL Process Manager 246
  Oracle Electronic Service Bus 246

Oracle Service Bus 246
Oracle WebLogic Integration 246
Oracle WebLogic Portal 246

T

target, Enterprise Manager Architecture
  about 23
  agent targets 23
  repository only targets 23
  types 23
target artefacts
  about 274
  target collection 277
  target metadata 274
target associations 42
target attributes 42
target collection
  about 49, 277
  metric thresholds 278
  operators 278
  schedule 277
target definition
  about 272
  attributes 273
target lifecycle
  about 43
  configuration, for monitoring 45
  discovery 43
  monitoring, stopping 46
  target updates 45
target metadata
  about 49, 274
  metric section 275
  properties section 277
  top section 275
target metrics
  about 42, 273
  status metrics 273
target subsystem
  building blocks 42
  target definitions 42
  target lifecycle 43
  target types 42
target types, OAS product
  Application Server Cluster 97
  Application Server Farm 97

Application Server Instance 97
OC4J 97
Oracle HTTP Server 97
WebCache 97
target types, target subsystem
about 42
target associations 42
target attributes 42
target metrics 42
tasks, Oracle Applications Server Administrator
configuration management 114
monitoring 106
notification methods, for metrics 114
patching 120
provisioning 99
thresholds, for metrics 114
thread
tracing, AD4J used 259
thresholds, for target
defining 114

Tomcat plug-in
installing 231
Tomcat Server, discovering 232
Tomcat Server
discovering 232, 233

U

UAT (User Acceptance Test) 76

W

WebLogic Server Cluster 61
WebLogic Server control job
scheduling 71-74
WebLogic Server Domain
about 60
architecture 60
Windows client
configuring 137

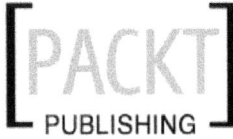

About Packt Publishing

Packt, pronounced 'packed', published its first book "*Mastering phpMyAdmin for Effective MySQL Management*" in April 2004 and subsequently continued to specialize in publishing highly focused books on specific technologies and solutions.

Our books and publications share the experiences of your fellow IT professionals in adapting and customizing today's systems, applications, and frameworks. Our solution based books give you the knowledge and power to customize the software and technologies you're using to get the job done. Packt books are more specific and less general than the IT books you have seen in the past. Our unique business model allows us to bring you more focused information, giving you more of what you need to know, and less of what you don't.

Packt is a modern, yet unique publishing company, which focuses on producing quality, cutting-edge books for communities of developers, administrators, and newbies alike. For more information, please visit our website: www.packtpub.com.

Writing for Packt

We welcome all inquiries from people who are interested in authoring. Book proposals should be sent to author@packtpub.com. If your book idea is still at an early stage and you would like to discuss it first before writing a formal book proposal, contact us; one of our commissioning editors will get in touch with you.

We're not just looking for published authors; if you have strong technical skills but no writing experience, our experienced editors can help you develop a writing career, or simply get some additional reward for your expertise.

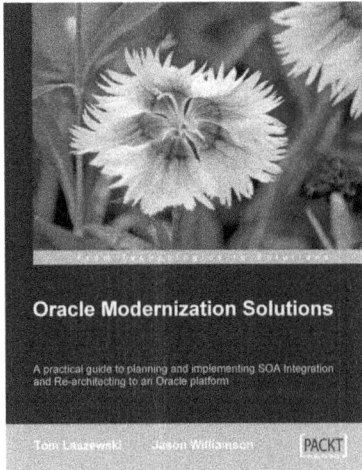

Oracle Modernization Solutions

ISBN: 978-1-847194-64-0   Paperback: 432 pages

A practical guide to planning and implementing SOA
Integration and Re-architecting to an Oracle platform

1. Complete, practical guide to legacy
    modernization using SOA Integration and
    Re-architecture

2. Understand when and why to choose the
    non-invasive SOA Integration approach to
    reuse and integrate legacy components
    quickly and safely

3. Understand when and why to choose
    Re-architecture to reverse engineer legacy
    components and preserve business knowledge
    in a modern open and extensible architecture

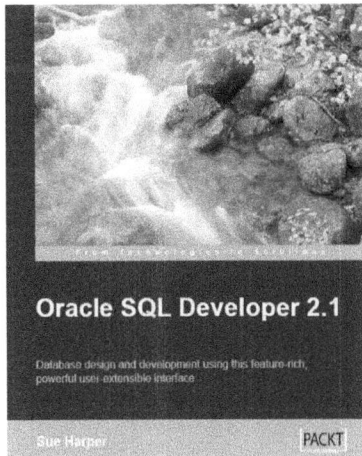

Oracle Modernization Solutions

A practical guide to planning and implementing SOA Integration
and Re-architecting to an Oracle platform

Tom Laszewski   Jason Williamson   PACKT

Oracle SQL Developer 2.1

ISBN: 978-1-847196-26-2   Paperback: 460 pages

Install, configure, customize, and manage your SQL
Developer environment

1. Includes the latest features to enhance
    productivity and simplify database
    development

2. Covers reporting, testing, and debugging
    concepts

3. Meet the new powerful Data Modeling tool
    – Oracle SQL Developer Data Modeler

4. Detailed code examples and screenshots for
    easy learning

Oracle SQL Developer 2.1

Database design and development using this feature-rich,
powerful user-extensible interface

Sue Harper   PACKT

Please check **www.PacktPub.com** for information on our titles

www.ingramcontent.com/pod-product-compliance
Lightning Source LLC
Chambersburg PA
CBHW080923220326
41598CB00034B/5660

* 9 7 8 1 8 4 7 1 9 8 3 4 1 *